2012 Saint Paul ALMANAC

ARCATA PRESS

Saint Paul

Community editors: Daunell (Nam) Barnwell, Maya Beecham, Mary Davini, Nimo Farah, Pamela R. Fletcher, Shaquan Foster, Andrew Hall, Barbara Haselbeck, Charlotte Kazlauskas, Patricia Kirkpatrick, Jewel Hill Mayer, Marianne McNamara, Arthur Nguyen, Sandra Opokua, Jennifer Syverson, Diego Vázquez Jr., Mai Yang Xiong, and Pa Yong Xiong

Copy editors: Sharon Parker, Jan Zita-Grover, Lucy Vilankulu

Cover art "Lowertown Saint Paul" © 2008 Tammy Ortegon

Cover designer: Ellen Dahl

Designer and typesetter: Donna Burch

History facts researcher: Steve Trimble

Proofreader: Sally Heuer

Publisher and managing editor: Kimberly Nightingale

Saint Paul city map and
Saint Paul downtown map © 2011 Roberta Avidor

ISBN 978-0-9772651-8-3

Printed by Friesens in Canada

Saint Paul Almanac
275 East Fourth St., Suite 735
Saint Paul, MN 55101
www.saintpaulalmanac.com

Saint Paul Almanac is a subsidiary of Arcata Press, a nonprofit publisher.

For Deborah Torraine
1951–2011

Like a force of nature, Deborah made furious passage through this life with love, wit, wisdom, humor, and compassion. In these days after her transition, we discover who she really was by the wide spectrum of humanity who tell loving, cherished stories of their personal encounter with this sistah-lady, mother, Ms. Deborah. To keep embracing the largeness of her spirit, we must now embrace the manifestations of nature and humanity that she loved with urgency and care. To keep her spirit alive, we must have our bold Deborah moments, days, weeks, or years to make this place better than we found it. Here's to the Life of Deborah Torraine! What a teacher, friend, activist, critic, lover of life. She guides, inspires, and loves us still as new ancestor, dancing through the elements earth, wind, fire, and water.

Louis Alemayehu

Contents

*For information on events listed in the
calendar section, see pages 298–315.*

Acknowledgments

Competing in a basketball game. Taking a bus for the first time. Visiting relatives in Skyline Towers. Digging neighbors' cars out of snowdrifts. These are some of the experiences tucked within the calendar of events and historical facts in the *Saint Paul Almanac*.

Unlike most books written by a single author or a few authors, the *Saint Paul Almanac* is a community endeavor that brings the essence of living in Saint Paul into a book each year. Stories about Saint Paul come from all over the world, but it's Saint Paul people who choose and edit the stories and poems you read here. While reading, you may smell mowed grass or breathe the Saint Paul winter air that dependably curls your nostril hairs.

And how many people does it take to put a book like this together? Lots. Seventeen community editors worked fourteen weeks on reading and choosing the stories in the *Almanac:* thank you to Daunell "Nam" Barnwell, Maya Beecham, Mary Davini, Nimo Farah, Pamela Fletcher, Shaquan Foster, Andrew Hall, Barbara Haselbeck, Charlotte Kazlauskas, Patricia Kirkpatrick, Jewel Hill Mayer, Marianne McNamara, Arthur Nguyen, Sandra Opokua, Jennifer Syverson, Diego Vázquez Jr., and Mai Yang Xiong. Their camaraderie and dedication was impressive, and they were very supportive of the process and of each other. Pa Yong Xiong, as our community photographer, beautifully recorded all of our meetings using still and film cameras. One hundred and twenty-nine authors' works were selected.

Two illustrators worked on the *Almanac*: Roberta Avidor and Andy Singer, who illustrated several of the stories and poems in the book. Roberta also brilliantly hand-illustrated our new full-color poster-sized maps of the City of Saint Paul and downtown Saint Paul. Our stunning cover art was created by Tammy Ortegon, with artist Ellen Dahl designing the cover. Seasoned artist Donna Burch took care of all interior design and typesetting work.

Nine visual artists' work was accepted into this year's *Almanac* through a competition managed by curator Patricia Hibbard: Rudy Arnold, Kara Hendershot, Jennifer LaCasse, Dana Maltby, Brenda Manthe, Tom Reynen, Shiny Thunder Productions, Cameron Torgerud, and Ernesto 'Neto' Ybarra. Their work shows the tremendous breadth and depth of Saint Paul's visual artists.

Saint Paul's Gordon Parks High School students continued their multi-year media documentation of the changes occurring on University with the building of the light rail. We include some of the students' photos taken for the project *Transitions: University Avenue*. Their teacher's photos are presented as well— acclaimed photographer Tobechi Tobechukwu. Tobechi has won many awards and much praise for his work, including a McKnight Photography Fellowship. Kathy Kelly, GPHS community coordinator, did much to make the *Transitions* project a success this year. Paul Creager, GPHS curriculum and media arts coordinator, and Micheal Thompson, GPHS principal, were also an integral part of moving this years' *Transitions* project forward. Read more about this project on page 381.

Thank you to our in-house photographers, Patricia Bour-Schilla, Henry Jackson, and Pa Yong Xiong, for their hard work running around town snapping photos for the *Almanac* stories. The artists' and photographers' work in this years' *Almanac* will be exhibited in September 2011 at the AZ Gallery in Lowertown. A considerable number of photos for this year's *Almanac* were kindly donated by photographers from the Flickr community, living in Saint Paul and around the world.

We also feature the fine poetry of the 2011 winners and honorable mentions of the Saint Paul Sidewalk Poetry Contest: winners Michael Murphy, Michael Russelle, Sara Clark, Lillian Rupp, and Louis DiSanto as well as honorable mentions Susan Steger Welsh, Destiny SaNaa' Carter, Gloria Bengtson, Megan Marsnik, and Charles Matson Lume. Marcus Young created and organizes this impressive celebration of poetry in the city with support from Public Art Saint Paul.

Thank you to a group of extraordinary people who work long hours for little pay to keep the *Almanac* thriving: Nigel Parry, web manager and photo editor; Tina Dybvik, calendar manager; Duncan, calendar assistant; Shelagh Connolly, administrative assistant; Betsy Raasch-Gilman, bookkeeper; David Unowsky, fundraising director; and Robert Smaller, director of sponsorships. We are very appreciative of CPAs Bernard L. Brodkorb and Scott Eekhoff, for keeping our nonprofit in good financial order.

Dan Tilsen is our much-needed, all-around fix-it, do-it, manage-it guy. We enlisted the expertise of Sharon Parker, Jan Zita-Grover, and Lucy Vilankulu as our three copyeditors, and Sally Heuer was our proofreader. Our three historians this year are Steve Trimble, Patrick Coleman, and Anura Si-Asar. Michelle Bierman managed our liaison with Saint Paul Public Schools. Nora Murphy wrote grants to help us pay our way. And thank you to Jay Dick at Dynamex for handling our books at the warehouse.

Anya Smith and Jessica Huppler provided important support as our American Sign Language interpreters at our readings. Thank you to Jen Ouellette-Schramm from the Minnesota Literacy Council for sending her students' stories to the *Saint Paul Almanac* and for the opportunity to teach about the *Almanac* in Erica Lehner's classroom at Hubbs Center. I don't know of a more engaging place than Hubbs Center in Saint Paul. It buzzes with activity.

Thank you to the Black Dog Café and owners Sara, Stacy, and Andy for showcasing our Lowertown Reading Jams and hosting our book-release party, and to Clouds in Water Zen Center for hosting our book-release party reading. Thank you to AZ Gallery, who opened their gallery doors to hosting our community editor project. A special thank you to board chair Todd Peterson for doing all the organizing to make it all happen.

Our community engagement director, Deborah Torraine, who passed away on June 10, 2011, skillfully collected stories from students, seniors, new writers in English, and others. She visited many classrooms and centers and living rooms. Deborah did whatever it took to help you feel safe and write your story and make it ready for publication. We will miss her.

Eight board members brought their partnership strengths to the *Almanac*: Carol Connolly, Poet Laureate of Saint Paul, Pamela Fletcher, Sooriya Foster, Metric Giles, Patricia Kirkpatrick, Ann McKinnon, Tim Nolan, and Uri-Biia Si-Asar. Lots of people donated to keep the whole effort afloat. And best of all: over five thousand readers will read this year's *Almanac*. PS: If you are reading this now, you are one of the 5,000. Thank you!

— *Kimberly Nightingale, Publisher*

More information about the events listed on the calendar pages is available by checking the event listings, pages 298–315. We try to be as accurate as possible with our event dates, but they are subject to change.

The *Almanac*'s website—found at www.saintpaulalmanac.com—has a greatly expanded and regularly updated Calendar that offers a diverse listing of events, and includes an online version of our City Guide. Bookmark these regularly updated resources on your mobile device, join us on Facebook at facebook.com/saintpaulalmanac, and on Twitter @ stpaulalmanac.

THANK YOU TO ALL OF OUR SUPPORTERS!

Black Dog Café
The City of Saint Paul Cultural STAR Program
Clouds in Water Zen Center
Common Good Books
F. R. Bigelow Foundation
Friends of the Saint Paul Public Library
KFAI Radio
Lowertown Future Fund of the Saint Paul Foundation
Lowertown Wine and Spirits

The McKnight Foundation
Mardag Foundation
Metropolitan Regional Arts Council
(whose support was made pos-
sible by the Arts and Cultural
Heritage Fund through the vote
of Minnesotans)
Minnesota Humanities
Commission
Minnesota Licensed Beverage
Association
The Ordway
Saint Paul Foundation
Travelers' Arts & Diversity
Grants Committee
Twin Cities Daily Planet

Aleli Balagtas
Richard Broderick
Mary and Stephen Budge
Richard J. Byrne
Gary Carlson
Sharon Chmielarz
Carol Connolly
Shelagh Connolly
Page and Jay Cowles
Gerald and Mary Devaney
Jeannie Dietz
Anne Field
Pamela Fletcher
Denise and Ane Fosse
Dyane Garvey
David George and
Carolyn Levitt
Rhoda Gilman
Eleanor Hall
Roger and Dana Hall
Cathie Hartnett
Barbara Haselbeck
Margaret M. Hasse
Mike Hazard
Nor Hall
Steven Horwitz

Jeannea Jordan
Karen K. Karsten
Nathaniel Khaliq and
Theresa Davis
Patricia Kirkpatrick
Evelyn Klein
Thomas Lacy
Faith Latimer and Josh Tilsen
Ethna McKiernan
Ann McKinnon
Roger Meyer
Jennifer Monaghan
Nora Murphy
Dave Ness
Dennis Nightingale
Edmund Nightingale and
Betts Carter
Timothy Nolan
Jean O'Connell
Deb Pleasants
Georgia Ray
Mary Kay Rummel
Barbara Schmidt
Kathleen Schuler
Karen Starr
Lisa Tabor
Janie Tilsen
Jocelyn Tilsen
Ken Tilsen and
Connie Goldman
Steven Trimble
David and Ruth Tripp
Cynthia Unowsky
David Unowsky
Lee and Stacy Unowsky
Everett Vanderwiel
Kathleen Vellenga
Jonathan Weiss
Irv Williams
Ronald Zaine
Hilary Ziols

Introduction

Walk in on a session of community editors for the *Saint Paul Almanac*. You are inside an art gallery located across the hall from the Black Dog Café. In this session in progress, watch the assembly that includes students, writers, readers, people of interest to their bankers and their preachers, people of interest to their neighborhood and to the city at large, people of interest to their family and friends, people of all walks gathered to select content for the forthcoming edition of the *Saint Paul Almanac*. What content are they selecting, and where does the material come from? Stories, poems, articles, biographies, all things Saint Paul are sent in for consideration during an open process that has a minimum of rules. We ask only that people write something of interest related to Saint Paul that is compelling enough to be published in the *Almanac*.

You are watching people of all shapes sizes, colors, heights, weights, desires, affiliations, philosophies. You watch a democracy in action in real time. The community editors meet once a week for three months; during this time they read all submissions for publication. At these weekly meetings the community editors discuss, haggle, bargain, read aloud, dismiss in whispers, plead, and bargain again; and eventually they vote. The scores help the process of determining the pieces of writing compelling enough to publish. This is a wild time, a time of much learning, much confusion, much reflection and acknowledgment, and it is a time worth witnessing. Better yet, it is a time worthy of participation. I am humbled and overjoyed to be a community editor. I have been a part of this process for almost four years. In the first years, we were a small group, yet we always had student representation on the panel. This year, on the first day of meeting, I was astonished at the size of the group, and exhilarated with the number of students. And with so many students on the loose, one may ask, "Where is the teacher?" Before each meeting, publisher Kimberly Nightingale conducts invaluable seminars on elements of publication. Not only does she review the salient features of advanced copyediting, she encourages further learning with shiny brand-new thick books known as the bible of book making in American English, *The Chicago Manual of Style*. Young and old alike, all community editors, were handed a copy of this luxurious red manual on all things book-creation related.

The community editors learn the full process of how to produce the *Almanac*. Intricate details, such as reading quotes from the printers, the guides and measurements, type of paper stock for the inside of the book, and the binding for the cover, are all covered in the weekly lessons.

Community editors are recruited from the city of Saint Paul. They are made responsible for the heart and soul and joy that eventually becomes the content inside the 2012 *Saint Paul Almanac*. The entire process of selecting the material for publication is a perfect combination of Dreamers and Achievers. The wonderful book in your hands is the result of skilled writers who submitted their work to a community of editors, who sought to shape lengthy discussions, tremendous energy, wonderful respect and desire into a product that is worthy of being called an *almanac*. And best of all, it is an almanac about Saint Paul, Minnesota.

—*Diego Vázquez Jr..*

2012

JANUARY
S	M	T	W	T	F	S
1	2	3	4	5	6	7
8	9	10	11	12	13	14
15	16	17	18	19	20	21
22	23	24	25	26	27	28
29	30	31	1	2	3	4

FEBRUARY
S	M	T	W	T	F	S
29	30	31	1	2	3	4
5	6	7	8	9	10	11
12	13	14	15	16	17	18
19	20	21	22	23	24	25
26	27	28	29	1	2	3

MARCH
S	M	T	W	T	F	S
26	27	28	29	1	2	3
4	5	6	7	8	9	10
11	12	13	14	15	16	17
18	19	20	21	22	23	24
25	26	27	28	29	30	31

APRIL
S	M	T	W	T	F	S
1	2	3	4	5	6	7
8	9	10	11	12	13	14
15	16	17	18	19	20	21
22	23	24	25	26	27	28
29	30	1	2	3	4	5

MAY
S	M	T	W	T	F	S
29	30	1	2	3	4	5
6	7	8	9	10	11	12
13	14	15	16	17	18	19
20	21	22	23	24	25	26
27	28	29	30	31	1	2

JUNE
S	M	T	W	T	F	S
27	28	29	30	31	1	2
3	4	5	6	7	8	9
10	11	12	13	14	15	16
17	18	19	20	21	22	23
24	25	26	27	28	29	30

JULY
S	M	T	W	T	F	S
1	2	3	4	5	6	7
8	9	10	11	12	13	14
15	16	17	18	19	20	21
22	23	24	25	26	27	28
29	30	31	1	2	3	4

AUGUST
S	M	T	W	T	F	S
29	30	31	1	2	3	4
5	6	7	8	9	10	11
12	13	14	15	16	17	18
19	20	21	22	23	24	25
26	27	28	29	30	31	1

SEPTEMBER
S	M	T	W	T	F	S
26	27	28	29	30	31	1
2	3	4	5	6	7	8
9	10	11	12	13	14	15
16	17	18	19	20	21	22
23	24	25	26	27	28	29
30	1	2	3	4	5	6

OCTOBER
S	M	T	W	T	F	S
30	1	2	3	4	5	6
7	8	9	10	11	12	13
14	15	16	17	18	19	20
21	22	23	24	25	26	27
28	29	30	31	1	2	3

NOVEMBER
S	M	T	W	T	F	S
28	29	30	31	1	2	3
4	5	6	7	8	9	10
11	12	13	14	15	16	17
18	19	20	21	22	23	24
25	26	27	28	29	30	1

DECEMBER
S	M	T	W	T	F	S
25	26	27	28	29	30	1
2	3	4	5	6	7	8
9	10	11	12	13	14	15
16	17	18	19	20	21	22
23	24	25	26	27	28	29
30	31	1	2	3	4	5

Calendar

Plus Saint Paul
Stories,
Facts,
Quotes,
and Poems

January

Photo © Rudy Arnold

Sleigh Ride

Homemade snow pants of thick wool, ice caked on my jacket sleeves and on my mittens: I head out with my best friend, Rita doll, who's decked out in her brown velvet cape my mother made. She has a shoebox for a sleigh and away we go to a magic winter land—over huge hills we ride, snow dancing in our faces.

"Time to come in!" my mother calls.

Always too soon.

Gerri Patterson

⇨ "There is no delight greater than the delight of creating something—something all your own which expresses you, apart from every other human being ... this satisfaction is what art does for the artist."—Alice Hugy, Saint Paul artist (1876–1971)

JANUARY

S	M	T	W	T	F	S
1	2	3	4	5	6	7
8	9	10	11	12	13	14
15	16	17	18	19	20	21
22	23	24	25	26	27	28
29	30	31				

26 Monday

27 Tuesday

28 Wednesday

29 Thursday

Photo © Gordon Parks High School, Isha

Snowy walk to school on University Avenue

30 Friday

31 Saturday   Saint Paul Winter Farmers' Market

New Year's Eve

1 Sunday

New Year's Day

🐚 January 1: Bryan Thoa Worra, a Laotian-American poet, was born today in 1973.

The University Club on Summit Avenue, which was modeled after the great city clubs of London, opened in 1912.

January 5

Photo courtesy Gayla Ellis

Ione's cousin, Elaine, and Ione, dressed in her work coveralls

Radio Crew

Gayla Ellis

Although I live in Minneapolis, I have a strong connection to Saint Paul. When I worked as a legal secretary in downtown Saint Paul, I could see across the Mississippi from my twenty-second-floor window to where my mother, Ione, worked in 1943 during World War II: Holman Field.

Born in Spicer, Minnesota, Ione moved to Minneapolis in her early twenties. During the war, she had a long commute from North Minneapolis to her job in Saint Paul: A bus took her to downtown Minneapolis, then a streetcar brought her to downtown Saint Paul, and a shuttle carried her across the Robert Street Bridge to the Northwest Airlines Modification Center, where she worked on a radio crew for the B-24 bomber plane known as the Liberator.

Designed by Consolidated Aircraft Company of San Diego, and mass produced by contractors like Ford Motor Company in Willow River, Michigan, over 18,000 Liberators were built from 1940 to 1945. The government contracted private companies like Northwest Airlines for final work. Ione's crew added radios, communications, and lights, then routed and clamped cables. A petite and agile twenty-year-old, Ione did whatever job needed doing, including work in narrow spaces, like under the cockpit.

Production went on twenty-four hours a day, and each crew had to rotate shifts every two weeks (8 a.m.–4 p.m., 4 p.m.–midnight, midnight–8 a.m.). After work, she rode home on the shuttle, streetcar, and bus, often falling asleep on the last leg of her trip; the driver would wake her at her stop. A fellow worker acquired a car, and after that she rode with him, a great relief after months of public transportation. One night, she realized he had forgotten her. The plant gate was locked, she couldn't return to the building, and she had missed the shuttle. Ione had to walk alone across the bridge in the dark to get downtown to catch the streetcar back, which was scary for her. That man didn't forget again.

After Ione had worked almost a year, Northwest management discovered that she was four months pregnant and they took her off the crew. The only other work available to her was in administrative offices as a secretary, but she didn't want clerical work; she was a competent mechanical laborer. She didn't find another job until after my brother Bruce was born. She was hired at a clock factory to make cardboard boxes but soon proved her ability and moved into clock assembly.

Three million women had worked in the defense industry.

Three million women had worked in the defense industry. After the war, men replaced women in the workforce. It would be years before women would again be hired for those kinds of jobs.

When her husband returned from the war, Ione struggled with his abuse and alcoholism until she finally divorced him. She had witnessed the effects her father's drinking had on her mother and family. After the war, she met Joe, a World War II veteran and a switchman on the Northern Pacific Railway. They married in 1948, raised Bruce, and had four children together, including me. Ione spent the next part of her life as a mother of five and a homemaker in Fridley.

Ione carries a certain pride from those days. She moved from small town to big city and also changed her life. She gained confidence in her ability to do skilled labor. She still learns as much as she can, reads avidly, and stays interested in new ideas and adventures. She was the family photographer, and recently we have been sorting and scanning her photos. New stories and old have emerged as we've gone through them, which brought forth these memories of Saint Paul. At eighty-eight, Ione continues to inspire me with her stories of survival during challenging times.

⇨ In 1896, conductor Walter Damrosch led a 170-member opera troupe in a performance of Richard Wagner's *Ring Cycle* in Saint Paul.

JANUARY

S	M	T	W	T	F	S
1	2	3	4	5	6	7
8	9	10	11	12	13	14
15	16	17	18	19	20	21
22	23	24	25	26	27	28
29	30	31				

2 Monday

3 Tuesday

4 Wednesday

5 Thursday

🕸 January 5: Adele Monfort, a leader of Saint Paul's Colony of New England Women, was born today in 1884.

Shopping at Aldi's on University Avenue

Photo © Gordon Parks high School, Emily

| **6 Friday** | Saint Paul Chamber Orchestra |
| | Land O'Lakes Kennel Club Dog Show |

7 Saturday	Saint Paul Winter Farmers' Market
	Saint Paul Chamber Orchestra
	Land O'Lakes Kennel Club Dog Show

| **8 Sunday** | Land O'Lakes Kennel Club Dog Show |
| | Minnesota Boychoir Winter Concert |

John R. Irvine obtained in 1850 to operate a ferry
across the Mississippi River at the Upper Landing.

The Dead of Winter

Richard Broderick

We speak of it
as though it were a place,
a battlefield strewn
with corpses,
a burial ground
of shattered statues
hooded with snow.
We picture something
grainy, gray-and-white,
crow-like figures
hunching inside capes,
frost working its claw
into the heart of trees.
In this zone we hear
an echo, a dread voice
that chills words to zero.
Over on the dark shore
branches snap like bones.
Scurrying across the ice,
we wait for the crack,
never looking down
into the depths, so close
but a lifetime away,
the final holding tank
of those we couldn't
hope to save.

Photo © Henry Jeckson

Saturday Morning

Michael Teffera

It was around 9:55 a.m. I was waiting for the library to open.

I saw a cute Ethiopian girl coming toward me. She had dark brown skin, short hair, and a pretty baby face.

"What time is it?" She asked me. Her English accent was very good.

"Five to ten," I said.

"Oh, five minutes more," she said, and she stood beside me.

"You know, you have a familiar face. By the way, what is your name?" I asked.

"My name is Queen," she replied.

"My name is King," I said with a smile.

"You are kidding! What is your real name?" she asked.

"My name is Michael, and my friends call me Micky. So where are you from, anyway?" I asked.

"Here," she said.

"No, I mean not where you live, but where did you come from?" I asked.

"Does it really matter where I am from?"

"Sorry. Do you speak Amharic?" I asked her.

"What are you talking about?" she said in scorn.

Then I realized my thinking was wrong, She was African American.

"Oh, my mistake," I said with broken sound.

"Excuse me, I want to go," she said, and she went inside the library.

I followed her in slowly.

▷ "A photograph can be as much a piece of fiction as it is a document of the real world. ... Indeed, the most compelling photographs shed light on reality in much the same way good fiction does."—Wing Young Huie, Saint Paul photographer

JANUARY

S	M	T	W	T	F	S
1	2	3	4	5	6	7
8	9	10	11	12	13	14
15	16	17	18	19	20	21
22	23	24	25	26	27	28
29	30	31				

9 Monday   *Saint Paul Almanac* Lowertown Reading Jam

🎖 January 9: Elizabeth "Betty" Musser, philanthropist and leader in arts and cultural institutions, was born today in 1911.

10 Tuesday

11 Wednesday

12 Thursday

Small memory of spring

13 Friday	Saint Paul Chamber Orchestra
14 Saturday	Saint Paul Winter Farmers' Market
15 Sunday	

The Karen community of Minnesota celebrated New Year 2750 on January 8 in 2011 at Washington Technology Magnet Middle School.

Photo courtesy Maya Beecham

Maya in second grade

My Second Grade Teacher

Maya Beecham

I was seven years old, in second grade, and tired on a daily basis. Most mornings I arrived at Highland Elementary School after limited sleep. I was robbed of sleep by bouts of eczema, an inflammatory condition of the skin. Rashes covered my skin, and in the middle of the night, half asleep, I removed the socks from my hands and dragged my wirey fingers and fingernails against my dry skin, scratching for relief that seemed unattainable. Endless scratching led to long mornings. By the time I settled at my classroom desk, I was not interested in arithmetic, reading, or writing. I was interested only in doing what I wanted to do, and school didn't make the list.

Mrs. Georgia Bulson, my classroom teacher, was interested in me. She saw potential in all of her students, including the sleep deprived. She encouraged us, believed in us, pushed us, and entertained us. My favorite moments in class included sitting on the classroom rug while she read Nancy Carlson books in an animated fashion. I was a challenging student, and in return, Mrs. Bulson challenged me to learn and be engaged. For example, I didn't qualify for gifted and talented programming, but I showed enough spunk, energy, and talent in pushing back against school that she found a way to redirect my energies. She made a deal with me: if I did my work in class, she would let me join Omnibus, the gifted and talented class. I was ecstatic. My self-esteem soared. I felt smart, relevant, and important. I helped to create the heady Omnibus newsletter, a good challenge that was both fun and exhilarating.

Mrs. Bulson singlehandedly changed my seven-year-old life. At the end of the school year, I was preparing to move to South Minneapolis with my family. Mrs. Bulson stopped me as I exited the classroom for the last time. She said, "I want to stay in contact with you." That was the beginning of a lifetime friendship.

The following school year, I started third grade across the Mississippi River in what seemed like a foreign land. I was shocked and disheartened that my new teacher didn't meet the standards set by Mrs. Bulson. One day, I phoned Mrs. Bulson with my concern. I said, "My teacher thinks I am dumb."

Mrs. Bulson singlehandedly changed my seven-year-old life. At the end of the school year, I was preparing to move to South Minneapolis with my family. Mrs. Bulson stopped me as I exited the classroom for the last time. She said, "I want to stay in contact with you." That was the beginning of a lifetime friendship.

She said, "Why do you think that? Do you do your homework?"
I said, "No, but can you talk to her?"

That was one of many conversations spanning childhood, adolescence, and adulthood. We went from yearly summer lunches to yearly phone calls and greetings cards to stay in touch. I still refer to her as Mrs. Bulson, my second grade teacher, although she often reminds me that I can now call her Georgia, my friend. When I deal with children in my line of work, I channel Mrs. Bulson, so I, too, can singlehandedly change the lives of children by helping them reach their full potential.

JANUARY

S	M	T	W	T	F	S
1	2	3	4	5	6	7
8	9	10	11	12	13	14
15	16	17	18	19	20	21
22	23	24	25	26	27	28
29	30	31				

⇨ Northland Ski Manufacturing Company, founded by Norwegian-born Christian Lund, was incorporated 100 years ago in Saint Paul. The company made skis, toboggans, and hockey sticks.

16 Monday

Martin Luther King Jr. Day

17 Tuesday

18 Wednesday

🌼 January 18: John T. Salminen, watercolor artist, was born today in 1945.

19 Thursday

Photo © Patricia Bour-Schilla

Winter swing

20 Friday   Saint Paul Chamber Orchestra

21 Saturday   Saint Paul Winter Farmers' Market

🐞 January 21: Louis Robert, pioneer Saint Paul businessman after whom Robert Street was named, was born today in 1811.

22 Sunday   Minnesota RollerGirls (Bout)

Saint Paul's Union Station served nine railroads in 1912. Each day, 35,000 passengers and 300 trains moved through the structure.

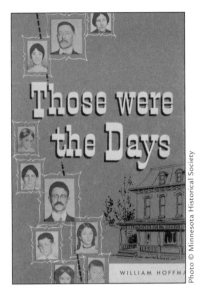

Photo © Minnesota Historical Society

Those Were the Days *by William Hoffman*

A Nostalgic Zephyr: William Hoffman on the Old Jewish West Side

Patrick Coleman

It is difficult to choose from Bill Hoffman's writings because they are all so compelling. Street by street and door by door and character by character he documented an important piece of Saint Paul—Jewish life on the West Side flats—that no longer exists. Hoffman should be required reading for recent immigrants and for those who have forgotten that their families were once immigrants.

William Hoffman, *Those Were The Days* (T. S. Denison and Company, 1957); pages 26–27, 29–31.

Do you remember the blacksmith shop on Texas Street where the mighty smithy, Mr. Reznick, labored diligently with peddlers' wagons and sturdy steeds? This was Texas Street: an impossible morass of mud after each rain. It was so bad that Chaim Greenstein (Peg Green's brother) wrote to the old *Daily News* asking for airplane service from State Street to his home at 320 Texas. There were other neighbors who felt the same way: The Senenskys, Blumstiens, Chases, Macarofskys, Hirschorns,

Hoffmans, Gransbergs, Dietzes, Rosenblums, Lynches, Zuckers, Skroopkas, and others I may have forgotten at the moment. But today, most of these families have left long since and Helen Gransberg Turner ("Hawtkeh"), with her own family, reigns as queen of a shrinking dominion.

To live on State Street, which was paved and had sewers and running water, was the Mecca and dream of my mother. It was not her own comfort she was concerned about, but rather that of her daughters. How would any eligible suitor in his right mind ever get down so far as the end of Texas Street to court her daughters? "Gott zu danken" (thank heaven), however, all was not lost, for the tennis courts were across the street on the Minnetonka playground, and my mother took advantage of the terrain to bait the trap. Most of the "Castle Garden" dandies in their white slacks came down often to play tennis and my mother made full use of her homemade root beer to lure the unsuspecting. Who could resist the cold foaming drink? Finally, it was "Shloymie" Solomon who asked my sister Annie for her hand. What a potent brew that was, full of yeast and probably the forerunner of today's atomic bomb. ...

Harriet Island, known to us as "Bading House," provided good swimming in the Mississippi River and the best picnic spot. There were cages with animals, slides, and sand boxes. For a hot shower or "vaneh" (bath) we went to the Wilder Public Baths for the weekly "Shabus" (Sabbath) clean-up—towel and soap for one penny. I would have written that even today one old patriarch makes the trip over the Robert Street bridge every Friday with a change of underwear bundled under his arm but now he is gone too.

Oh, that first delicatessen store, Levoonehs (Lebanon) on Fairfield. Do your nostrils quiver with the mixed, intriguing smells of herring, "shmookfleish," Russian candies, halvah, and pickles? Can't you see coming out from the back room, portly and genial, "Mr. Levooneh," father of the Stacker boys and proprietor of the store? He also sold us our "chedar" writing tablets, "gragers" (noise makers) for Purim, and monkey nuts. And on one side on top of the glass counter were stacks of Jewish newspapers: *Der Tag, Morgen Journal,* and the *Forvitz.* ...

Take hold of my hand and walk along with me. The day is clear, the sun bright, and there is a nostalgic zephyr which whispers softly of the promise along this winding path. This is the little world of our beloved West Side, and who can blame others who wish to claim it, too, for their own. We invite them also, and even those who are reluctant because for some reason or other, in the length and depth of their lives, have once wished to disclaim their childhood and the legacy of their parents.

⇨ "A working woman gets just as hungry as a working man. She has as many dependents to support. She must demand equal opportunity to earn her living."— Sarah Colvin (1865–1949), Saint Paul suffragist, speaking in 1934

JANUARY

S	M	T	W	T	F	S
1	2	3	4	5	6	7
8	9	10	11	12	13	14
15	16	17	18	19	20	21
22	23	24	25	26	27	28
29	30	31				

23 Monday

Chinese New Year

24 Tuesday

25 Wednesday

26 Thursday   Saint Paul Winter Carnival

Photo © Patricia Bour-Schilla

Spring fever

27 Friday

Holocaust Memorial Day

Saint Paul Winter Carnival

Fourth Friday at the Movies

🐞 January 27: Tim Rumsey, Saint Paul physician and author, was born today in 1948.

28 Saturday

Saint Paul Winter Farmers' Market

Saint Paul Winter Carnival

Global Hot Dish Variety Show

Minnesota Opera, *Werther*

Saintly City Cat Show

29 Sunday

Saint Paul Winter Carnival

Saintly City Cat Show

The Gleam, Johnson High School's literary magazine, first appeared in 1912. It ceased publication in 1926 but was revived in 1992.

January 21

When Everything Was Everything

Saymoukda Duangphouxay Vongsay

1. Food stamps in my pockets. Two dollars' worth of Now n Laters. Green saliva, couldn't swallow quick enough. Standing nervous. Red light on Dale Street. Crossed the bridge over Hwy 94. Trekking back to St. Albans. Candy wrappers clenched tight. Waved good-bye to Tiger Jack.

2. Every Friday Bhet opens the screen door and announces, "Pahw mah la, pahw mah la!!" All afternoon we've waited. In my father's tan Isuzu truck we drove to Hudson. Mom buys lottery tickets for her, bags of Funyuns and a giant Slurpie for us. Bhet likes the blue ones—they stain his tongue so good, makes a point to show me every time. On the way home, mom spends imaginary millions in out-loud daydreams. Blue-lipped smiling, Bhet tells me we are like kings in Dad's gold chariot. I agreed.

3. Bowl cuts. Red-handle scissors.

4. Holding my Korean blanket, rolled under my arms. Dad carried trash bags, everything we owned, slung over his shoulders. Tiny feet tired from walking, twelve blocks to our new home. Stopping every other he asks, "Ee la, nyang die yoo baw?" Every time, looking up, forcing smile, "Doiy, ee pahw."

5.
692 North St., St. Paul.
250 Oxford St. North, St. Paul.
308 North St. Albans, St. Paul.
3634 15th Ave. South, Mpls.
1090 York Ave., St. Paul.
130 Bates Ave., St. Paul.

6. "Mah nee, ee Thoun," Bhet says. I follow him to his first grade classroom, passing cubbies, water-color family portraits, and a picture of Jesus the Christ. He lifts up the lid of his school desk, no. 2 pencils with bite marks, color crayons, and two small boxes of Sunmaid raisins. He hands me one and smiles, showing teeth.

7. I interrupted my class when I walked in, returned from an ESL session. Mr. Smith made everyone read out loud, stopping when they want to. No one ever reads more than three sentences from *The Cay*. They giggled and snickered on my turn. That day, I read two chapters without stopping to breathe. The snickering, ridiculing, and ESL sessions stopped after that.

8. I went to Head Start preschool. Bhet went to Saint Mark's Catholic school.

9. I killed my father's lawn one summer with my blue plastic pool. Fresh-out-of-the-bag Disney underwear and bare chested, grass blades speckled my feet and ankles, I watched as the grinning crocodile begins to swim, hidden sometimes by the sun's reflection, until water spills tiny waterfalls over the brim.

10. Hand-me-down jeans, ripped, and dirtied at the knee. Working in cucumber fields. Picking only the ones as big as my five-year-old hands.

11. Grocery store. Pharmacy. Welfare office. Parent-teacher conferences. All are unmaneuverable without your double tongue, looking up to your right, up to your left, at adult mouths moving and adult ears, waiting, listening to everything lost in an eight-year-old's interpretation.

12. Carrying a roll of toilet paper in a wrinkled over-used plastic bag, I jumped into my father's Isuzu. Seldom visible at 3 a.m., the moon can't hear Father singing during the hour drive to a Christmas wreath-making factory, suspended between awake and weary. Mother cups my face with her sap-dried hands, dirt under her nails, plants kisses before unrolling 6, 8, 10 sheets to blow the dust out of her nose. Her hand rakes my hair and neck leaving dried flakes of sap, the smell of pine, the residual optimism she still has.

13. The art of haggling with the Hmong grandmothers at the Farmers' Market is not for the meek minded.

14. Be the first to line up in front of the food truck before its back door slides up, thundering over the murmurings. Everyone wonders if they'll get a bag of frozen chicken this time. Or angel food cake, two days past the expiration date. I exchange all of my cheeses for boxes of rice with anyone who doesn't look like me.

15. Mrs. Jaquelin traded cassette tapes with mom every week. Roy Ayers, Sade, and Dolly Parton for Thai singers I only knew by face.

Notes

2. Pahw mah la, pahw mah la!! (Dad is here! Dad is here!)

4. Ee la, nyang die yoo baw? (Babygirl, are you okay to walk?); Doiy, ee pahw. (Yes sir, Daddy.)

6. Mah nee, ee Thoun. (Come here, Thoun.)

Thirty Degrees Below Zero

Mary Wlodarski

I like the cold so brisk and fresh
it cuts through clothes
and crimps nose hair. I like

the winter mornings, dark at first
giving way to crystallized trees and pastel
sunrises. I like waking up

under six heaped blankets so deep I crawl out
of the mattress depression. The creep
of traffic and grumble of weather

is the Minnesota song. I feel the pinpricks
on my spine, the attention of every hair follicle
to tasteless air.

Holding on to morning in winter
with mittened hands, I like to greet
the day that steals

   my breath.

Photo © Media Mike Hazard

Nimo

Your Body Grows Alert When You Hurt

Media Mike Hazard

Nimo is real. The debate about health care is abstract. Real is when you hurt and you need care and Nimo is there.

A nurse at United Family Practice Health Center, Nimo teams with Tim Rumsey, my doctor. I bring them apples. After we clicked this picture, and she moved on to help another patient, I asked Dr. Rumsey about Nimo.

"A couple years ago a woman came in the clinic in the middle of winter. It was twenty below. She did not have a coat. When she left, she was wearing a jacket. Nimo gave her the coat off her own back."

Nimo says, "Your body grows alert when you hurt."

Rumsey says, "She is wise."

Photo © Minnesota Historical Society

Laying the cornerstone at the new St. Ambrose Church in 1956

The Center of My Life

Margaret Anzevino

There had been rumors for the past six months, but Father Pingatore would soothe them, saying that they were just the result of misinterpretation. "Don't believe what you overhear," he'd say. In January 1997, when I opened the letter saying that St. Ambrose Church would be closed, I was numb. Here was the place that had been a huge part of my existence, particularly in the early years of my life.

My world hadn't been very big when I was growing up on the Lower East Side of Saint Paul in the middle '30s and '40s. I could walk to Morelli's store or to Kornmann's store to pick up any grocery item that my Mom had forgotten to purchase on her weekly grocery trip, or to Lincoln School where all of us kids on the block went to school or just to play ball on the playground. There were the occasional Saturday walks up the hill to Payne Avenue to shop at Hartman's Dry Goods store or spend the afternoon at the Capitol to see a movie. The two most important influences in all of our lives, however, was the Christ Child Community Center, now Merrick, and St. Ambrose Church.

Much of the lives of the Beaumont Street residents were centered on these two places. To this day, I can name the families living on Beaumont Street. On the south side of the street were Rossis', Savinos', Gene Corbos', Nick Corbos', Anzevinos', John Dinzeos', Katherine Dinzeos', Skipons', Scalzes', and Pete and Tilly. On the South side were Benson's, Ritchie's, Mike Corbo's, Erickson's, Procino's, Pilla's, and Carletta's. The church was located on lower Payne Avenue just a block up from East Seventh Street—an old red brick structure. I remember there were wooden kneelers and when Mass was over, our knees had deep horizontal indentions in them caused by their rigid edges. A wedding on a Saturday was the most fun; we kids would get to the church just in time for the wedding party to exit. Guests would throw sugared almonds and rice. We had a great time scrambling for the candy.

My father's devotion to and love of St. Ambrose Church had brought our family to that part of the city in the first place. It was the smaller of the two Italian settlements in St. Paul, and my father and the other immigrants who had come from Benevento, Calabria, and the surrounding towns did not have the money, political clout, or know-how to plead for their own pastor. From its earliest history, 1919 to 1955, St. Ambrose was considered a mission church, with the pastor from the Upper Levee, Father Pioletti, in charge. When he came once a month to say Mass, church lasted much longer; Father would preach first in Italian and then he would give the same sermon in English.

St. Ambrose was the center of our spiritual lives and, to a great extent, our social lives as well. I remember the great St. Anthony festivals held in the unpaved church yard. There always were parades with a statue of different saints being honored at different times of the year. There were games of chance and raffles, hot dogs, and ice cream for the children. It was a day of only fun, and I was allowed to spend the pennies and nickels I was given in any way I wanted.

After 38 years, the Archdiocese finally named a pastor for St. Ambrose church. For those old-timers still living, it was a great accomplishment and a cause for great celebration. A new church was built on the corner of Minnehaha and Burr streets. As always, that small group of immigrants, now with grown children and grandchildren, worked so hard that by the time the church was ordered closed, it was totally paid for.

As I became an adult, I realized that the church was the first line of defense for our immigrant parents and grandparents; it was central in their efforts to organize and preserve their identity. It is the place where I learned about the importance of understanding what a heritage actually meant in a changing world.

And so when that church was ordered closed, it was like a part of us was being taken. There was a small effort to fight the edict, but it was ignored. Plans proceeded to sell the church; its present members were to attend the new St. Ambrose Church in Woodbury. Not many of us did so.

I spent a long time trying to find a new spiritual home. I found a wonderful one in St. Pascal Baylon on the East Side of Saint Paul. St. Ambrose had given me that true sense of community, but I am finding that St. Pascal's is giving me a wonderful new community with new friends, new commitments, and new challenges.

Speaking

Suzel Aburto

I am from Mexico, and then I came to live in Las Vegas, Nevada. When I started to work, I needed to pass the criminal record. I went with my cousin to the office because he could speak English, but the person who was at the front desk said that only I could ask for the record. But I didn't understand English and I didn't speak. She was angry and yelling at me, and I was scared and cried. So I decided to go to school to learn English. When I came to Saint Paul, I learned English, and now I can speak English a little bit and people don't get angry with me, and I don't live scared to speak with people.

A Big Change in the U.S.

Maria I.

When I got here in the U.S., I felt so happy because I met with my family and we were all together. It was very nice , but then time passed. I started missing my country—the weather and the food. On one hand I was happy with my family; on the other hand I was missing my country. I didn't like the weather. But one day, I said to myself, "When you were in your country, you wished to live in the U.S."

So, I encouraged myself. Then I started thinking in a different way. Finally, I am very happy now because I live with my husband and my kids and love Minnesota.

February

Midway Motel

You might find yourself here unexpectedly, with neither direction nor intent. Say you are just passing through, no fixed address, and the less you say about where you're from the more at ease others seem to be. Say your wife found the letter you had intended for the eyes of another, or that other received the words intended for no one. Now you lie in the in-between, locked out of that other part of yourself. Down the hall you can hear coughing, muffled conversations from TV screens, the clack-clacking of typewriter keys like tiny gunshots echoing. You lie in a bed worn down by others, the desire of others, green-gray light from the free-way below framing the edges of windows and doors. Sipping lukewarm beer at three in the morning, you wonder where it all went; and who or what it might be heading toward now.

Greg Watson

From *What Music Remains*, Published by Nodin Press, 2011.

☞ "When we die we get buried in a casket with our best suit, no money in our pockets, and none of the material things we craved in life. All we have is our honor."—Herb Brooks, hockey player and coach

FEBRUARY

S	M	T	W	T	F	S
			1	2	3	4
5	6	7	8	9	10	11
12	13	14	15	16	17	18
19	20	21	22	23	24	25
26	27	28	29			

February

30 Monday

Saint Paul Winter Carnival

🐛 January 30: Mary Copley, a Mechanic Arts High School literature teacher, was born today in 1884.

31 Tuesday

Saint Paul Winter Carnival

Minnesota Opera, *Werther*

1 Wednesday

Saint Paul Winter Carnival

2 Thursday

Groundhog Day

Saint Paul Winter Carnival

Minnesota Opera, *Werther*

Getting ready for urban gardening at Gordon Parks High School

3 Friday	Saint Paul Winter Carnival
	Saint Paul Chamber Orchestra

🏺 February 3: George Benz, early distiller and wholesale liquor dealer, was born today in 1862.

4 Saturday	Saint Paul Winter Farmers' Market
Mawlid Al-Nabi	Saint Paul Winter Carnival
	Minnesota Opera, *Werther*

5 Sunday	Minnesota Opera, *Werther*
	Saint Paul Winter Carnival
	Saint Paul Chamber Orchestra
	Minnesota RollerGirls (Bout)

A century ago, Saint Paul grocer Walter Deubener invented the grocery bag with handles, which he patented seven years later.

Photo Courtesy of Sisters of St. Joseph of Carondelet

Frank Hetznecker, school police superintendent, and Sister Carmella Hanggi speak to young recruits to the new Saint Paul Police Force

The First School Patrol

Margie Hendriksen

On February 17, 1921, Sister Carmella Hanggi, principal of the old Cathedral School in Saint Paul, organized the first school patrol crossing in the country, at Summit and Kellogg. Recent years had seen a huge increase in automobile traffic, which led to a large number of accidents involving motor vehicles hitting children on their way to and from school. So in 1920, Sister Hanggi, with the help of Lt. Henry Winterhalter of the Saint Paul Police Department, persuaded the City Council to pass an ordinance establishing the School Police Force, as it was then called. The practice quickly spread across the country as other cities adopted similar ordinances following Sister Hanggi's example.

My 101-year-old Aunt Lorene Geheren, née Rademacher, still remembers her days in the school patrol at the old Van Buren Elementary School, located then in the Dayton Bluff neighborhood. Members wore Sam Browne belts, which is a wide leather belt with a strap that goes over the right shoulder for support; these belts were widely used by police and military at the time. The school patrol members had an official badge displayed on the cross-piece of the belt. Originally, the patrol was only for boys. Lorene still remembers with pride being the first girl chosen for the city's patrol in the 1920s, shortly after it was started. Her assignment was to guard the area in front of the fire barn near the school and keep children away so that they would not be run down should the doors open and the firefighting rig come racing out.

Yes, it was called a fire barn, not a fire station. Back in the 1920s, horses, not internal combustion engines, powered the firefighting rigs. Lorene recalls that the fire barn was not as big as a modern fire station—but there was a pasture around back for the horses. Firemen (not called firefighters back then when there were only men) used a pole to slide down from their quarters on the top floor of the barn. But instead of jumping in a fire truck and taking off, they had to hitch up the horses.

Lorene still remembers with pride being the first girl chosen for the city's patrol in the 1920s, shortly after it was started. Her assignment was to guard the area in front of the fire barn near the school and keep children away so that they would not be run down should the doors open and the firefighting rig come racing out.

Lorene remembers that the other children obeyed her when she told them to stay away from the fire barn doors. Of course, there was that one rascally boy who would not, and she would have to chase him away.

Thanks to Sister Hanggi, Lorene, and her fellow school patrol members over the years, there have been no reports of children ever being killed in a crossing or area that was guarded by the school patrols. To honor Sister Hanggi for her role in establishing the first school patrol, a little monument stands on a knoll overlooking Kellogg Boulevard, and a commemorative plaque is mounted on a large cement base that holds a U.S. flag, across from the Saint Paul Cathedral, on the corner of John Ireland Boulevard and Dayton Avenue. It would be fitting to pay a visit and say "thanks" for this life-saving program.

↪ "Saint Paul presents to the eye the spectacle of a huge city clinging tenaciously to the east and alarmed over the danger of falling into the west."—Thomas Boyd (1898–1935), writer, Saint Paul bookstore owner

S	M	T	W	T	F	S
			1	2	3	4
5	6	7	8	9	10	11
12	13	14	15	16	17	18
19	20	21	22	23	24	25
26	27	28	29			

February

6 Monday

7 Tuesday

🏵 February 7: Robert E. Hess, labor union leader, was born today in 1918.

8 Wednesday

9 Thursday

Delivery of the Pioneer Press
A car coughs
gray exhaust
into the early morning.
In a hooded parka,
someone big
as a grizzly bear
plods through snow
to our door
and drops a bone.
A motor revs.
Red eyes of rear lights
blink, disappear.
Inside our warm house,
the newspaper thaws
to room temperature
releasing smells
of ink and oysters,
cold motor oil,
and a whiff of wet fur.
Margaret Hasse

Flamingo co-owner and author Shegitu Kebede answering the phone

10 Friday

🏛 February 10: Dr. Thomas R. Potts, president of the first Saint Paul Town Council, which became the City Council in 1854, was born today in 1810.

11 Saturday   Saint Paul Winter Farmers' Market

12 Sunday

Frederick McGhee, Saint Paul African American attorney, gave a speech this month in 1902 at the city's Lincoln League dinner.

Photo courtesy Kitty Gogins

Olga Zoltai

Saint Paul, a New World for Refugees

Kitty Gogins

Olga's breath condensed and froze as she briskly walked from the parking lot into the airport terminal. On this subzero February day in 1976, she was meeting a Laotian refugee family. A refugee herself, she had long ago adjusted to the frigid prairie winter.

My mother, Olga Zoltai, had fled Hungary near the end of World War II, minutes ahead of advancing Russian troops. After several years of struggling to survive in war-ravaged Europe, she immigrated to North America in 1949 as an indentured agricultural worker. Through perseverance and creativity, she learned to survive and even flourish. She was now case manager at the International Institute, and had resettled many Southeast Asian refugees since the Vietnam War ended in 1975. At the terminal, Olga joined two women from the sponsoring churches, their arms loaded with warm blankets and jackets; they were there to welcome the first Hmong family to resettle in Minnesota.

The family of ten huddled together, as if to ward off the unfamiliar surroundings. The head of the extended family, a young man, was dressed in a summer-weight suit; the women wore thin shirts, skirts, and sandals; the toddlers only tee shirts.

"Welcome to Minnesota," the three women said, smiling.

"It's nice to meet you," the young man replied. Having worked with American forces, he spoke fluent soldier English. The others looked shyly at their hosts, appearing somewhat bewildered.

"How are you?" Olga asked.

"Fine."

"Would you like a jacket?" she offered.

"No, thank you."

These were the Institute's first refugees from Laos, and Olga inquired about their background.

"We're Hmong," the young man said. Olga later learned that the Hmong had been important U.S. allies in Vietnam, rescuing downed American pilots in the mountainous jungle and serving as foot soldiers.

"We're Laotian citizens," he continued. "Our people live high in the mountains."

Before going outside, the women persuaded the family to put on jackets or blankets. Even with the added protection, the cold was painful and frightening. The newcomers tried to breathe, but the arctic air froze their windpipes.

Sights, smells, clothes, weather, language—nothing was familiar.

"Is this the ancient part of the city?" the head of the household asked on the ride to the Saint Paul apartment the sponsor had prepared.

"Yes," answered the sponsor.

"Where are the leaves on the trees?"

"The trees don't have leaves in winter. The sun only shines on us at an angle, so it's colder. Soon it'll be spring and the sun will shine on us more directly. It'll be warmer and the leaves will return."

Years later, the Hmong family told the sponsor that this explanation had sounded so bizarre at the time they thought she must be lying. They believed she had been too ashamed to admit that Agent Orange, a Vietnam War defoliant, had destroyed the foliage in Minnesota.

The apartment was ready with food, pans, beds, blankets—everything. But the building with central heat, indoor bathrooms, and an electric kitchen was strange and confusing to the refugees. Olga knew that, even with generous material support and ongoing help, the family's adjustment was going to be extremely difficult. She remembered how hard hers had been, and she hadn't come from a remote jungle, arriving in deep winter, in an enormous city with no residents of her ethnic group.

With time, the refugee family adjusted, even helping newer Hmong arrivals adapt to life on the prairie. By 2000, the census reported 38,000 Hmong in Minnesota, with two-thirds settling in Saint Paul.

I'm grateful that for over a century, Saint Paul has been a haven for refugees from many countries, and I'm proud of my mother's role in helping welcome newcomers who've come from ever farther reaches of the world.

Adapted from *My Flag Grew Stars* by Kitty Gogins
(independently published, 2009)

↪ "There were moments when I was bartending at O'Gara's and I would get another rejection letter and I'd think, what am I doing. Why am I doing this?" —Vince Flynn, writer and teacher

S	M	T	W	T	F	S
			1	2	3	4
5	6	7	8	9	10	11
12	13	14	15	16	17	18
19	20	21	22	23	24	25
26	27	28	29			

February

13 Monday
Saint Paul Almanac Lowertown Reading Jam

🐞 February 13: Mary GrandPré, illustrator of the Harry Potter series and other books, was born today in 1954.

14 Tuesday
Valentine's Day

15 Wednesday

16 Thursday
Saint Paul Chamber Orchestra

🐞 Feb 16: Ferdinand Willius, German American banker, was born today in 1830.

Light painting in Saint Paul tunnel

17 Friday	

18 Saturday	Saint Paul Winter Farmers' Market
	Saint Paul Chamber Orchestra
	Ordway Family: Children's Corner
	A Scottish Ramble

19 Sunday	A Scottish Ramble

🌸 February 19: Matt Morelli, Italian American grocer, was born today in 1916.

Pearson's Candy Company introduced
the Nut Goodie a century ago.

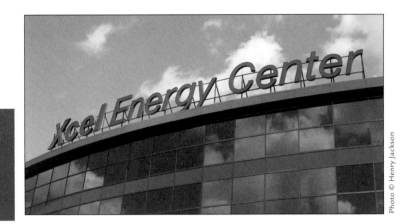

Xcel Energy Center

Oliver Swingen

Swoosh! A man in black, white, and yellow glides down the ice. As he reaches the defending zone, the small black puck he is handling is intercepted by the Minnesota Wild in green, red, and white. They pass it back and forth then finally shoot and score! This is the Pittsburgh Penguins vs. the Minnesota Wild at the Xcel Energy Center. And if you get tired of hockey, head down to the gift shop and get some ice cream in a helmet at a concession stand. And if you're lucky, you may even catch a hockey puck!

The St. Anthony Park Neighborhood

Noah Johnston

The St. Anthony Park neighborhood is a wonderful place. The Finnish Bistro is alive with the smell of fresh-baked cookies. SAP Elementary's spider tree reaches up toward the sky as if to embrace it, a beautiful sight. The Saint Paul Public Library looms over the Como and Carter intersection, its vast bookshelves and countless volumes beckoning. College Park's gigantic crater-like valley pulls you down like a huge vacuum. This is my home. This is where I live. This is St. Anthony Park.

Photo © Axel

1986 Saint Paul Winter Carnival ice palace, taken from Cherokee Heights

Carnival

Susan Solomon

I was a young Philadelphian, freshly divorced, and looking for a new city in which to start my new life. I was tired of rat-filled alleys and dirty heaps of black snow that lined the streets like piles of coal. At a library, I happened upon a travel magazine. And on those glossy, full-color pages, I spotted a picture of the Saint Paul Winter Carnival. The photo stopped my heart. The ice castle lit up the night like a neon rainbow. The air around the castle glowed brilliant colors, and the blocks of ice were impossibly beautiful, translucent, and heavy as God. This was nothing short of a winter masterpiece. The frozen palace promised wonderful possibilities and magical thinking. Plus, it was surrounded by clean, soft, *fresh* snow. I made up my mind then and there: I had to live in Saint Paul, because any city that would build a sparkling ice castle every year was definitely the place I would want to claim as home.

Fifteen years later, I am still here. And though our city most definitely does *not* build a pretty ice palace yearly, it does not matter. It does not matter.

➪ On Feb. 20, 100 years ago, William Boss, founder of the Specialty Mfg. Co., which still operates in Saint Paul, received a patent for a clothesline reel. Boss's other inventions include a lawn mower grass collector and a garden hose reel.

FEBRUARY						
S	M	T	W	T	F	S
			1	2	3	4
5	6	7	8	9	10	11
12	13	14	15	16	17	18
19	20	21	22	23	24	25
26	27	28	29			

20 Monday

World Day of Social Justice

Presidents' Day

21 Tuesday

International Mother Language Day

Mardis Gras

🐾 February 21: Josias King, first Civil War volunteer, was born in 1832.

22 Wednesday

Ash Wednesday

Minnesota State High School League Girls' Hockey Tournament

23 Thursday

Minnesota State High School League Girls' Hockey Tournament

Photo © Tobechi Tobechukwu

Genocide Moms Project—Ms. Angel

24 Friday

Fourth Friday at the Movies

Minnesota State High School League
Girls' Hockey Tournament

Saint Paul Chamber Orchestra

25 Saturday

Saint Paul Winter Farmers' Market

Minnesota State High School League
Girls' Hockey Tournament

Global Hot Dish Variety Show

26 Sunday

Saint Paul Chamber Orchestra

Rose Ensemble

The hip-hop group Heiruspecs, which started at Central High
School, performed a benefit concert in 2010 for a scholarship
fund they established.

Photo courtesy Nimo Farah

Nimo with her mother, sister, and niece

The Titanic Tower

Nimo Farah

"*Dakhaso, dhakso,*" my mom is screaming, standing at the door of her Minneapolis home.

"*Hooyo,*" I whine, "You can't rush tea! You know that, *Hooyo.*"

It is going to be a long day, and I need tea to keep me going. Every Sunday I'm dipped into Somali stories and rituals with my mom, my "*hooyo,*" and her lady relatives and friends. I'm finally old enough to hang out with my mom, sit in on her chats, and maybe even say a few words. My Sunday roles are well defined: I am the driver and the tea maker. And if any of the extended relatives needs help with translations and filling out paperwork, I'm good for that too.

Our final Sunday destination is Mama Warsan's apartment on the ninth floor of a place we call the Titanic but which is really the Sky Line Tower in Saint Paul. Tall and visible from Highway 94 at Lexington, the Titanic is truly a village in the sky. Many East Africans, predominantly Ethiopians and Somalis, reside there. I have relatives living on many of the floors, taking care of each other and raising their children together. My mom would love to live there, too, if she were not terrified of elevators and escalators.

Mama Warsan is an elderly aunt who was a prominent businesswoman in Somalia. She doesn't like anyone making tea besides me and says I have a sweet tea-making hand. If I could, I would live in a cup of sweet Somali tea! And even though Mama Warsan is eighty-three years old, she has a girlish laugh and a young, generous spirit that brings everyone together. She says I bring out the young girl inside her, and I think she's the most elegant woman I've ever met.

As usual, the Titanic's telecom is broken, so someone has to come down to let us in, and the elevator is slow. While we wait, I get a call on my mobile phone from Mama Warsan. She tells me to go buy tea ingredients from the *halal* grocery store across the street, then to pick up an aunt named Faduma and three of her daughters, who've just arrived in the country.

In the store, I gather cinnamon, ginger, cardamom, cloves, and Lipton tea bags. I also grab some *xalwo* and *sambus*. Normally I ask the cashier to write the bill on Mama Warsan's page on the tab book. But today I have a little cash and feel generous, so I pay. Today is also a potluck feast to welcome a newly arrived relative to the country.

We will be at Mama Warsan's apartment, furnished with imported cushions and Turkish carpets, until the late evening. *Uunsi* incense mingles with the scent from spicy tea, lingering throughout the apartment and the whole ninth floor. The women will be buying and selling imported garments and exchanging gifts and gossip. They celebrate, sing, dance, recite poetry, talk, and chant away their worries. I keep the tea boiling and being served. The door to Mama Warsan's will remain open.

Some time ago, a rumor spread that the Sky Line Tower had reached its expiration date and was about to collapse.

The rumor got people so frightened that they showed up at the next resident meeting, which none of them had attended before. The building's community room was filled to capacity, and the overflow of people lined up in the hallway. My aunts had invited me to come and translate, so I was there as rants and concerns reached all corners of the room.

An American woman who works there stood up to greet the residents. "We are surprised by this attendance. Normally we have an agenda, but this evening we want to listen to your concerns and answer your questions." An elderly Somali woman stood up, cleared her throat loudly, and began speaking.

"Me lived in this building ten years, come Saint Paul, live here. Now me, friends, family, all scared!" She looked around, scanning and circling the room with her hands. "We here because we hear story, the building go down soon." She gestured collapse with her hands.

"Like *Titanic* go down, the tall building go down soon. We afraid of sleep, like *Titanic,* we die, finish! Sorry, English broken, but me have to speak for self because me scared, understand?"

Everyone applauded in agreement with her.

It turned out that because the elevators had been getting slower and slower, people's fears turned into stories and rumors of collapse. At the meeting, residents were assured that the building was not going to go down. Since that day, among Somalis, the building has been called the Titanic Tower. Every Sunday , the Titanic, a village in Saint Paul, keeps me connected to Somalia.

Photo © Media Mike Hazard

Rick Cardenas

The Knife

Media Mike Hazard

Nicknamed "the knife," Rick Cardenas cuts through crap.
He helps people see disability oppression and how to fight it. He connects civil rights, disability rights, and self-advocacy. Co-director of ACT since 1998, if you look behind most of Minnesota's key legislative victories for people with developmental disabilities, you'll probably spot this rabid gray-haired activist rolling round.

"There's no budget crisis, there is a crisis of values."

Pel Ray Moo

My First Day in Saint Paul

Pel Ray Moo

February 17, 2009, was my first day in Saint Paul. When I arrived here, on the first day, I was very surprised because I saw snow, and I saw that the trees didn't have leaves. In my country I never saw snow. When I saw snow, I felt surprised and happy. In my country, there was always a war. We didn't have freedom. I like the United States of America because people have equal rights. But living in the U.S. is not easy. People speak very fast and it's hard to understand English. There are many new words to learn. My goal is to understand 80 percent of the English I hear. English is very important in my life. Right now I improve my English in the Intermediate class at Arlington Hills School.

Blanket toss, Saint Paul Winter Carnival parade, circa 1956

Winter Carnival Parade
Leslie Walters

My family always loved the Saint Paul Winter Carnival. From the coronations of Boreas Rex and Aurora, his Queen of the Snows, to the parades, treasure hunts, and sled dog races, we took it all in with great relish and excitement.

Since January was my birthday month, the carnival held special appeal for me. So, in 1960, it was a huge thrill when my father, the chief fundraiser for the March of Dimes, secured me a ride on that organization's float in the Torchlight Parade as a surprise gift for turning six years old.

Like a lot of little girls, I dreamed of being a princess and riding on one of the beautiful floats that glided through the snowy streets each winter. Aching with anticipation for the big night to arrive, I envisioned myself in a beautiful gown and tiara, practicing my wave and smile in front of the mirror.

My mother followed the treasure hunt clues religiously in the city's daily newspapers. We kids accompanied her where we joined scores of treasure hunters churning the snow, searching for that hidden medallion. My father, slightly oblivious to this great ritual, continued to walk our two golden retrievers near Warner Road every evening. When one of the dogs fetched Dad a crumpled paper bag, he tossed it away without thought. How exasperating when, four days into the carnival, Boreas's treasure was found in a ratty paper bag just off Warner Road.. The prize was $2,500.

At last the big night, one of the winter's coldest, arrived. My mother bundled me for sub-zero temps including insulated boots and a swath of scarves. This attire was not what I had fantasized when dad promised me a ride on that magical float.

When we arrived at the State Capitol staging area, we were met by a trailer wrapped in purple streamers, carrying a princess in stretch pants and ski jacket, who was trying to keep her teeth from chattering. She was accompanied by a feisty dairy cow the March of Dimes would raffle off to bolster their fundraising efforts. I was to ride up front with the truck driver as he towed this homely "float" along. I was crestfallen, and my father promptly gave me a pep talk and a promise of pie and hot chocolate after we met back up at the finish line,

Amidst the glitter and sparkle that made for an enchanted winter night, the parade made its way down St. Peter Street. As clowns and vulcans cavorted through the crowd, school marching bands blared and bouncing girls were tossed high in the air.

As we reached the holding area, our prize cow butted our pretty princess hard into the trailer's sideboards. Parade workers gathered around the injured princess. This was scary, but when I didn't see my parents, panic set in. Now I was a little girl alone in the big nighttime city. Fortunately, March of Dimes volunteers Natalie and Court took me on a search of downtown establishments, looking for my parents.

First on the tour were the Saint Paul and Lowry hotels, both royalty headquarters, where we searched party room after party room. Members of the Royal House were imbibing and carrying on with festive gusto. What a dazzling dream come true as the Prince of the South Wind pulled me up on his lap and gave me a special carnival button. A bevy of visiting princesses provided glamorous comfort and assurance to me. And local television personality Mel Jass patted my head on his way out the door. Maybe things weren't so bad after all.

It was approaching midnight when we made the rounds of Saint Paul cafés and night clubs packed with revelers. We scouted Jimaty's Bar on St. Peter. No luck. On to Gallivan's where we were rushed by Vulcanus Rex, who planted greasy kisses on Natalie and me. Frightened and excited, I vowed to never wash off the black grease paint.

I was getting mighty sleepy, wanting to go home with my folks. The evening's luster began to wear off. Court thought another thorough check of the Saint Paul Hotel was in order. Finally, I spotted my mother frantically calling out to me, rushing to sweep me into her arms. We joined my father, always the fundraiser, working the room at the Old Gopher Grill.

The Winter Carnival was so magical for me that year that it didn't even matter that there wasn't an ice palace. It turned out that the March of Dimes princess was not badly hurt, just a bit shaken up. And, fittingly, a dairy farmer won the cow.

Talk

Sharon Chmielarz

To say something
and have someone near enough
to hear,
maybe even comment,

something small
like, "it's windy out"
when closing the bedroom blinds for the night—

what was once so possible,
common, redundant,
seems to be now
some passionate miracle.

Tomorrow is Divine Mercy
a woman tells me
standing outside the locked church.
Tomorrow the door will be open.

(Venu: St. Agnes Church in Frogtown)

March

March

it is impossible to miss the red bird
the only ember alive
this snowy March
this gray March
this bitter March
this windblown
    dismal
    pewter
    listless
    day

Carol Pearce Bjorlie

⤳ "For each of us who appear to have had a successful experiment there are many to whom their own experiments seem barren and negative."—Melvin Calvin (1911–1997), Saint Paul native and 1961 winner of the Nobel Prize in Chemistry

S	M	T	W	T	F	S
				1	2	3
4	5	6	7	8	9	10
11	12	13	14	15	16	17
18	19	20	21	22	23	24
25	26	27	28	29	30	31

27 Monday

28 Tuesday

🏵 February 28: Sidney Applebaum, well-known businessman, was born today in 1924.

29 Wednesday

1 Thursday   Minnesota State High School League
                          Boys' Wrestling Tournament

Protest display concerning small business survival with light rail construction

2 Friday Boys' Wrestling Tournament

March 2: Jerome Hill, filmmaker and philanthropist, was born today in 1905.

3 Saturday Saint Paul Winter Farmers' Market
Minnesota Opera, *Lucia di Lammermoor*
Boys' Wrestling Tournament

4 Sunday Minnesota Opera, *Lucia di Lammermoor*

Eight-year-old Josephine Labon of 566 Rice Street celebrated her
birthday Feb. 29th in 1916 with a party attended by 14 children.

Keg delivery wagon, Hamm's Brewery

Meridel LeSueur Recalls
Swede Hollow Before Prohibition

Patrick Coleman

LeSueur was perhaps Minnesota's most famous proletarian writer, so it is not surprising that she wrote about the humble people of Saint Paul's Swede Hollow. The following selection was written during Prohibition, ushered in by passage of the Volstead Act in 1919.

Meridel LeSueur, "Beer Town," *Life in the United States: A Collection of Narratives of Contemporary American Life from First-Hand Experience or Observation* (Charles Scribner's Sons, 1933); pages 31–33, 40.

I should have had a bad life. Any reformer would say so. I was bred, born and raised in the shadow of the old-time, pre-Volstead brewery. Below it, in the shadow, lived the Germans, the Irish, the Swedes, and it rose upon the hill like a castle and from it night and day came the yeasty odor of beer....

The resemblance to a feudal castle was increased when later Mr. Hamm's sons took unto themselves wives, and his daughters were wedded and he built beside his own Rhine mansion other preposterous edifices looking down over the town and the Mississippi.

Below across the tracks on the other side lay what was called the Hollow. Here lived the man-power that manned the brewery. They lived in homemade houses that looked as if they were built from scraps like a family quilt, but they had an intimate aspect, for each man had put his house together like a piece of embroidery, with the color of an old sign and a flash of tin, but they were tight and neat with smoke curling cosily [sic] from the slanting chimneys in winter. A stream ran through the Hollow, and over this lovely thread of water sat the outhouses, each delicate and crazy shamble propped over the stream on planks. They tipped over easily in a wind or when pushed. In the back of each house there was a small patch of garden set out crookedly, and usually a rickety fence marked the boundaries of a tiny square of "lawn" in front. The streets were unpaved and in spring full of water. ...

In the morning we were awakened by the rumbling of the beer-wagons going out loaded to the town. The streets leading to the brewery were of cobblestones because the huge beer wagons were death on ordinary pavement. The clatter of horses and the rumble of the heavily burdened wagons made a fierce rumble and clanging, and half in our dreams we started up seeing the splendid horses treading sparks and hearing that strange sound of hoofs beating out and away in the morning. We ran to the windows and looked up the hill and saw the brewery rising all safe and stable with the cattle in the barns, the men climbing up to work, the animals waking and lowing, the drivers driving out their wagons of beer, cracking their whips, crying out to each other, swearing full-mouthed oaths, the horses snorting and backing and galloping off, rumbling the great wagons into town. We saw the complete, the substantial, feudal city flashing up in the morning air. ...

The Hollow and its wreckage still lie below the track, the outhouses still over the stream. Hamm's Brewery is still there, its Rabelaisian power greatly reduced by what is called the Eighteenth Amendment.

March

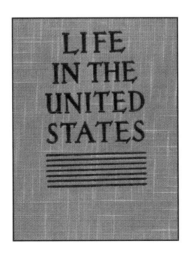

⇨ "As we sacrifice our protections under the Fourth Amendment and our civil liberties on the altar of fear, we move closer to George Orwell's vision of an all-knowing government that uses surveillance to control its citizens."—Christopher Valen, Saint Paul mystery writer

MARCH

S	M	T	W	T	F	S
				1	2	3
4	5	6	7	8	9	10
11	12	13	14	15	16	17
18	19	20	21	22	23	24
25	26	27	28	29	30	31

March

5 Monday

Minnesota RollerGirls (Bout)

6 Tuesday

Minnesota Opera, *Lucia di Lammermoor*

🏵 March 6: Elizabeth Decourcy, first woman on the Saint Paul City Council, was born today in 1899.

7 Wednesday

Minnesota State High School League Boys' Hockey Tournament

8 Thursday
Holi (Hindu)
International Women's Day
Purim

Minnesota Opera, *Lucia di Lammermoor*
Minnesota State High School League Boys' Hockey Tournament

Border Tacos truck on University Avenue

9 Friday

Purim

Minnesota State High School League
Boys' Hockey Tournament

🐾 March 9: Frank J. Dixon, internationally known immunologist, was born today in 1920.

10 Saturday

Saint Paul Winter Farmers' Market

Minnesota Opera, *Lucia di Lammermoor*

Minnesota State High School League
Boys' Hockey Tournament

Saint Paul Chamber Orchestra

11 Sunday

Daylight Saving Time begins

Minnesota Opera, *Lucia di Lammermoor*

Irish Day of Dance

Henry A. Castle—merchant, newspaperman, and historian—
published his three-volume *History of St. Paul and Vicinity* in 1912.

March 57

"Centennial gesture"; men for whom certain Minnesota lakes were named: Max Shulman, Daniel D. Mich, Herman Salisbury, Sig Michelson with Governor Orville Freeman

How Max Shulman Got to College

Steve Trimble

Max Shulman (1919–1988) grew up in a Jewish community in Saint Paul's Selby-Dale neighborhood. After graduating from Central High School, he earned a journalism degree from the University of Minnesota. His writings were invariably humorous and were published in novels and magazines. He eventually became a successful writer for theater and television. His novel *Potatoes are Cheaper* was a portrayal of life in the city in the late 1930s.

Max Shulman, *Potatoes Are Cheaper* (Doubleday and Company, 1971): 1–4, 23

Oh sure, potatoes were cheaper all right, and so were tomatoes, just like Eddie Cantor kept singing on the radio, but who the hell had money to buy any except maybe Eddie Cantor?

But finally, thank God, we got a break. On March the 14th, 1936, Pa went down to the St. Paul Public Library just like he did every day as usual. Not that he was such a great reader; in fact he could hardly read at all, not English anyhow, except maybe for eviction and foreclosure notices. He could read Yiddish all right, but that didn't help because there were no Yiddish books in the St. Paul Public Library. But Pa went every day anyhow. What else could he do? He didn't have a job to go to, and if he stayed home Ma would give him the whammy all day long. So where else could he find that was (a) warm; and (b) free?

So on this March the 14th, 1936, we're talking about, Pa started walking into the library as usual, but he never got inside because he slipped on an icy step and fractured his tailbone. Or as my mother told the whole neighborhood, "He fell and broke his ass, my smart husband."

Naturally we sued the city. My cousin Herbie who got out of law school five years ago took the case—his first case, as it happened. But he was confident. "Don't worry, Aunt Pearl," he told my mother. "We got 'em dead to rights. You'll collect fifty thousand minimum."

Herbie figured a little high. The actual settlement came to $125 of which the doctor grabbed twenty. Still and all, it was the biggest chunk of money we'd seen since my father took up unemployment back in 1929, and we had a family conference at five o'clock one evening to decide what to do with it. ...

"So who got a suggestion?" said Ma.

Pa stepped forward. Pa used to be a house painter back in the olden days when he was working and this is what he suggested: He'd take the hundred dollars and get his Plymouth back from the finance company. Then he'd drive around St. Paul looking for houses that needed painting and when he found one he'd try to sell the people a paint job.

Ma gave him a look. "Very intelligent," she said. "But I got a question. When a house needs painting, it's because they ain't got money to paint. So how are they gonna pay you, Dr. I.Q.?" ...

Now my sister Libbie stepped forward. ... "I think I should have the money," said Libbie, "so I can buy some decent clothes and get invited to nice parties and meet the right kind of people."

Ma gave Libbie a look. "Very intelligent," said Ma. "But I got a question. Who among your shlepper friends is gonna invite you to a nice party?"

Libbie couldn't think of an answer so naturally she started in crying. Ma turned to me next. "Well, breadwinner," she said, "I suppose you think you should have the money too?" ...

"This is gonna be better than you think," I said. "I will go to college."

What a bombshell! College? Who ever heard of such a thing? First of all I was twenty years old and already two years out of high school. Second, the highest mark I ever got in high school was a B-minus and that was in tin shop. And third, even if you were a genius and came out of college with a lawyer degree or a doctor degree you'd still starve to death these days like everybody else.

They gave me a look, all of them, not just Ma, but Pa and Libbie too. They just stood and stared at me like they couldn't imagine where in the world I got such a nutty idea. ...

"In college I will have a chance to meet rich girls," I said, "and let's face it, the only way this family is ever gonna see any money is if I marry it."

Then I stepped back and waited for Ma to give me the whammy.

But she just stood and rubbed her chin for a couple minutes. "Makes sense," she said finally.

⇨ "How did the writing bug bite me? Maybe this way. My father was first a high school teacher, then a librarian. ... My mother is a born teller of folk-tales. So I started life with a book in my hand and well-said words in my ear. "—Mabel Seeley (1903–1991), Saint Paul mystery writer

MARCH

S	M	T	W	T	F	S
				1	2	3
4	5	6	7	8	9	10
11	12	13	14	15	16	17
18	19	20	21	22	23	24
25	26	27	28	29	30	31

12 Monday   *Saint Paul Almanac* Lowertown Reading Jam

🐞 March 12: Patricia Hampl, writer and teacher, was born today in 1946.

13 Tuesday

14 Wednesday

🐞 March 14: Maud Borup, purveyor of fine chocolates, was born today in 1877.

15 Thursday   IMDA St. Patrick's Day Celebration

The new Frogtown Square at University and Dale

16 Friday

17 Saturday   Saint Paul Winter Farmers' Market

St. Patrick's Day   Saint Paul Chamber Orchestra

St. Patrick's Day Parade

St. Patrick's Day Irish Ceili Dance

18 Sunday

In 1942, Saint Paul's Seeger Refrigerator Company stopped making refrigerators and began to manufacture war materials instead.

Keys Café in downtown Saint Paul. Keys is also on Raymond Avenue.

Keys Café

Arlo Beckman

When I lived in California, my favorite restaurant was Tomatina's. Then I moved to Minnesota, and I went to Keys. Keys is on Raymond Avenue, and it is my favorite breakfast restaurant in Minnesota! Usually, we only go there for special events. Once, my friends from California visited us, and we went to Keys. That was the second time I had been there, and it was better than the first time

Every time I have been to Keys, I've ordered buttermilk pancakes with eggs and a sausage. Their pancakes are soft, buttery, golden, and huge! Whenever I get the pancakes, I always expect them to be smaller than they are. They're practically as big as the plate and almost as thick too. Though, for some reason, it just makes them taste better.

I also like their side of bacon and their cinnamon caramel rolls. The bacon is super good and has just the right amount of fat. The caramel rolls are tall and puffy, with caramel and butter oozing down the sides. The people there make their own strawberry jelly to go on toast, and the flavor goes well with the toast.

When you order eggs, they let you choose if you want your eggs scrambled, over easy, etc.

Keys is a great restaurant and I recommend it for any restaurant outing. Don't be afraid to try something new every time. Don't worry, I bet you'll love it!

A Listing of Gravelly and Numinous Items at Carol Bly's House, Juno Ave., St. Paul

Eric Charles Hansen

Over her unmade cot	Xeroxed copies of the brain and its six creasy folds.
Tacked up in the WC	several theories competing all at once on moral development.
The framed poster of	the weeds painting we remember means our dumb, rainy lives can be beautiful, too.
The dining room table	whose leaves could draw out to fit twenty-seven social workers and writers.
Across the unimportant linoleum in the kitchen	the back door's bright glass: spruce trees.
All gone. The house has been listed and emptied—except for	the books
on shelves built with	third-rate do-it-yourself carpentry. Gorgeous,
gorgeous. Still, who will get the books?	Maupassant? D.H. Lawrence? *Tomcat's Wife* and Country Letters?

➯ "Who are we and where do we come from? I consider myself fortunate that we are coming to the U.S. as a community. People are starting to learn how important it is to keep memories of where you come from and that they add a lot to this country."—Bryan Thao Worra, Laotian American writer in Saint Paul

MARCH

S	M	T	W	T	F	S
				1	2	3
4	5	6	7	8	9	10
11	12	13	14	15	16	17
18	19	20	21	22	23	24
25	26	27	28	29	30	31

19 Monday

March Melt
Bereft snow geese clutter
the brilliant blue above,
ravenous warmth sucks
the snow beneath my skis,
Crosby Lake ages into
mottled colors of old lady skin.
My own arms shed
their cashmere cocoons.
Kathleen Vellenga

20 Tuesday

Spring Equinox

🐝 March 20: Dr. Arthur B. Ancker, longtime superintendent of the City and County Hospital, was born today in 1851.

21 Wednesday

International Day for the
Elimination of Racial Discrimination

Naw-Ruz (Baha-i)

22 Thursday

World Water Day

Entrance to the Saint Paul Farmers' Market plaza

23 Friday   Fourth Friday at the Movies

World Meteorological Day

🐾 March 23: Arthur Farwell—composer, conductor and music publisher—was born today in 1872.

24 Saturday   Saint Paul Winter Farmers' Market

Saint Paul Chamber Orchestra

25 Sunday

🐾 March 25: Mabel Seeley, popular mystery writer, was born today in 1903.

The Twin City Protection League, which eventually became the Twin Cities branch of the NAACP, was organized on March 25 in 1912.

Patricia Black at Aurora/St. Anthony Neighborhood Development Corporation offices

Oreo Cookie
Ms. Patricia Black

I am proud to make Saint Paul my home, as I feel the African American people of Saint Paul are strong, proud people.

The first sixteen years of my life were spent in Minneapolis in a poor White neighborhood. My siblings and I were the only Black children in the schools we attended. Yes, there was a great deal of prejudice in our community. Little children don't know hate; they have to be taught. Even though my White friends' parents may not have liked their children being friends with us, most of them accepted it because they loved their children more than they hated us.

Some families were not accepting and forbade their children to be friends with us, and would beat their kids when they found that they had played with us anyway. I was really hurt when my best friend showed up totally bruised because of our friendship. Nevertheless, she refused to end our friendship.

Even though I enjoyed my childhood and had lots of friends, I longed for the day I could be with and associate with Black people. That day came when I entered Minneapolis Central High School. To my surprise, I found I was not welcome into their group. I felt like the little lion cub, Elsa, who was raised by humans and longed to be with her own kind when she came of age. She was not welcome because the wild lions could smell the humans on her and her behavior was different. I was not accepted because my speech and mannerisms were White. I was an Oreo cookie, Black on the outside and White on the inside. The Black kids detected it right away. I had to learn to be Black. For two hard years I worked at becoming Black.

In 1953, there was an upheaval in my family, and my siblings and I were separated and went to different foster homes. I came to Saint Paul as a foster child. My new foster parents were very nice people with a son and a daughter. They introduced me to their friends who were reluctant to accept me. I just couldn't go through trying to fit in with people who didn't accept me again.

I played the piano and my foster family didn't have one, so I used to go over to St. James AME Church, on Central and Dale Street, to use the piano. I met a group of teenagers that hung out there. They were very friendly and accepted me. That was the beginning of the happiest years of my life. I have a hard time understanding people who put down foster homes, but maybe mine was unique. Maybe God blessed me with a really nice foster home and a personality that gets along with most everyone. I remained in my foster home until I was twenty-one and got married. Later, I found that that is very unusual, as foster children are required to leave at age eighteen.

My new friends and I spent many happy hours hanging out at Field's Drugstore, Hallie Q. Brown Center, and St. James AME Church. St. James had a youth program, which kept us occupied.

It was a wonderful time of life. I look back on those days when Black people did not have equal opportunity and were forced to live in the "Black Belt," now known as the ghetto. There was freedom in our community. Our community was free of crime, drugs, and prostitution, and no one would bother you if you were walking down the street late at night.

In 1980, burglaries, drugs, and prostitution moved in to our community. Ron Pauline founded Aurora/St. Anthony NDC (Neighborhood Development Corporation), to address the problem. He taught us pride in where we live. He pointed out that we have prime property in this city because you could get on the bus and go anywhere in the Twin Cities you wanted to go. Everything we needed was within our reach by bus. I am proud of my neighborhood, and raised two fine children in this community.

When people recognized de facto segregation, many Black people moved out of the neighborhood and into White neighborhoods and suburbs. I stayed right here, because I never wanted my children to grow up not knowing their own people or feeling that the only way they can achieve is through White people. Ghetto is a word that means a place where people live because of race, creed, or color. It does not mean that you are ignorant, uneducated, or poor. No one should feel shame because they live in a ghetto. The shame is on the people who put you there.

I continue to work with Aurora/St. Anthony NDC because not only is it working to preserve this historic community, but, also, it teaches Black people pride in themselves. That is very important.

Cynthia (right) and her sister on the way to Pig's Eye Island City Dump

Pig's Eye Island Adventure

Cynthia Schreiner Smith

When I was growing up near Mounds Park during the fifties and sixties, fresh milk was delivered to our stoop like clockwork; however, no one came to haul away the refuse. A big, rusty metal drum in our back yard received the trash instead. When it got full, my father lit it on fire. Items you couldn't burn—bottles, cans, old plastic toys—were driven to the Pig's Eye Island City Dump.

My brother almost always got to go with Dad to the dump, a fact that he lorded over his little sisters. But sometimes we got to go too. Dad would throw the trash in the trunk of his Chevy and we'd fly down steep Warner Road toward the Mississippi River. At the bottom of the hill, he'd take a hairpin left turn onto the gravel road that led to Pig's Eye Island and the dump. My father paid fifty cents at the gate for the privilege of adding to the mountain of trash.

Afterward, we'd continue farther onto the island to visit the farm of my Uncle Mickey. We called him Uncle Bum-Bum because he lived on an Island called Pig's Eye, beyond the dump, past the municipal sewage treatment plant, and across many railroad tracks with boxcars hiding hobos. I remember one visit when all three of us kids were in the car. As we passed the sewage treatment plant, we somehow convinced Dad to stop and see if we could take a peek inside. Being young children, we were fascinated by all things pertaining to toilets. I'm sure the man inside was surprised to see our little family asking for a tour. Most people had no interest in the graphic details of disposing with bathroom waste. Receiving a warm invitation to come inside, we were met by an enthralling maze of pipes, vats, and spigots—and an unpleasant odor. The worker kept up a running patter of mesmerizing facts regarding Saint Paul's sewage system. Eventually we were led into a huge room with a gigantic open pool that glistened a beautiful golden yellow. It took us a moment to figure out what it was. My brother gleefully threatened to dunk his little sisters in it. We screamed with appropriate giggling and fear.

The tour ended with a trip to the office, where the man kept a strange collection in a little glass case. He saved unusual items that people accidentally flushed down the biffy—most commonly coins, rings, and false teeth. The most interesting thing was a glass eye. The thought of some poor person's eyeball popping out and flushing away horrified and delighted us all at once.

The tour ended with a trip to the office, where the man kept a strange collection in a little glass case. He saved unusual items that people accidentally flushed down the biffy—most commonly coins, rings, and false teeth. The most interesting thing was a glass eye. The thought of some poor person's eyeball popping out and flushing away horrified and delighted us all at once.

At home, we breathlessly told our mother about our exciting trip to the Pig's Eye sewage treatment plant. Mom just shook her head, giving Dad that "What were you thinking?" look. But all she said was: "Sounds wonderful, kids. I hope you remembered to thank the nice man."

Aghast, I realized I had not. I felt horrible the rest of the night. He had been so nice, so proud of his unappreciated job. Lying in bed, I fretted and fretted, thinking about the nice man and his collection of flushed items. Suddenly, inspiration hit! I jumped out of bed, wrote him a neatly printed thank-you note, carried it to the bathroom, and flushed it. Confident he would get my note in the morning, I fell blissfully asleep.

Mounds Theatre today

Photo © Pa Yong Xiong

The Mounds Theatre and Me

Greg Cosimini

I've lived in Dayton's Bluff just a few blocks from the Mounds Theatre all my life, but not for the whole life of the Mounds Theatre. It was built in 1922, and I was born twenty-nine years later.

The Mounds started out as a silent movie house. It was billed as "The Pride of Dayton's Bluff." It had a small stage for vaudeville acts. Local musicians played in an orchestra pit.

The first "talkie" was shown at the Mounds in late March 1929—on what would eventually become my birthday. The movie was *My Man,* starring Fannie Brice. The Mounds was remodeled in the 1930s, receiving air conditioning, an exterior ticket booth, and a fancy marquee.

The theater had a close call in the late 1940s, when Highway 12 cut through Dayton's Bluff, destroying all of the businesses and homes across the street from it. Surviving that, the Mounds underwent a major renovation in 1950. Its brick exterior was covered with stucco, its vertical sign and marquee were replaced with a horizontal, twinkling "MOUNDS" sign and lighted attraction board, and most of its interior was "modernized."

I'm pretty sure the first movie I saw at the Mounds was the original *Shaggy Dog* in 1959. After that I saw so many movies there that it is difficult to remember many specific ones. At first they were mostly Disney flicks. One Sunday in 1962, our family hiked over to the Mounds in a snowstorm to see Disney's *Babes in Toyland.* Eventually, I graduated to more grown-up movies, including the first James Bond films, *Dr. No, From Russia with Love,* and the greatest of them all, *Goldfinger.*

I don't remember the final movie I saw at the Mounds, but it was on a rainy night and a section of the auditorium was roped off because the roof was leaking. The Mounds had fallen on hard times. It finally closed in July 1967.

The Mounds sat empty for decades but there were rumors something was going on inside. Strangest of all, it was always listed in the phone book. I'd occasionally call the number, but no one ever answered. Finally, in 1988, I wrote to Don Boxmeyer, a columnist for the *St. Paul Pioneer Press*, asking him if he knew anything about it. To my surprise, he wrote an entire column in reply. The building was owned by George Hardenbergh, a former Ramsey County commissioner and a genuine character. He collected old theater organs and had moved them into the Mounds, planning to get them assembled and working. But he never did.

At a 1997 neighborhood meeting about a new streetscape for the area, architect drawings showed the Mounds restored to its former glory. But these were just drawings. There were no actual plans to do anything. When I asked about the current state of the Mounds Theatre, someone said it was infested with rats and would be torn down very soon. But it wasn't.

The Mounds started out as a silent movie house. It was billed as "The Pride of Dayton's Bluff." It had a small stage for vaudeville acts. Local musicians played in an orchestra pit.

In early 2000, I attended another neighborhood meeting and met Raeann Ruth, the executive director of the nonprofit Portage for Youth. She mentioned George Hardenbergh was donating the Mounds Theatre to her organization, and she was in the process of raising money to renovate it. I wrangled a tour of the building. Amazingly, the interior of the theater was still intact, buried under an incredible number of organ pipes and other stuff. Only a couple of light bulbs illuminated the interior. I started working on getting more lights fixed and have been volunteering at the Mounds ever since.

The Mounds officially reopened in October 2003 as a general-purpose venue for movies, plays, dinner theater, and other activities. I once again started watching movies at the Mounds, and finally got to see *The Wizard of Oz* on a full-sized movie screen.

The Mounds will probably still be going strong long after I am gone. Or maybe I won't be—gone, that is. The Mounds is purported to be the most haunted place in the Twin Cities. If so, I might drop in for a visit.

Life in the United States and Life in My Country

Paw Ree Say

March

My name is Paw Ree Say. I was born in Burma in Bo Ka Lay City, and I have two brothers and four sisters. I have been in Saint Paul since January 30, 2008.

When I arrived at the airport my sister and her family came to the airport to pick up my family, and when I saw them, they said "Welcome to Saint Paul." My first surprise was the snow. Before I came to the United States, I heard people talk about snowfall. I thought, *if I go to America, I will eat snow and I don't need to do anything—just put it in a cup and mix it with sugar and milk, and then we can eat it, because in my country we eat ice a lot in the summer.* But in the U.S., no one eats snow.

I grew up in a poor family. I remember when I was ten years old, I liked to climb trees like coconut and mango trees. Usually people in my country grow rice and plant vegetables and fruit to eat. In my country, we have three seasons. We have summer time, raining time, and winter time. We don't have snow in winter, just a little bit of cold. We don't have enough clothes, especially families who have a lot of children, because they have no money to buy clothes for their children. But we have enough food and we eat fresh food everyday. Usually our villages and houses are near the river. One thing that I liked is everybody takes a bath in the river—no one takes a bath at home. I liked the river, and I liked swimming. There is no electricity or refrigerator and everybody uses candles or lamps at nighttime.

Now I live in Minnesota—just my older sister and me. I am married and have two kids, and my sister has four kids. We are lucky that we had the opportunity to come to the United States. My parents and my two brothers and two sisters stayed at the Thailand-Burma border.

My life in the United States is much better. I have learned a lot of good things. Even though I couldn't speak English or understand when I came, now I can do it. I can drive, I have a car, and I can use the computer too. The government in the U.S. and the governments in Asia are different because I saw a lot of people in Thailand and Burma where the education for kids is so poor. There is no public assistance, and no opportunities for poor people. But here in the United States, it is different. Everybody, every kid can go to school without money, and our kids can get public transportation for school. People who have low incomes can get benefits from the government like food support and health insurance. That is why I would like to say "Thanks, America."

April

April

nature abhors
taxation
as does the
populace,
yet rain showers
and sunshine
blend well this month
as do last minute
important
imaginative
deductions
that give us
a running chance
to refund
ourselves.

Diego Vázquez Jr.

⇨ Macalester president James Wallace resigned from the college's Neutrality and Peace Association in 1917 because he supported America's entry into WWI.

APRIL

S	M	T	W	T	F	S
1	2	3	4	5	6	7
8	9	10	11	12	13	14
15	16	17	18	19	20	21
22	23	24	25	26	27	28
29	30					

26 Monday

27 Tuesday

28 Wednesday

Summit Avenue
One thing is true—
St. Paulites
Really love Summit Avenue
With its grand old edifices
It transports you
And anyone
Who has grown up here
Has driven down the Avenue
And picked out a house
His favorite
Her fairy house
French doors and cupolas
For their own.

Linda White

29 Thursday

🐾 March 29: Rev. Floyd Massey Jr., African American teacher and minister, pastor of Pilgrim Baptist church in the 1940s, was born today in 1915.

April

*Gordon Parks High School students supporting Minnesota's
Arts and Culture Heritage Fund*

30 Friday

31 Saturday   Saint Paul Winter Farmers' Market
                                    Global Hot Dish Variety Show
                                    Saint Paul Chamber Orchestra

1 Sunday   Saint Paul Farmers' Market
April Fools' Day
Palm Sunday

African American leader W. E. B. DuBois gave a lecture
in Saint Paul in 1920, sponsored by the local NAACP.

Springtime in Minnesota

Rashidah Ismaili AbuBakr

In the spring of 1994, I was a writer in residence for Consortium of Associated Colleges in the Twin Cities. This meant that participating campuses would house me for seven days, and during this time I would do individual and group writing critiques, a workshop, and a formal reading for the entire campuses at St. Thomas University, Macalester College, Augsburg College, Hamline University, and College of St. Catherine.

I'd been to the Twin Cities before, mostly in the summer to visit my godson and his mother, but I had not been during the winter. The cold of Minnesota is infamous, and I am extremely sensitive to cold weather. My friend Charlie Sugnet assured me that the worst of winter would be over in March and April, and that it would be not much colder than New York.

I arrived fully prepared for the onslaught of biting winds and head-high snow mounds. The campus at St. Thomas University was set on the banks of the Mississippi, but when I arrived, I did not know this nor had I fully grasped the geography. The next morning on my way to meet the English faculty, covered from head to toe in a new long coat and knee-high boots, I encountered a young man in shorts, a hooded sweat jacket, and Birkenstock sandals hurrying across campus to class. I asked if his mother knew he was courting pneumonia. He smiled and said it was balmy today compared to the previous week when the temperature had been below 30 degrees. I asked him about the lake, and he told me with a big smile that it was the Mississippi River. I had no idea of the vastness of the river, because what I'd seen in New Orleans was muddy and resembled a lake. After a few days, the weather changed and became Minnesota winter.

Next, I went to Augsburg, where I stayed in a big apartment that normally housed at least three students. While at Macalester, I was able to walk across the street to a bus stop and travel around Saint Paul. There were lots of Vietnamese restaurants. I was taken to dinner by various faculty members and later to the lovely home of Cass Daglish. In fact, we continued to stay in touch for many years afterward.

It was also at Macalester College that I encountered some multicultural exchanges. The first came from a few students who were Asian adoptees. In private sessions, they talked about their growing interests in their Asian heritage and, in a few cases, the resistance to this by their parents. They were all from South Korea. Only one had actually been back because he'd been able to trace the adoption agency that handled him. Two of the others were taking language classes at a nearby cultural center. I stayed in touch for a while with one of the young men because he later came to Columbia University. All were having problems with their adopted parents understanding their cultural needs. All of the students said they sometimes felt guilty when their parents said they felt rejection.

In another class, I made an observation that in their stories all the characters seemed identical: blonde with varying lengths of hair, blue eyes, and very slender figures. This was true whether the characters were male or female. This did not seem to be an issue for the class. In fact, one of the students said it would probably be the same if I described my tribe: everyone would be black, wooly hair and, you know, full lips. I said not everyone looks alike no matter where they come from.

One young woman spoke up saying she'd never been in close contact with someone who was—there was a significant pause as she searched for the word; I supplied African. In her town, all the families knew each other. Most were from Scandinavian immigrants. She was the first person in her hamlet to attend college in Saint Paul, and felt it important to return home and share her experiences. Some did have racial reservations about—again a pause—African people, but, she defended they were all good people, not racists. I am not sure of her age but I would venture to guess less than twenty-one. My observation about the characters had by now been lost.

I met lots of Somalis and they seemed to have adjusted, coming from an extremely hot and dry country to a state with severe cold weather. Some said they had experienced racism. Others said that Minnesota residents lived in isolation and didn't interact with people who looked different, other than on TV. There were also some intra-racial problems with Blacks. They evidenced disdain for African Americans while many of the youth, especially the boys, imitated postures and dress codes associated with young African Americans. They all said they were proud to be Somali and loved America.

I continued to wrap myself in my layers of long coats and shawls. Sometimes I went for rides with Charlie and my new friend, Don Belton. Don and I became very close, and it was a great tragedy when he was brutally murdered four years ago in Indiana. When we spoke, two days before Christmas, he wished me a pleasant Kwanzaa. Before going out to Indiana, he used to come up to New York and spend time with me.

I have since gone back many times to Saint Paul and Minneapolis. I attended a few of the Juneteenth events put on by my late friend, DeJunius Hughes, and his wife, Karen Starr. Charlie and I have a very close friendship and he has been here many times. I have really fond memories of the shops, especially a yarn shop, because I am a knitter. That writing residency gave me a geographic and cultural education, and lasting friends.

APRIL

S	M	T	W	T	F	S
1	2	3	4	5	6	7
8	9	10	11	12	13	14
15	16	17	18	19	20	21
22	23	24	25	26	27	28
29	30					

▷ "Place is prevalent, as is the working class. The characters sort of take over. I write from that perspective. It's what I know."—Suzanne Nielsen, writer from Saint Paul's East Side

2 Monday   Minnesota RollerGirls (Bout)

3 Tuesday

4 Wednesday

5 Thursday

🏵 April 5: Mike O'Dowd, Saint Paul–born Irish American boxer, Middleweight Champion of the World from 1917 to 1920, was born today in 1895.

April

Hartland Shoe Repair owner, Gene, from series Small Business as Community Catalyst

6 Friday

Good Friday

Passover begins

Saint Paul Chamber Orchestra

April 6: Vince Flynn—Saint Paul native, graduate of St. Thomas (academy and college), and best-selling author of political thrillers—was born today in 1966.

7 Saturday

World Health Day

Saint Paul Farmers' Market

Saint Paul Chamber Orchestra

Living Green Expo

8 Sunday

Easter Sunday

Saint Paul Farmers' Market

Living Green Expo

April 8: Ruby H. Hunt, former Saint Paul City Council member and Ramsey County commissioner, was born today in 1924.

Future Supreme Court Justice Harry Blackmun won the city oratorical contest for Mechanic Arts High School in 1924.

Elephant joke lunches

Elephant in the Room

Susan Koefod

Illustration © Andy Singer

One day, Darby and Marcella were quietly having lunch at a Galtier Plaza skyway table. Both worked at Cray Research, he in testing and she in quality assurance. Marcella had just unwrapped her jelly sandwich when Darby popped his question. "What's the difference between an elephant and a flea?"

Marcella opened the small spiral notebook she brought every day to lunch, and began to write the question down, but then paused. She removed another notebook from her purse and flipped through it rapidly.

"Aha," she announced. "October 14th."

"You're sure about that?"

"An elephant can have fleas, but a flea can't have elephants." She snapped the notebook shut.

"Noooo!" he moaned. "You have to give me another chance. According to the rules, right?"

Marcella located another notebook, even more ragged than the one she'd just shut. "After the first joke repetition, Darby is allowed to tell another elephant joke. If he repeats himself with the second joke, he has one last question."

Darby thought long and hard. Marcella took a bite of her sandwich.

The elephant jokes had begun a few years earlier, when Darby came across Marcella during the noon hour. She was sitting exactly where she was now, quietly crying into her jelly sandwich.

They'd been acquaintances, but not yet friends, and that day she needed a friend. She told him she'd just been dumped by her fiancé, a junior executive in the marketing division. Darby removed a clean tissue from his pocket protector, handed it to her, and offered to marry her on the spot.

He was more serious than she knew, but made the offer sound like a joke. She sniffled that he must be joking, but thanked him anyway. It was then he told the first elephant joke.

She laughed harder than she'd ever laughed at anything. "Well, now," she said. "You're welcome to join me for lunch any day, as long as the elephant jokes hold out."

"There are literally trunks of elephant jokes," he quipped. "So you won't be rid of me anytime soon."

Now it seemed he had finally run out of material. Mustard dripped from his Braunschweiger sandwich onto his shirt. Finally, a joke came to him. "How can you tell whether you're eating elephant or peanut butter?"

"How can you tell whether you're eating elephant or peanut butter?"

"Elephant doesn't stick to the roof of your mouth!" she said, triumphantly, without referencing her notes.

Darby gasped and turned pale. "I have one final shot. Right?"

"Right. You remember what happens if the jokes run out?" Marcella dabbed at Darby's mustard stain.

Yes. He knew. It would be time to get serious. Her broken heart had long since healed, yet he was the one dragging his feet, unwilling to take a risk.

All he'd ever asked of her was one more day, one more lunch, another new joke. Why get serious? Wouldn't that end it for them? Still, he'd agreed to the rules.

He'd told all the elephant-in-the-refrigerator jokes, all the jokes about how many elephants you can fit in taxis and Volkswagens. Why elephants have blue shoes (white shoes get dirty too fast), why they float upside down (to keep their blue shoes dry), all of the jokes about elephants crossing the road—with and without chickens. All of the wordplay jokes: elephones (how elephants communicate), elecoptors (what's big and gray and can fly straight up?), elevision (what elephants do for entertainment).

There was really only one question left.

Darby got down on his knees and held Marcella's hand. "I'm out of elephant jokes. Will you marry me anyway?"

Happy tears accompanied her answer. "Yes!"

⇨ On April 10 in 1912, Charles Bainbrigge, an English horse trainer headed for Savage's International Stock Farm in Minnesota, boarded the Titanic in Southampton. He died when the doomed ship sank, and his body was never recovered. His sister, Ethel, lived at 214 Dayton Ave. in Saint Paul.

APRIL

S	M	T	W	T	F	S
1	2	3	4	5	6	7
8	9	10	11	12	13	14
15	16	17	18	19	20	21
22	23	24	25	26	27	28
29	30					

9 Monday   *Saint Paul Almanac* Lowertown Reading Jam

10 Tuesday

11 Wednesday

12 Thursday

April

Walking along the Mississippi River in spring

13 Friday

14 Saturday

Saint Paul Farmers' Market

Minneapolis-Saint Paul
28th Annual Film Festival begins

Minnesota Book Awards Gala

Minnesota Opera, *Madame Butterfly*

🕯 April 14: Tiburcio (Joseph) Lucia Sr., a founder of Our Lady of Guadalupe
Church, was born today in 1909.

15 Sunday
Orthodox Easter

Saint Paul Farmers' Market

Minnesota Opera, *Madame Butterfly*

🕯 April 15: Stanley Gordon West, novelist, was born today in 1932.

Rebuilt fireplace at Como

My Dad's Love for His Parks

Pat Kaufman-Knapp

My dad, William LaMont Kaufman, was superintendent of Saint Paul Parks for thirty-four years. He dearly loved his job, and because he did, approximately one-third of our childhood was spent in his beloved parks. Como, our favorite, offered so much to children as well as to adults. Our dad taught us the name of each plant in the conservatory and the outside gardens, not only in English but also in Latin. Many Sunday nights were Como Nights, when we sometimes brought a picnic and raced to find Dad's name on plaques in the zoo and conservatory. But his love for Como extended to other parks: Harriet Island, Phalen, Highland, and his smaller treasures—Hidden Falls, Rice, Irvine, Kellogg, Lilydale, Indian Mounds, Mears, and Newell, among others.

My father left Owatonna to enter World War I when he was twenty-one. While hiding in trenches in the Argonne Forest of France, he became close friends with Hesley Jensen, a small soldier from Wisconsin. Hesley was so little that he quickly earned the name "the little Swede" from his army platoon. All of these men fought valiantly, using their spare minutes to discuss and plan their dreams of when—and if—they came home. My dad had a passion for nature even then—trees, flowers, landscapes, animals—and these became a dream for him in the cold, muddy trenches of the forest. Hesley was suddenly hit by a German sniper and gravely injured. Dad picked him up and prayed while Hesley died in his arms. The dreaded mustard gas took a devastating toll on my father's lungs and health, and a bullet from a German sniper struck his leg.

After World War I ended, Dad spent time in the Minneapolis Veteran's Hospital. He never completely regained his health. But now he could put his dreams and love of nature into action. He and my mother moved to St. Louis, Missouri, where he enrolled in and completed his studies in landscape architecture, an intricate piece of his lifelong ambition. He worked alone, designing gardens and yards for many clients, including some who lived on wealthy estates. He designed walkways, plantings, woods, flowerbeds, and statuary. Very soon he combined his talents with politics and was hired as the superintendent of Saint Paul Parks, the position that fulfilled his dreams.

As the superintendent, he was once invited by the Veterans of Foreign Wars (VFW) to speak at the dedication of a burial section for World War I veterans in the Bayport, Minnesota, cemetery. After his speech, a parade, and an emotional playing of "Taps," a woman asked if she could say a few words. She asked if anyone present had known her son, Hesley Jensen, who had died in the Argonne Forest in France. Dad walked to the podium, extending his hand, and told her that her son had died in his arms. This brought closure for both of them.

Seventy-five years ago, Dad designed a tall brick fireplace in an open field of his beloved Como Park. On it he had inscribed Joyce Kilmer's poem "Trees." He was a member of the Joyce Kilmer VFW, and the poem was always dear to his heart. When I was ten years old, I memorized "Trees" and recited it to him. That fireplace is now being rebuilt. Kaufman Drive signs are an integral part of Como Park. Each time I am in Saint Paul, we drive those streets, and I think of a young soldier's dream when he was far away in the Argonne Forest of France.

➪ "If you get an idea that does good for others and you really believe in it, you draw to you the right people who can grab onto it and carry it forward."—Olivia Irvine Dodge (1918–2009), philanthropist and environmentalist

16 Monday

Saint Paul Chamber Orchestra

17 Tuesday

Minnesota Opera, *Madame Butterfly*

🐞 April 17: Roberta Davis, African American jazz singer, was born today in 1937.

18 Wednesday

Minnesota Opera, *Madame Butterfly*

19 Thursday

Minnesota Opera, *Madame Butterfly*

April

The Mississippi River flooding in Saint Paul, April 2011

20 Friday
Saint Paul Chamber Orchestra
Minnesota Opera, *Madame Butterfly*

21 Saturday
First Day of Ridvan (Baha-i)
Saint Paul Farmers' Market
Minnesota Opera, *Madame Butterfly*

🦋 April 21: Bedros Keljik—Armenian-American writer, activist, and rug importer—was born today in 1874.

22 Sunday
Earth Day
Saint Paul Farmers' Market
Saint Paul Chamber Orchestra
Minnesota Opera, *Madame Butterfly*

In 1865, Saint Paul celebrated the end of the Civil War.
The city of 12,976 had sent 1,470 men into battle.

Photo © Sascha Grant/ibuildrockets.com

Three monkeys in the zoo

The Telepathic Monkeys at Como Golf Course

Scott Bade

In 1989 on the first tee at the newly reopened Como Park golf course, after watching my grandfather's drive slice across two fairways and bank off a tree, I learned that golf is as much educational as it is recreational.

"Grandpa, you missed," I said, playfully jabbing at my hero.

"Yeah, but that's alright," he replied with a smile. "Hitting a tree is good luck for your next shot."

"Oh!" I gleefully said, while altering my aim for a majestic birch 100 yards away.

"Wait," my grandfather said while he corrected my stance. "It doesn't work if you *try* to hit it. It's like a lucky penny. You can't put it down and then pick it up." This made perfect sense to my eight-year-old brain.

I'd run mindlessly into the woods or jump into piles of mud after every errant ball, getting myself covered with dirt and scrapes in the process. After one of my shots plunked into a pond, I started removing my shoes, fully prepared for an underwater expedition.

"Hold on there, Mr. Spitz. Let that one go. It's feeding Okee," my grandfather said with a hand on my shoulder.

"Who's Okee?" I asked with genuine intrigue.

"He's an alligator, named after the Okefenokee swamps where your grandma is from. He loves to eat golf balls." His straight face and nonchalant demeanor sold it.

"Wow, can I see him?"

"You can try." The lovable jerk let me stare for a good five minutes.

"Where does he go in winter?"

"He roams from house to house, eating food when no one is looking. That's what happened to an apple pie Grandma made last Christmas." I could barely wait to share this inside information with Mom and Dad.

"Just wait," the old man said. "On the next hole, you can see the supernatural monkeys."

At the next tee box I became nearly uncontrollable, desperate to sprint ahead.

"Now, just you wait," Grandpa said in a calming voice. "They won't come out unless you're golfing."

I watched his drive hook drastically more than the slight dogleg to the left and disappear into the lush forest that bordered the hole.

"They're mad at me," he said with a fake frown.

"Who's mad at you? The monkeys?" I had a million questions that needed answers.

"Take your shot first, Mr. Palmer." *Whack!* The only good shot of the round landed 100 yards away in the middle of the fairway. Through a beaming grin, Grandpa said, "Those telepathic monkeys must really like you. They're just around the bend here."

Grandpa said, "Those telepathic monkeys must really like you. They're just around the bend here."

Off the left corner of the green, a few hundred yards away, was a visible portion of the zoo next to the golf course, including a large outdoor cage with three rhesus macaques bouncing around inside.

Fascinated, I asked, "What's *telepathic* mean?"

"It means they can move things with their minds. They pull some shots into the woods to get them later."

"What do they want golf balls for? Do they eat them too?"

"No, they use them. They play out here once everyone leaves."

I was certain this was true. It was too incredible not to be. As soon as my grandfather entered the portable bathroom, I pulled my pitching wedge from the rental bag and flung it deep into the trees. I smiled and waved toward the monkeys, knowing they'd appreciate the gift.

At home, my grandfather's internal rage at the $50 it would cost to replace the wedge was perfectly counteracted by my grandmother's uproarious delight.

"Serves you proper," she said.

➪ "On a hike, pupils and teachers meet on a human basis … the relation that grows out of a walking expedition entirely prevents any future necessity for discipline."—Dietrich Lange (1863–1940), Saint Paul teacher, writer, and naturalist

APRIL

S	M	T	W	T	F	S
1	2	3	4	5	6	7
8	9	10	11	12	13	14
15	16	17	18	19	20	21
22	23	24	25	26	27	28
29	30					

23 Monday

World Book and Copyright Day

🐞 April 23: George Avaloz, bebop and jazz drummer, was born today in 1937.

24 Tuesday

25 Wednesday

26 Thursday   Saint Paul Chamber Orchestra

Minnesota State Capitol at night

Photo © Henry Jackson

27 Friday

Fourth Friday at the Movies

Saint Paul Art Crawl

28 Saturday

Saint Paul Farmers' Market

Saint Paul Chamber Orchestra

Saint Paul Art Crawl

🐾 April 28: Ka Vang, Hmong writer and poet, was born today in 1975.

29 Sunday

Saint Paul Farmers' Market

Saint Paul Art Crawl

A rabies epidemic began after a black-and-tan dog attacked
horses and other canines in 1901 on the West Side.

April 91

The basketball rim at school

The Game

Elena Cisneros

The kid loved basketball. He never had a basketball to speak of, but the school had plenty. The kid had a favorite. It was old, smooth, and had the feel of rough paper. It bounced as high as any of the new ones. The kid felt alive when it bounced back perfectly.

The kid knew the concrete playing field—all the broken spaces and the cracking cover of the court. The kid knew how to angle and fly by the arms and legs of others. All for that beautiful sound: *swoosh.*

On the court, the kid was calm and in control. On the court, the kid was happy.

Looking forward to school days put a target on the kid's back. Enjoying the quiet of the library put a target on the kid's back. Finishing homework put a target on the kid's back. Not being dark enough put a target on the kid's back. Writing clearly, knowing answers, being quiet, everything put a target on the kid's back.

But on the court, the kid was free. The kid had skills that shamed them all. And one day the kid beat the best. One day, one hour, one game, the kid was king.

Lunch hour was almost over. All the white bread, crackers, and apple juice—over. The focus for the kid was the court. The court was broken in places, pieces here and there, grass growing through the concrete. Torn nets on the rims. The backboards, bruised metal, were older than anybody on the court.

The kid saw Sam waiting at the other side of the court. The teams were made over lunch, the kid on one, Sam on the other. It was a long rivalry, a heated rivalry, played out every day on the court. The kid and Sam were never on a team together. Never.

A penny was flipped and the kid's team got the ball. The game began.

It was a whirl of arms and legs, of torn jeans and busted shoes, of dirty hands and long hair. The fouls were flying, hits on the head with elbows, slaps on the arms leaving red marks.

Sam got the ball, his team was on the lead, and Sam made a three shot. The kid was getting angry; had to focus, just needed two threes to get ahead.

It was a whirl of arms and legs, of torn jeans and busted shoes, of dirty hands and long hair. The fouls were flying, hits on the head with elbows, slaps on the arms leaving red marks.

The kid got the ball from the out and headed for the rim. Sam came out to the left and attacked, almost got the ball, but the kid passed it and his teammate made a shot. Now the kid felt a rumble. Sam had the ball and the kid watched. Sam's wrist spun as he bounced the ball, a weakness. Sam ran for the rim, and the kid slid by and reached in, sliced the ball away from Sam and headed for the rim. *Swoosh.*

The call: five minutes left for recess.

Sam stood in the court dumbstruck. No one ever took the ball from him. His team had the out and the kid took it from Sam again, another slice and pass, a three shot made.

Time.

The kid walked away from the court.

O'Shea Irish dancers

Photo courtesy O'Shea Irish Dance

O'Shea Irish Dance

Fiona McKen

O'Shea Irish Dance is my Irish dance school. It is part of the Celtic Junction building. O'Shea teaches Irish dance for kindergarteners to adults. The dance company moved to the Celtic Junction two years ago. It has three studios. O'Shea participates in the St. Patrick's Day celebration at the Landmark Center, the Irish Fair at Harriet Island in August, and Minnesota feishes (dance contests). They also go to the championships. There are many types of Irish dances. They include slip jigs, single jigs, treble jigs, and hornpipes. There's another dance that has a name, but at O'Shea we just call it a jig. Irish dancers also do reels, but reels are actually Scottish. Jigs and reels are done in soft shoes, which are black and look a little like ballet shoes. Treble jigs and horn-pipes are done in hard shoes—black shoes with buckles that are similar to tap shoes. For performances, we wear blue dresses with blue bloom-ers. Bloomers are like underwear, except you wear them like they are shorts. There is also ceili dancing. Ceili dancing is a dance done with a partner. Usually when you dance, your hands and arms are down at your side. In ceili dancing, your arms are up and you hold your partner's hand. O'Shea Irish Dance teaches all of these dances. Once you are in the advanced classes, it's amazing what you can do. Performing with O'Shea is a lot of fun. I love doing Irish dance. There are many other reasons O'Shea is one of my most favorite places in Saint Paul!

Tom

T. K. O'Rourke

Tom was an old experienced hand.
He was catching a line out at the head
from one barge of soybeans to another,
was stepping across to secure the line,
drop another wrap on it and dog it off.
I've caught that line a few times myself.

There are soybeans spilled on the wing tanks,
hard and round as ball bearings
and Tom slipped, got his foot caught in the line,
was dangling between the barges as they come in.

Young Paul was with him,
signaled to the captain to hold the barge out,
and the Old Man shipped up the *Itasca*'s engines
to flank that barge midstream as much as she would go,
and Paul put a ratchet in between the barges
hoping to hold them apart

but this line was caught upstream
and the river was a torrent after the rains
and Paul was hacking that line with his rigging knife in one hand
and trying to situate that ratchet with the other
and the Old Man just couldn't hold the *Itasca* out any longer
and that ratchet slipped and sank into the water.

Tom was looking up at Paul, no more fear,
when the barges came together.
Paul cried out "Tom! Tom! Tom!"

We gave him a Riverman's funeral.
Rivermen carried the coffin and put him in the ground
by the church above the levee at Hastings.

Rivermen got drunk at the wake,
and now when the shore wires
are mysteriously pulled up at the fleet where he died
in the Harbor of Saint Paul,
wrapped around the kevels with the right leads
going upriver and downriver,
the crows in the cottonwood cry
" Tom! Tom! Tom!"

Saint Paul Central Library at night

April

My Haven at the Saint Paul Central Library, 1959

Karen Karsten

"We're closing now," the librarian says softly, passing quietly along the polished reference tables. I love this room, with its long tables and sturdy oak chairs—the quiet soaks into me. I even feel smarter here in this calm oasis. I gather my books, take them to the checkout, have them stamped. I step out into the night, leaving behind the quiet, elegant beauty as I close the shiny brass-and-glass doors. I walk down the marble stairs—like a star arriving at a quiet event. The April wind is sharp, I breathe the damp air, the smell of books—lots of books packed tightly on their shelves—still in my lungs. Old scholars still talking to me in papery whispers.

I decide to walk the few blocks to our pink house next to my mother's restaurant, Dotty's Diner, the same way I came—down the long staircase, past the Saint Paul Milk Company and up Chestnut Street. I walk slowly, thinking about the library back in teeny Russell, Minnesota, where we lived until five years ago. Every other Saturday morning I would hear the *slap, slap, slap* against the wall next to my bed. New books! Miles Winter's barber shop next door was the town library—one tall bookcase next to the wall of mirrors that reflected every male face in town on a regular basis. The bookmobile guy would pull old books off the shelves, slam new ones in, then head back to Marshall, thirteen miles away. I would rush over, excited to see what had arrived—maybe a new Nancy Drew!

It is quiet in Saint Paul—Rice Park is deserted, except for a few men who are staking out a bench for the night. I smell the new greenness, look up at the night sky, searching for the blazing star that was always to the right of Russell's water tower. There are lots of stars, many of them bright, and I have lost track of where the star should be without the tower to guide me.

Then I am home. It is not quiet. Music blares from the open door. Mother has gone to our lake cabin for the weekend with my little brother, Kenny. My older sister, Kathy, and I begged to stay home and study. "Finals are so close," we said.

Kathy is not studying. The house is filled with teens drinking beer, slow dancing to "Love Me Tender," and talking or making out on the floor. Kids are everywhere, in the hall, in the kitchen; potato chips are everywhere, smashed into the carpet; and pizzas are coming in the front door, lots of them. Good thing I got most of my final paper done at the library—this is bedlam.

I know that bright and early Monday morning, Mrs. Barbato down the street will tell my mother what was going on tonight, and we will both be grounded forever. My sister knows that, too, but she is surrounded by thirty or so of her best friends, wearing her tightest jeans, long dark hair pulled back into a ponytail. They are looking at records and arguing about what to play next, fast or slow? She doesn't even notice me.

I go up the stairs, holding my books and papers, and head for my room. A blond guy is coming out of the bathroom, stumbling a bit, still sculpting his greasy hair into a duck tail as he walks. He looks at me.

"Who are you?" he says. "Do I know you?"

"Me? I live here," I say, and slam the door to my room.

At Home on Grand Avenue

Diane Helander

Writing can be a lonely business. Most people don't understand you. They think that because you have a disagreement with a fictional character—and lose the argument—that, well ... you're odd. To other writers, though, these kinds of conversations are normal. They also know how to tell you that your piece stinks without making you feel you should never attempt to write even a grocery list again. Needless to say, it's not easy to find these folks and, once you do, it's even harder to find a common place where you can all meet.

Our writer's group may have been born at The Loft in Minneapolis, but we grew up on Grand Avenue. We decided to meet there because it was centrally located, so we'd all have to drive about the same distance; but, to be honest, I wasn't so sure that this was the place for us. Let's face it, when you think Grand Avenue, you think expensive boutiques and upscale restaurants, which doesn't exactly sound like a place where folks can sit around all afternoon trying to figure out how to kill people, or debating whether dragons can fly over mountains. But, that's exactly what we did.

Now, some ten years later, we're still meeting at Axel's Bonfire, where the staff welcomes us like old aunties. For creative people, we seem to be creatures of habit when it comes to lunch—they just bring us "the usual." Then, depending on who waits on us, we have a little chat about their college classes, or what their kids are doing, or that they won't be there the next Thursday because they are going on vacation.

People in the group have come and gone, too, but a few of the charter members are still there. Through the years, we've watched our baby-faced children morph into alien teenagers, temperamental college students, and, finally, into the wonderful young adults we always knew they'd become. We've planned weddings for our kids and funerals for our parents. We've said goodbye to grown children moving away, we've turned into in-laws, and we've welcomed beloved grandchildren. Oh, and somewhere in between, we've not only become writers, we've become sisters. We may live in suburbs around the city, but on Thursday afternoons, our writing family is at home on Grand Avenue.

Photo © Henry Jackson

Axel's Bonfire interior sign

May

A Song Apart

Ceres, Goddess of Corn, grieved and raged
for her stolen daughter. They say she withheld
the harvest. But corn was already here.
The first cornfield was the beginning of settled life on earth.
"Spirit grain," the Anishinaabe called it.
Then blades of a steel plow dug short-cuts
to fortune. Settlers came. *Soon the plow dug*
deep into the hunting grounds, the children died,
and their fires went out from shore to shore.

Zeus let Persephone visit each year. Shared custody.
Seeing her child, Ceres returned to green fields.
The attorney wrote: *She still retains a great deal of anger.*
Dakota tribes were driven from the river.
The sound of their weeping / comes back to us.

Patricia Kirkpatrick

May

The first cornfield... —Edith Hamilton, *Mythology* (Little Brown and Company, 1942)
Soon the plow... —Meridel Le Sueur, *North Star Country* (University of Minnesota Press, 1998)
The sound of... —Gerald Vizenor, translator, *Anishinaabe Lyric Poems* (University of Oklahoma Press, 1993)

⇨ "I wanna hang a map of the world in my house. Then I'm gonna put pins into all the locations that I've traveled to. But first, I'm gonna have to travel to the top two corners of the map so it won't fall down."—Mitch Hedberg (1968–2005), Saint Paul comedian

MAY

S	M	T	W	T	F	S
		1	2	3	4	5
6	7	8	9	10	11	12
13	14	15	16	17	18	19
20	21	22	23	24	25	26
27	28	29	30	31		

30 Monday

I can't remember
all the flowers she taught me.
Her pansies worry.
Michael E. Murphy

1 Tuesday

May Day

🕷 May 1: Brooks Henderson, early radio personality, was born today in 1908.

2 Wednesday   Circus Juventas

🕷 May 2: Pinky Lee, comedian, was born today in 1907.

3 Thursday   Circus Juventas

World Press Freedom Day   Festival of Nations

🕷 May 3: Wing Young Huie, photographer and author, was born today in 1955.

Shiloh Baptist Church: Grand opening of new church at 501 West Lawson Avenue

4 Friday

Circus Juventas
Festival of Nations
Ballet of the Dolls
Cinco de Mayo Festival

5 Saturday

Cinco de Mayo
Wesak Day (Buddhist)

Saint Paul Farmers' Market
Circus Juventas
Festival of Nations
Cinco de Mayo Festival
Summer Flower Show begins

6 Sunday

Saint Paul Farmers' Market
Festival of Nations

May

Civil Rights activist Roy Wilkins, a 1919 graduate of Mechanic Arts High School, was given the Distinguished Alumni Award in 1960.

May 101

Lyceum Theater, 479 Wabasha, in 1954

Triumph at the Lyceum

Louis DiSanto

It was the "Ugly Betty" of the seven downtown Saint Paul movie houses, a dungeon where rats ran under the seats and bats flew past your head. At least that's what I had heard about the Lyceum Theater on Wabasha Street. So on my first visit there in the fall of 1960 to see *Abbott and Costello Meet Frankenstein* and *The Creature from the Black Lagoon,* I had this terrible sense of dread.

Well, no vermin gnawed on my feet, and the only bat flying around was Dracula chasing Lou Costello on the screen. Once I began to relax and throw popcorn with my friends from St. Pascal's grade school, I thought the Lyceum was a pretty neat place, especially the big stage with the ornate red curtain. Little did I know that I would soon be on that very stage in one of the most memorable experiences of my life.

It began when Principal Sister Sophia announced that she wanted five "intrepid" police boys to represent St. Pascal's in a short skit competition at the Lyceum to celebrate school patrol week. Her idea was to tell the story of Lt. Henry Winterhalter and Sister Carmella Hanggi, who helped develop the Saint Paul school patrol program. After playing a lowly shepherd in the Christmas pageant, this was my chance for the big time. At tryouts, I did an impression of a tough-talking policeman that had Sister in stitches and won the role of Lt. Winterhalter. The role of Sister Carmella went to Keith Brown because he was the only one willing to wear a nun's habit! For my part, I scrounged up a rumpled hat, pipe, and Dad's bulky army overcoat—the perfect outfit, or so I thought, for an important police official.

After several chaotic weeks of rehearsals that left Sister Sophia totally frazzled, there we were, the intrepid five, standing on the stage of the Lyceum Theater and staring in sheer terror at this huge audience. And now it was show time! At first, my voice was cracking and I could barely move in that bulky coat. Then Keith almost tripped on his habit as he showed Joe Duncan and Greg Blees how to use a patrol flag. But even with all the nerves and being awestruck by the bright lights and big stage, we bravely carried on and somehow made it through without any major gaffes, although I was afraid I looked ridiculous strutting around in an army coat and rumpled hat.

As the ornate red curtain closed, none of us had the slightest idea how we did. I couldn't even remember if the audience applauded or threw tomatoes. We were just glad it was finally over. When it came time for the audience to vote for the best skit, the thought of winning never crossed our minds. In fact, I was anxious to get home and watch *Axel* and *Huckleberry Hound*. As it turned out, we vastly underestimated ourselves.

"The ballots have been counted," the man at the microphone said, "and the winner in a landslide is St. Pascal's!"

We were so stunned, it took us a moment to realize he was talking about us! When we made our triumphant return to the stage, Lt. Winterhalter himself presented the award, then gave me a wink and pat on the back. It was like a dream, going from a bunch of nervous seventh-graders to basking in the glow of victory at the Lyceum Theater. And now I could definitely hear the applause. But what I remember most, other than the award, was kids coming up to the stage and telling Keith and me that they voted for St. Pascal's because of us and our great costumes.

Then came the best part: Sister Sophia took us to Bridgeman's for ice cream cones (two scoops!).

In the years that followed this monumental achievement, I saw *Psycho, Hud,* and a few other movies at the Lyceum. And each time I smiled as I pictured our little troupe on that big stage, especially the kid in an army coat and rumpled hat.

Then, in 1972, everything changed. After sixty-one years of providing good entertainment (my grandpa said he saw vaudeville acts there), the aging Lyceum was turned into a garish adult venue called the Las Vegas Cinema, a sad fate for an iconic Saint Paul landmark. Four years later it was gone, replaced by a parking lot.

Maybe this oft-maligned (some called it the Lice) symbol of a past era wasn't as elegant as the Paramount or Orpheum theaters, but to me it was a very special place. And I will always cherish the memories of our triumph at the Lyceum.

May

⇨ "The discomfort of wanting to be an actor, but the desire to write for the theater has plagued my waking and sleeping hours from my sixth birthday."—James Gray (1899–1984), writer and critic

S	M	T	W	T	F	S
		1	2	3	4	5
6	7	8	9	10	11	12
13	14	15	16	17	18	19
20	21	22	23	24	25	26
27	28	29	30	31		

7 Monday

🐝 May 7: Dr. Burnside Foster, public health advocate and editor of *St. Paul Medical Journal*, was born today in 1861.

8 Tuesday

International Migratory Bird Day

World Red Cross Day

9 Wednesday

10 Thursday   Circus Juventas

🐝 May 10: Eoin McKiernan, scholar of Irish culture, was born today in 1915.

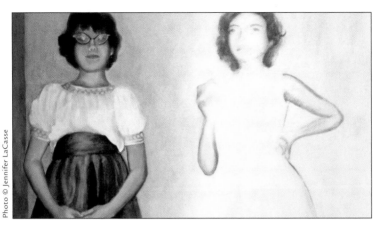

Photo © Jennifer LaCasse

Sisters II (Detail)

11 Friday

Friends School Plant Sale

Circus Juventas

12 Saturday

Saint Paul Farmers' Market

Friends School Plant Sale

Circus Juventas

Bonsai Show

13 Sunday

Mother's Day

Saint Paul Farmers' Market

Friends School Plant Sale

Saint Paul Civic Symphony

Mother's Day Celebration

Bonsai Show

🏵 May 13: Sharon Sayles Belton, African American activist and Minneapolis mayor, was born today in 1951.

Mount Zion Rabbi Isaac L. Rypins spoke on "The Glories of America" in 1907 at a settlement house established by Mount Zion's founders.

Forest

Elena Walczak

I hear whispers as the leaves gently move,
A canopy of greenish yellow.
Tints of periwinkle show through the autumn leaves.
A golden-brown twig splinters beneath my feet.
A sea of green appears before me as the trees thin out,
Flowers dotting the earth, like minnows in the shallows.
A beetle crawls along my shoe, and I think,
There's no better place to be.
Rocks pop up like mountains in this city of nature,
A quiet rustle in the bushes as two fat gray squirrels play a game of tag.
Splashes of color—the beautiful brown of bark,
The many shades of green,
Gray rocks the color of the moon,
Yellow and white flowers hide among the leaves,
And I think,
There's no better place to be.
I smell the wood, the bark, it smells like maple syrup.
An army of small black ants march single file,
Surrounded by the enemy—early falling leaves,
But the ants don't stop.
I do,
And I think,
There's no better place to be.

Mears Park

Martin Devaney

Where I first put my arm around you.
Clad in red coats
and autumn hats,
we walked from the Farmers' Market,
bags of basil in hand,
then arm in arm.
The dog waited.

Where so much music has been made.
Echoing through Lowertown
where the shade of the stage
and the wind and the leaves
made sense of that Saturday.

Where a fine cup of coffee
cut through foggy minds.
We spread our blankets on grass
and listened.

Later, on rocky terrain near the river
we climbed and laughed
as we carried the dog.
We'd left the basil behind

but I had a foreign feeling
that everything was all right.

⇨ A monument featuring a bronze bust of writer Henrik Ibsen, designed by Jacob Fjelde and donated by the Sons of Norway, was dedicated in Como Park on May 19, 100 years ago.

S	M	T	W	T	F	S
		1	2	3	4	5
6	7	8	9	10	11	12
13	14	15	16	17	18	19
20	21	22	23	24	25	26
27	28	29	30	31		

14 Monday

Saint Paul Almanac Lowertown Reading Jam

15 Tuesday

International Day of Families

🌑 May 15: Kristen Vigard, Broadway theater and television actress, was born today in 1963.

16 Wednesday

Tyrannosaurus
Tyrannosaurus so big and wide
Can gulp you up in one big gulp
He is one big fat guy to hide
Poor tyrannosaurus with big
tears
when you cry
What am I going to do with you?
Destiny SaNaa' Carter

17 Thursday

Gordon Parks High School students plant in their raised-bed urban garden

18 Friday

---

19 Saturday   Saint Paul Farmers' Market

Saint Paul Chamber Orchestra

May 19: Louis W. Hill, railroad executive and philanthropist, was born today in 1872.

---

20 Sunday   Saint Paul Farmers' Market

Automobile license number 1 was issued in 1903 for
a Packard owned by R. C. Wright of Saint Paul.

Rebuilding

John Lee Clark

My grandfather spanked her. Half of the time
my mother didn't know why. He didn't have the signs
to tell her. After she got married and gave birth
to three deaf children, he wanted to say something
to us. His hands creaked to life. Buildings
were all he could tell us about. The sod hut
he was born in. The red barn on the farm.
The basement he put his family in while building
a house above their heads. The Ramsey Hospital
where he was foreman and where I and my sons were born.
The Ramsey County Jail we always pointed out
on our way to visit Grandma and Grandpa.
The bird houses in his green garden.
It didn't matter what kind of building
it was, as long as it was with his hands.

Square Dance

Phebe Hanson

Dancing is a sin, my father told me.
That's all there is to it. No ifs, ands, or buts.
No exceptions. Not even for the Square Dance Unit
Murray High, St. Paul, Minnesota, May 1943.
So he wrote a note to my gym teacher,
A far-too-long note, explaining
the reason I must be excused from participating:
dancing was against our religion.
I read the note as I walked down Larpenteur to Cleveland,
past the fields of the U of M farm campus,
where the little shoots of barley and oats and flax
were just beginning to push through the moist black soil.
The note didn't mention how embarrassed
I was at having to ask to be excluded
From square dancing. The note didn't implore Miss Miller
To try not to call attention to me in front of all the other girls.
I was miserable enough in gym where we had to wear bright
Blue one-piece bloomer-like outfits that I would often leave in my
locker for months until they emitted unspeakable odors.
We had to stand naked with all the other girls under icy cold
or scalding hot water of the showers whose sprays burst forth
with military vigor and before we entered we had to step into
a tall pail filled with oily yellow disinfectant to prevent athlete's foot.
But horrible as gym was, to be excused was worst of all.
The square dance unit lasted four weeks so I couldn't possibly
pretend I was squatting on the sidelines, my butt pressed against
the ceramic tile wall in a futile attempt to make myself invisible,
because I had "The Curse." Even the most sympathetic
wouldn't believe my period lasted four whole weeks.
Then the Sunday after the unit was over, dad took us all
To Sytennde Mai Celebration in Minnehaha Park where
Native-costumed Norwegian-Americans squared danced merrily
 to sprightly fiddle music and for a few minutes after the concert
 as we sat eating potato salad and summer sausage sandwiches
at the park picnic table, my dad was silent. But then he spoke:
"Well, I guess square dancing isn't so bad after all. Maybe
next year, Phebe, it would be all right for you to take a class."

From *Why Still Dance*, Nodin Press, 2003

☼ "I consider myself a painter, muralist, and an art activist. My art reflects the many facets of how I think and the experiences I have had. My work is deeply based in the promotion of positive mental and spiritual attitudes."— Ta-coumba Aiken, African American artist

MAY

S	M	T	W	T	F	S
		1	2	3	4	5
6	7	8	9	10	11	12
13	14	15	16	17	18	19
20	21	22	23	24	25	26
27	28	29	30	31		

21 Monday

World Day for Cultural Diversity
   for Dialogue and Development

🐞 May 21: Larry Rosenthal, professional baseball player, was born today in 1910.

22 Tuesday

International Day for Biological Diversity

23 Wednesday

24 Thursday

May

Dandelion field

Photo © Tobechi Tobechukwu

---

25 Friday   Fourth Friday at the Movies

26 Saturday   Saint Paul Farmers' Market

🌼 May 26: Mary Thygeson Shepardson, cultural anthropologist, was born today in 1906.

27 Sunday   Saint Paul Farmers' Market

Shavuot

May

People gathered in 2008 on the former Wadena
Avenue to celebrate renaming it Aguirre Avenue.

Photo © Deborah Torraine

Muriel Tate

The Good Ole Days All Over Again

Muriel Tate

Hi there! Everyone talks about the good old days—how they used to be—what a difference from today. Remember when gas was 25¢ a gallon? And cigarettes 26¢ a box with a 1¢ tax? Wow! But of course young teens didn't smoke. Before I forget: White Castles were 12¢. A dollar really went far! There were no gangs, or at least we didn't know about them. Life wasn't so complicated. You could walk early morning or late evening and be safe.

Do you remember Field's Drug Store? Yes, the place where the teenagers hung out. I remember it quite well. It was a place where you could go and parade with your new or old boyfriend, but *he had to be cute*. If he wasn't, we thought he was anyway. He'd carry your books if you had some. Boy, we were young. We could get a coke and have two free refills. This place was the hub for gossip. Mister Field knew all the teenagers by name. His daughter was one of us. We knew how to socialize. This was our fun!

The corner opposite Field's still stands, now a shack called Tiger Jack's. He sold candy, pop, ice, coal, and fishing licenses. He was a jack-of-all-trades. He was on the corner of Dale Street, at one time called St. Anthony Street, for over forty years. A little farther, about two or three blocks from Tiger Jack's, was the Hollow. This is where the guys played football and showed off for the ladies. Excitement and testosterone were heavy.

One of the other spots to go and have fun was the Arts and Science Museum, located on Tenth Street. (It has since moved to Kellogg Boulevard). Oh yes, the museum! We would go and wander through the Eskimo and the American Indian displays. We would stay for hours on end—I said we were young. Then we would go to Bridgman's Drug Store to have that cup of coffee that never ran out and rum-cherry ice cream—delicious! There were movies downtown, but we went to the ones in our area; the two main ones were the Faust and the Center. We no longer have theaters here.

Oh, before I forget about my boyfriend, now don't you get jealous! I have always liked tall men because I'm kind of short and that way I feel protected. Kirk had curly brown hair and hazel eyes. He was caramel brown, and he liked me! I was a little heavy, but I carried my weight well. I had long black hair. My mom wouldn't let me cut my hair, so I had to wear a ponytail or two braids pinned on top of my head. Oh well—but on Sundays I had it curled into a pageboy style, so I looked good. I felt I did. Kirk was my teen heartthrob. He joined the Air Force, and during that time, I cried a lot and wrote a lot of letters. Time heals all things, even my feelings for Kirk. I guess it was puppy love.

Mechanic Arts and Central High were rivals: Mechanic Arts' football team was better, but Central High was academically superior. There was a little friendly rivalry between the two schools—a little competition is healthy. I graduated from high school, and yes, you probably guessed: I graduated from Central High School.

Six months later, I met another tall, dark, and handsome man; this one was a keeper. He made me feel whole, and we clicked. Nine months later, we got married. This lucky man was David, and he is still my husband today. We've been married for forty-nine years. Just saying his name still makes me smile. We have three very bright children: one girl, Lonetta, and two boys, David and Anthony. I would never stretch the truth—they are intelligent!

Lonetta is a doctor and married, but she doesn't have any children yet. David is a lawyer and the proud parent of two boys: Charles and David Jr. Anthony, my youngest, is a mailman; he's still just looking and looking. As I look at my children now with pride, I wonder how they turned out so well. I have spoiled them, loved them too much, and given them things they didn't want or need. I know this was probably the wrong approach, but I did it because I didn't have those things as a child.

Our children are the better part of David and me: the goodness, the stubbornness, the wonderful smile—the thrift. I could go on and on. My friends keep me in line when I get too outrageous. They tell me about myself when I'm wrong and also when I'm right. I'm blessed; with David by my side, I will continue to learn and grow. When we talk about the Good Ole Days, I think to myself: I'm still living them. With the grace of God, I hope the Good Ole Days will last forever.

May

Young fiddle player performs with a piano player around the corner from her school, the Saint Paul Conservatory of Music

The Saint Paul Conservatory of Music

Beth Fryxell

The Saint Paul Conservatory of Music is where I take violin lessons. The building is made of bricks and it is very old, with ivy crawling up the sides. When you step out of the small, old-fashioned elevator that has mirrors around the inside, you almost always can hear a violin or a cello or any other instrument. My teacher is Wendy Tangen Foster and she teaches violin and is the president of Suzuki. When you leave the building, the door creaks closed and you get a sense of loneliness, missing the comfort of the building. The walls of Wendy's room are brown, and there are many lamps and colorful boxes decorating the room. If I could choose a place to go on a rainy day, it would be to the Saint Paul Conservatory of Music.

Fog

John Minczeski

Think of Jimi Hendrix blurring the notes
of *Purple Haze* without the purple.

A bottle of white-out
with grass starting to peek through.

Climbing out on top, a jumbo jet can see
we've gone all pillowy here.

No matter how one shifts the narrative,
the neon exclamation atop the 1ˢᵗ National

Bank Building still shines, once the ooze lifts,
with its first person singular.

But how thrilling, as the world fades
at fifty feet, to think the void may have

found us, that you or I may materialize
as though reinvented

in front of the library on Market
and 4ᵗʰ, in last week's clothes,

fresh from a solo wilderness trip,
bewildered at civilization. Crows

settle out of the muck, a pigeon slips
into a swirl of wind above the storm sewer grate.

I can neither contain nor console myself.

Sheldon

Greet and Grin

Media Mike Hazard

"Good afternoon, welcome to Ordway. Good afternoon, welcome to Ordway."

For ten years, Sheldon has greeted visitors to the Ordway Center for the Performing Arts with a grin that is larger than his face.

"My voice is hoarse after."

Stormy Wedding

William Fietzer

The saying goes that everybody complains about the weather, but nobody does anything about it. Maybe so, but four years ago, my future daughter-in-law, Nicki, had done everything in her power to minimize the impact weather would have on her wedding day. Hoping for a June wedding, she and Alex opted for the day closest to it: May 31. Given the fickle Minnesota climate, they nixed an outdoor wedding at the Chanhassen Arboretum in favor of Black Bear Crossings in Como Park, where the Outdoor Promenade with its sweeping vista of the lake could protect the festivities of their special day from even a late-season snowstorm.

The morning of the wedding broke clear and as crisp as the scent of the new-mown fairways at the golf outing planned for the early-arriving relatives. The weather forecast predicted a calm, sunny day in the low 70s with only a slight chance of a late afternoon shower. Leaden clouds were passing toward the northern horizon, however, by the time we completed nine holes, changed into our tuxedos, and headed toward Como Park. The wedding photographers already had captured the wedding party's joy ride through downtown Saint Paul, so all that remained to be done before the ceremony started were the photos of the bride and groom with their respective families.

Photo © Joyce Orr

Tornado clouds threaten wedding couple Alex and Nicki Fietzer in front of Como Conservatory, May 31, 2008

The penetrating sun had turned the cool, feathery air sticky and damp by the time we reached the pavilion parking lot. The northerly clouds grew more menacing, yet the blue sky to the east seemed to indicate that any showers in the area would hold off

Tornadic vortex hovers over Como Conservatory, May 31, 2008

Photo © Joyce Orr

until after the ceremony. The participants took their seats while the local justice of the peace—a wizened, vigilant man—spoke in hushed tones with the bride's father and Alex's best man, his brother, Nick. As a precaution, Nick moved the microphone and the bridal flowers away from the ivory balustrade overlooking the lake.

A moment later, a gust of wind sent the bridal bouquet crashing onto the cement floor. The shards were soon swept up, but the bride refused to emerge from her dressing room behind the promenade stage. While Nicki's father settled her nerves, those seated on the benches in front of the altar gaped at the lightning strikes hammering the north end of the lake.

The bride appeared with an unsteady smile, arm in arm with her resolute dad. As wind whistled through the doorway, her veil billowed like a fan behind her while her father led her up the aisle. Lightning crackled and hail danced across the parking lot. The justice pulled his suit lapels across his chest and proceeded with the vows. Nicki and Alex kissed chastely while a double rainbow arced over the lake behind them.

The newlyweds headed for the reception at the Como Conservatory to the howls of warning sirens. Cell phone plastered against his ear, Nick reported that three twisters already had been reported and that his date was stalled at the side of the road in west Minneapolis because of the storms. My wife and I climbed into our car under the twisting, sulfurous sky accompanied by a second blare of warning sirens. If this day was destined to be our last, we decided to spend it celebrating Alex's and Nicki's new lives together, however brief. Halfway to the Conservatory, the deluge came.

Within fifteen minutes, the sun re-emerged. The perilous wind, thunder, and hail seemed never to have occurred. Everyone partied into the night and beyond, doubly gratified by the newlyweds' and their own good fortunes.

May

June

Photo © Media Mike Hazard

Camel Bells

Said Salah Ahmed is the Fred Rogers of Somalia.

Poet, playwright, filmmaker, community elder, reconciler, and teacher, Ahmed builds bridges between and within communities.

"I use camel bells to bring together the Somali people who are dispersed throughout the world."

Media Mike Hazard

June

➪ Louis LeRoy, a Native American player for the Saint Paul Saints baseball team, compiled a 20–10 record while pitching 277 innings in 1912.

JUNE

S	M	T	W	T	F	S
					1	2
3	4	5	6	7	8	9
10	11	12	13	14	15	16
17	18	19	20	21	22	23
24	25	26	27	28	29	30

28 Monday

Memorial Day

🌼 May 28: Stanley S. Hubbard, local radio executive, was born today in 1933.

29 Tuesday   Saint Paul (Seventh Place) Farmers' Market

International Day of United
   Nations Peacekeepers

🌼 May 29: Steven D. Levitt, economist and author of *Freakonomics*, was born today in 1967.

30 Wednesday

31 Thursday   Saint Paul (Seventh Place) Farmers' Market

World No-Tobacco Day

June

In the neighborhood walking home from school

1 Friday	

2 Saturday	Saint Paul Farmers' Market
	Saint Anthony Park Art Festival
	Flint Hills International Children's Festival

3 Sunday	Saint Paul Farmers' Market
	Flint Hills International Children's Festival
	Grand Old Day

June

In 1997, Ila Borders became the first woman to pitch in minor league professional baseball, as a reliever for the St. Paul Saints.

Como Park Conservatory

Life in Saint Paul

Mehari Baheru

I have been living in Saint Paul for the past two years. Saint Paul is a historical place and it has many lakes and parks. Como Park is my favorite place to walk with my wife during the summertime. In addition in 2009, I met new classmates at the Hubbs Center. The Hubbs Center is a good place for adult learners. I learn English writing, listening, vocabulary, and grammar. Also, I took a nurse assistant class in 2009, and I passed the exam and got a job at a nursing home as a nursing assistant!

In my opinion living in Saint Paul is good but sometimes it is hard because of the culture, the food, the weather, and the social life. In Saint Paul we have to shovel the snow, and we have to scrape the ice from our cars and we don't see much sunshine except in the summer. As far as social life, it starts from talking to your neighbors, asking them to have some coffee at your house.

In Saint Paul, there are schools, colleges, and universities. There are so many opportunities to go to college.

Living in Saint Paul gives a lot of people many opportunities to learn and grow. I feel Saint Paul is more peaceful and convenient for bus transportation and has a lot of shopping centers that are not far away. There are grocery centers in the Midway area, for instance, which is convenient for a lot of people who live in that area.

June

Mural at Midway Stadium

Midway Stadium

Eli Pattison

My favorite place in all of Saint Paul is Midway Stadium. It is where the St. Paul Saints play their baseball games. The Saints are very fan-friendly, and between innings they have hilarious game shows and contests. If you get bored of watching the game, you can go to the Kids Zone, where they have a bounce house, a playground, and a baseball-hitting game. They also have great concessions like frozen root beer, frozen lemonade, and of course the regular delicious concession items. The seats are always good because you're very close to the action. One time in the summer of 2010 at a night game, my brother, my friend, his brother, and I went to a USA vs. Canada game. They were the best high school players from all over the United States and Canada! There was basically no one at the game besides us, so whenever a foul ball was hit, we ran behind the stadium to get it. We all got a foul ball from Midway Stadium that game. Afterward, we got to run the bases and get autographs from the players. Midway Stadium is so fun.

June

↪ The parish of St. Agnes, established by Archbishop John Ireland for the city's German-speaking immigrants, dedicated its grand baroque revival building at 548 West Lafond Avenue on June 9 in 1912.

S	M	T	W	T	F	S
					1	2
3	4	5	6	7	8	9
10	11	12	13	14	15	16
17	18	19	20	21	22	23
24	25	26	27	28	29	30

4 Monday

International Day of Innocent
   Children Victims of Aggression

5 Tuesday   Saint Paul (Seventh Place) Farmers' Market

World Environment Day

6 Wednesday

7 Thursday   Saint Paul (Seventh Place) Farmers' Market
                          Music in Mears Park

🐞 June 7: Edward Payson Bassford, architect, was born today in 1837.

June

Pier at Como Lake

8 Friday	Saint Paul Chamber Orchestra

9 Saturday	Saint Paul Farmers' Market
	Saint Paul Chamber Orchestra

10 Sunday	Saint Paul Farmers' Market

Four feet tall and poised,
glove on, front row, third base line,
yearning for the foul.
Michael Russelle

The Town and Country Club's new nine-hole golf course was opened in 1898.

Mears Park creek

Peace in the City

Wendy Brown-Baez

In winter, Mears Park looks forsaken and small. The snow piles up on the benches and sidewalks, and seen from the protective warmth and laughter spilling out onto the sidewalk from the Barrio Tequila Bar, even the Christmas lights do not entice anyone to attempt to cross it.

But in summer, going to Mears Park is like walking through Alice's magical Looking Glass. Only a block long, the gurgling stream lined with colorful flowers and green leafy trees becomes an enchanted brook in a forest. The sounds of the city drift away, and a cool breeze sweeps along my forehead. Removing my sandals, I dangle my bare feet in the water (not caring if this is allowed or healthy) and pretend that instead of walking to the corner to catch a bus, there is nothing else to do with my day but dream.

When the Slam Poetry Festival came to Saint Paul, I chose to attend the poetry slam for loss and grief. Here the rules were relaxed; there would be no judging. As each one of us stood up to share poems that articulated our love and grief, anger and incredulity at some of the senseless deaths we had experienced; as we faced the audience of our poetic peers, the air shimmered with tears and we were woven into an intimacy that is rare amongst strangers. We had written poems about death from cancer, overdoses, drive-bys, suicide, old age, and car accidents. We recited poems that wept, howled, raged, and forgave. To be heard in such an environment is healing. I shared my poem about my son's death, one that I have spoken aloud only once before, right after it happened. So often I have felt my grief too strong, too naked, too deep for ordinary poetry readings. So often I felt the audience wouldn't know how to respond to such depth of raw feelings. But in this two-hour session, I was held and succored by those who had a glimpse into my own entangled emotions because they had not only been through something similar, they had chosen to transform it with words.

Afterward, I felt full and exhausted at the same time. I knew that Mears Park was only a few blocks away and there, surrounded by nature, the gurgling stream would replenish me. Under the sheltering shade of the trees, I ignored the bustle of the city around me and was quiet and still. In the midst of Lowertown, where cars and buses chugged past, people stopped to buy hot dogs from a cart on the corner of the park and met in restaurants with TVs blaring the daily news, where the neighbors walked their dogs and business meetings were conducted, I found a tranquility that eased my heart. A little miracle in the midst of concrete, an oasis where I could rest.

Photo © Pa Yong Xiong

Mears Park benches

⇨ "I discovered one way to get the pain out of me was to write. I wrote and wrote and wrote."—Darina Siv, Cambodian American activist and writer, who died in Saint Paul in 2002 at the age of 44

S	M	T	W	T	F	S
					1	2
3	4	5	6	7	8	9
10	11	12	13	14	15	16
17	18	19	20	21	22	23
24	25	26	27	28	29	30

11 Monday
Saint Paul Almanac Lowertown Reading Jam

🐞 June 11: Emma L. Brock, writer and illustrator of children's books, was born today in 1886.

12 Tuesday
Saint Paul (Seventh Place) Farmers' Market

13 Wednesday

🐞 June 13: Robert A. Smith, Saint Paul's mayor 1887–1892, 1894–1896, and 1900–1908, was born today in 1827.

14 Thursday
Saint Paul (Seventh Place) Farmers Market

Music in Mears Park

Back to the '50s Car Show

Twin Cities Jazz Festival

June

Rice Street sign at intersection of Rice and University

15 Friday   Back to the '50s Car Show
                                 Twin Cities Jazz Festival

16 Saturday   Saint Paul Farmers' Market
                                 Back to the '50s Car Show
                                 Twin Cities Jazz Festival
                                 West End Neighbors' Garden Tour

17 Sunday   Saint Paul Farmers' Market
Father's Day
World Day to Combat
  Desertification and Drought

🐞 June 17: Elmer L. Andersen—writer, editor, and 30th Minnesota governor—was
born today in 1909.

June

Star Wish

Marilynne Thomas Walton

For Barbara Kast-Walton

Far from the shoulders
of Superstition Mountain
or the palms' wild-man haircuts,
black pirate ships held
against desert dusk,
and a crew of saguaro,

We live where rivers converge
like veins in a wrist;
waves twinkling blue
off new car roofs on sunny
University Avenue lots.

Or look out again at a green park:
yellow dogs, four feet flying in the air
to field frisbees, with jack o' lantern grins,
hold the moon between jagged teeth.

Remember little mom-and-pop cafés you favored?
Hot oil smell of yeast, fennel, sausage
funneling into a strip mall.
Cool vapors of ice cream shops
on sweet Sunday afternoons.

At the end of the dock
sunny fish come snapping,
tame-looking as baby coots.
Saxophones spoon
liquid sound, lazy syrup
from the Como Park Pavilion.

Oh, little Loved One.
We all wish to be here
where stars heat
the heart of cold nights,

And we can almost hold them,
still warm Christmas cookies
in this safe home
you've come to.

Illustration © Cindy Berglund

Fishing Time

Sybil Smith

Dishes in the sink,
Laundry basket's overflowing,
Garage needs cleaning
And the lawn needs mowing,
It's time to go fishing.

Bills piling up.
House is falling down,
Got no money
For going to town.
I want to go fishing.

Dog's run off
Kids got the flu
Too little time
And too much to do.
So, I'm going fishing.

Sitting on the lake
In an old rowboat,
Bailing half the time
Just to stay afloat.
But I'm fishing.

Bass in the lily pads,
Crappie in the hole.
It doesn't even matter
That I'm getting old
Let's just go fishing!

⮫ "It's nice when they call on the old warhorses to come out and talk. … I've been involved in this issue for almost 40 years, trying to reduce the blight of billboards in our wonderful city."—Ruby Hunt, former Saint Paul City Council member, speaking at a 2009 meeting

JUNE

S	M	T	W	T	F	S
					1	2
3	4	5	6	7	8	9
10	11	12	13	14	15	16
17	18	19	20	21	22	23
24	25	26	27	28	29	30

18 Monday

19 Tuesday

Saint Paul (Seventh Place) Farmers' Market

Juneteenth

20 Wednesday

Summer Solstice

World Refugee Day

🐞 June 20: Mary Allen Whedon, editor of *Farmer's Wife* magazine, was born in 1862.

21 Thursday

Saint Paul (Seventh Place) Farmers' Market

Music in Mears Park

June

Urban Lights Music at 1449 University Avenue

22 Friday	Fourth Friday at the Movies

23 Saturday	Saint Paul Farmers' Market
United Nations Public Service Day	

24 Sunday	Saint Paul Farmers' Market

June

Noon Time Express, starring Roger Awsumb as Casey
Jones, first aired on local television in 1954.

Photo © Tobechi Tobechukwu

Kofi Bobby Hickman

The Brawl in Saint Paul

Kofi Bobby Hickman

During the Civil Rights movement, most youth felt that the leadership of their community was inadequate and didn't speak to their concerns, and therefore they would "take matters into their own hands." Little did they realize that their methods and tactics were causing more problems than they were solving, that they had the effect of polarizing the community; as a result, there were constant disputes and conflicts, stemming from those who thought they knew the most about what to do, how to do it, and who would do what about the problems that were plaguing the community.

These disputes would sometimes turn into ugly fights between opposing families, groups of friends, girls against girls, boys against boys, blacks against whites, etc. Every day there would be reports of clashes that were mostly instigated by people who held personal grudges that often bordered on petty jealousies, mistrust, fear, hatred, and uncertainty. This brought negative attention to the African American community, which gave rise to a lot of police presence. Much of that presence resulted in police brutality, arrest, and injuries that further caused parents who were formerly good friends to turn against each other in defense of their children.

In Saint Paul in 1967, we formed an organization called The Inner City Youth League, and immediately set about to change this behavior, and persuade the combatants that there is a better way to deal with their frustrations. All across the nation, there were youth organizations cropping up to teach the young people about the civil rights movement, and,

June

more importantly, how their help was needed, and how violent actions were detrimental to the cause.

The youth responded to our call to have meetings and tell us "older folks" what their concerns were. Could they justify their behavior? Their arguments were as follows: "We don't have any decent places to go, no activities for us, and there are no jobs available, we have to go out of our neighborhood to school. The police are brutal and disrespectful to our whole community. We have no black businesses. We're crammed into houses that are not decent to live in, our so-called leaders are someplace else, and don't listen to our concerns. Who is here to teach us what we need to know?"

No one could deny or dispute the stories they told or the arguments they made. In fact, we agreed with most of the things they were saying, but we couldn't agree with the way they were dealing with the problems. There *was* a void in leadership in the community; in many cases, adult members of the community were frightened by the youth.

We attempted to convey to the youth that we understood and in most cases agreed with their arguments, but there was still a need to embark upon different approaches to solve these problems. They could get involved with the movement, go to meetings where these things were discussed, engage in peaceful protest, learn some trade skills. They could show more love and concern for family and community. But the problems were so well entrenched that no amount of words were going to get them to fully understand and change their attitudes and behavior. That meant that a new approach was necessary, but what? How could we persuade our youth to try our way of doing things?

One answer came in the most unexpected way. A rumor was circulating around the community that a long-simmering feud was about to boil over into some serious violence involving two families and their friends. These families contained two well-known and influential "street guys," known as Billy P. and Chum, whose reputations were all about unrest and keeping tensions up in the community. Due to our credibility with most of the youth, we were expected to help squash this problem.

Part of the program at ICYL was to go out and break up fights and skirmishes in the streets. We often took the fighters to our gym where we had a boxing ring, and we would fit them with boxing gloves and make them fight it out under the supervision of Rock White, a professional boxer. No one was admitted who might be there to instigate in a negative way. In this case, we confronted the two men who were threatening each other. We asked them if they would be willing to fight it out in a boxing ring, at

June

a recreation center with the community in attendance. We would charge three dollars admission and they would split the proceeds between them. When they agreed, they were told that they would be required to train for the event every day at the Inner City Youth League under the watchful eye of our trainers. We embarked on a serious advertising campaign with pictures, flyers, and posters. This would be a takeoff from the Muhammad Ali vs. Joe Frazier "Thrilla in Manila." We called it the "Brawl in St. Paul," and we promoted it just like the professionals do, we had a doctor at ringside, three judges, and a "trainer" in each corner, in the personages of Dennis Presley and David McCall, who were up-and-coming boxers at Inner City. Lansing Thompson, a.k.a. Kokayi Ampah, was the announcer. There was a timekeeper to ring the bell, and some sisters sold tickets at the door. Robert McLain took pictures. Inner City's video class was on hand to record the fight.

On the night of the fight, a large crowd of almost two thousand people showed up to the gym at Oxford playground. It seemed as if the whole neighborhood had turned out, and there were people of all descriptions. We couldn't be sure of what might happen, but we kept our fingers crossed, and I remember thinking of how beautiful a gathering it was of our community. The lights were lowered, and the fighters entered the ring. The crowd went wild, and they were given instructions by the referee. The bell rang and after forty-five seconds of wildly swinging, ducking, and dodging they were so tired that they could not continue. In fact, they looked more like lovers than fighters the way they were leaning on each other at the bell. (A strong indication that street fighting is quite a bit different than organized boxing.) After the fight, we all went back to The Inner City League, where a celebration was held. The money was split up as we had promised. Billy P. and Chum became good friends and are still good friends to this day.

A few days later, a large group of youth came to The Inner City Youth League and wanted to know if they could start some programs there and get involved in learning more and being active in the civil rights struggle. Through this process, the youth learned that there are more viable solutions to problems than they had heretofore experienced. This creative approach was valuable instruction to both the youth and the community as a whole.

What mode of persuasion will we use to deal with the problems of today's youth? How will we reach conflict resolution? My conclusion is simply this: Conflict can't always be resolved by talking alone. Persuasion often calls for creative action.

June

The Title Game

Michael E. Murphy

Again the seminal season and fungoed moonshots
pause above the gloves tracking them before
the school wall in right. Infield finished
our kids sprint out there for the title game.

Two of our kids are riding the far end
of the bench. They're dreaming of girls and Nook burgers;
they joke about the old guys in worn-out loafers
lined up there behind the wrought iron fence

on Randolph. The one with his foot on the fence rail nudges
his buddy when our kid lines home a run in the third:
Schmidty's grandson, he says, young Eddie's boy.
Yes, and didn't young Eddie marry a Melady?

The dreaming carries one kid off to the back seat of
his buddy's moon-lit Ford and the sweet wet heat
in the lake night air, the scent of alyssum in her hair.
The dreaming brings the other a walk-off homer.

With our kids down one in the fifth the old guys seem
to remember this game: You took second on the balk.
Yes, and when their coach came out for a jaw
at the ump, Warner got you up to hit for Monk.

But for all the pensive spitting into the cleat-clawed dirt
we're still down one, two out, and Muff's been sitting
on second for something like sixty years it seems.
So Jimmy goes to his bench for a kid with a dream in the

bottom of the seventh. Better to hear than to feel
your hit. As their kid tracks it toward the wall in right
the old guys remember this small May moon in a steel
blue sky, this arc of hope in its seamless flight.

Beverly and her parents at their home at 1120 West Iowa Avenue

Theresa's Peonies

Beverly Schultz Golberg

Every June of my childhood, when our peonies were in their most voluptuous bloom, my mom planned an evening outing to Calvary Cemetery to visit her mother's grave.

In preparation, she'd put an empty two-pound Folger's coffee can in the trunk of our dark green 1950 Packard. As soon as we finished dinner, she would pick an armful of peonies, which she held on her lap in the passenger seat while my dad slid in behind the wheel for the five-minute drive to the cemetery. I sat alone in the back seat.

For me, visiting this beautiful but mysterious land of entombment was a trip of uneasy intrigue. My parents' demeanor was solemn, and they barely spoke when we pulled into the cemetery and wound our way around the slope to my grandmother's grave at the far end. I felt no emotional connection with my grandmother, who had died weeks after my birth.

My dad edged the car to the side of the quiet road and parked next to a faucet, where we filled the red and white coffee tin with water and stuffed it tightly with peony stems. I carried the enormous bouquet to my grandmother's grave, and before placing it beside the flat granite marker engraved with the name "Theresa Cufer," I tipped my face toward the blossoms. The pink flowers, softer than velvet, were cool and soothing when they touched my nose and cheeks. I closed my eyes and nestled my face farther into the moist cushion of petals and inhaled deeply, losing myself momentarily in their sweetness.

My parents knelt—my dad on one knee, my mother on both knees—and bowed their heads over the shiny gray stone. I wasn't certain whether

Calvary Cemetery

they assumed different fashions of kneeling because my dad struggled with back pain and my mother didn't or because my mother was Catholic and my father an atheist. Or perhaps, I reasoned, it was a gender preference. Since I was strong-backed, Catholic, and female, I knelt on two knees like my mother.

I imitated my parents' reverent manner, our heads bent over the gravestone for a long few minutes. My mother, her eyes glistening, softly prayed the "Hail Mary." My father engaged in silent contemplation. I did not like to see my mother cry or my father brought to his knee. I stared at the ground, trying to conjure up an image of the skeleton in my grandmother's grave. How different from the fleshy, fresh, and luscious flowers we brought from our sunny garden.

Because a BNSF track ran adjacent to the back of the cemetery, inevitably a train or two would roar by, quite near to us, behind a dense screen of trees and underbrush. Interrupted, we would stop and face the direction of the terrible clatter, quietly waiting for the sound to fade to a distant rumble. I caught only glimpses of the cars as they thundered by, obscured by foliage. The ground shook beneath us, and I envisioned bones shuddering in their graves for those few moments and then settling back to their eternal sleep.

Before we returned to our car, we meandered across the lovely grounds, exploring the final earthly homes of countless other Saint Paul Catholics who, I understood to my relief, had no concern with us anymore; they were wholly turned to experiencing their everlasting rewards or punishments. An enormous stone fireman carrying a rescued toddler towered high from its base over the graves of Saint Paul firefighters. Standing in Bishops Circle, the highest point in the cemetery, my parents directed my gaze to an expansive view of Saint Paul. The domes of the Capitol and the Cathedral of Saint Paul shared the city's airspace, just as secular notables like Hamm, Butler, and Bremer were neighbors in Calvary with churchly luminaries like Cretin, Grace, and Ireland.

When the sun sank and the elongated shadows of ancient elm trees blended with those of century-old marble angels and obelisks, we strolled back to our car. Sensing my discomfort in this land of the dead, my dad often reached down to wrap his large fingers around mine. With my hand secure inside his, a hand that worked sheet metal, I knew all would be well for me.

When we pulled our car doors shut around us and headed toward the exit, the horizon was tinted the same shades of pink as the peonies we had left behind. Our car's wheels rolled faster, speeding up from a dirge to the rapid and rhythmic hum of life as we turned out onto Front Street. We traveled north on Lexington and through Como Park toward home. My parents chatted. Mundane matters again picked up our attention. The dome of the Como Conservatory glowed in the night sky over the far edge of the golf course. Beyond that flashed the red "1ˢᵗ" sign of downtown's preeminent bank, visible all the way to the northern border of the city. The lights of our neighborhood shone from bright neon store signs and softly lit house windows. Porch lights glowed in front yards where kids were still outside. Their quick, long shadows darted across lawns and sidewalks with them as their final games of tag were played out. I had little inclination to think about graves for another year.

Now in my sixties, I realize I'm in the last third of my life. I still visit my grandmother's grave every summer, offering the gift of one peony stem. I honor the memory of my parents in the same manner. These last few years, along with my reverence, I bring a wary attention that mimics my childhood curiosity. Really, I know little more about death now than I did then. For most of my adult years, my imagination was occupied with more timely diversions than pondering my mortality. I've come full circle; my mind's eye again visualizes the possibilities of that last journey.

I still live in Saint Paul, only blocks from my childhood home, and just a few miles from the railroad track that passes by Calvary. Sometimes when I lie in bed on a summer night, and the breeze that drifts in through my open bedroom window is soft and quiet, I hear the faintest rumble of the train rolling along toward the cemetery. I close my eyes to recall the cool, silky touch and the sweet redolence of peonies, evening shadows cast by tall monuments on a grassy hill, and my girlhood imagination depicting skeletons jiggling inside dark coffins. And against that delicious melancholy, I can almost feel my dad's warm, strong hand reaching down to enclose mine.

June

July

Photo © Pa Yong Xiong

City of Alleys

Saint Paul is a city of alleys
that if you haven't visited before
causes you to wonder at
the blocks on blocks of houses
all neat rows, no driveways, no garages in sight.

And if this was your first introduction to
a city—the State Fair anticipated
for weeks, calendar squares crossed off
in a twelve-year-old girl's shorthand
for kisses—those rare visits would have trained

you to find most other cities and their suburbs
troubling. Other places with their houses hidden
behind oversized garages seem to have
no delicacy, no subtlety,
no rhythm of home home home.

Kathryn Knudson

143

➪ "Today there is not a city or government that does not fully comprehend the importance and value of public parks for its citizens ... chiefly by their benefits in ministering to the health and pleasure of the masses, who cannot afford the expensive outings of the rich."—Frederick Nussbaumer, Superintendent of Saint Paul Parks from 1891 to 1922, writing in 1903

JULY

S	M	T	W	T	F	S
1	2	3	4	5	6	7
8	9	10	11	12	13	14
15	16	17	18	19	20	21
22	23	24	25	26	27	28
29	30	31				

25 Monday

Why must we wait 'til we die
And fly to our home in the sky
And endure resurrection
To find such perfection
As a week in St. Paul in July

Garrison Keillor

26 Tuesday   Saint Paul (Seventh Place) Farmers' Market

International Day Against Drug Abuse
  and Illicit Trafficking and International
  Day in Support of Victims of Torture

27 Wednesday

🎂 June 27: George Bannon, founder of Bannon's Department Store, was born in 1843.

28 Thursday   Saint Paul (Seventh Place) Farmers' Market

Music in Mears Park

Photo © Ernesto "Neto" Ybarra

Viva Mexico

29 Friday

30 Saturday   Saint Paul Farmers' Market

1 Sunday   Saint Paul Farmers' Market

The first celebration of Rondo Days, then called
Remember Rondo, began in 1983.

Photo © Nina Hellman, flickr.com/sedagenvakna

Spinning a record

Record

Katrina Vandenberg

Late night July, Minnesota,
John asleep on the glassed-in porch,
Bob Dylan quiet on a cassette

you made from an album
I got rid of soon after
you died. Years later,

I regret giving up
your two boxes of vinyl,
which I loved. Surely

they were too awkward,
too easily broken
for people who loved music

the way we did. But tonight
I'm in the mood for ghosts,
for sounds we hated: pop,

scratch, hiss, the occasional
skip. The curtains balloon;
I've got a beer; I'm struck

by guilt, watching you

from a place ten years away,
kneeling and cleaning each

with a velvet brush before
and after, tucking them in
their sleeves. Understand,

I was still moving then.
The boxes were heavy.
If I had known

I would stop here
with a husband to help me
carry, and room—too late,

the college kids pick over
your black bones on Mass. Ave.,
we'll meet again some day

on the avenue but still,
I want to hear it,
the needle hitting the end

of a side and playing silence,
until the arm gives up,
pulls away.

From *Atlas*, published by Milkweed Editions in 2004.

↪ "I grew up in a really cool neighborhood… It had the best dump in the world. A dump mall."--Stephen Capiz, an artist from the West Side flats

JULY

S	M	T	W	T	F	S
1	2	3	4	5	6	7
8	9	10	11	12	13	14
15	16	17	18	19	20	21
22	23	24	25	26	27	28
29	30	31				

2 Monday
International Day of Cooperatives

Hmong International Sports Tournament and Freedom Festival

3 Tuesday
Asala-Dharma Day

Saint Paul (Seventh Place) Farmers' Market

Hmong International Sports Tournament and Freedom Festival

Nine Nights of Music Series

4 Wednesday
Independence Day

Hmong International Sports Tournament and Freedom Festival

Saint Anthony Park Fourth of July Parade

🐞 July 4: Mother Seraphine Ireland, educator and school founder, was born today in 1842.

5 Thursday

Saint Paul (Seventh Place) Farmers' Market

Music and Movies

🐞 July 5: Anna Arnold Hedgeman, African American activist and first Black woman graduate of Hamline University, was born today in 1899.

Cafesjian's Carousel at Como Park

6 Friday

7 Saturday   Saint Paul Farmers' Market

He's fat
My fault
No walks
Lily Rupp

8 Sunday   Saint Paul Farmers' Market

Brian Brunette of Saint Paul made his professional boxing debut in 1980, winning with a second-round knockout.

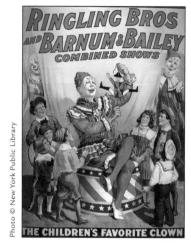

Photo © New York Public Library

Ringling Bros. and Barnum & Bailey Poster

The Last Big Top

David McKay

It was a hot, humid stretch in July 1956. Ringling Brothers, Barnum and Bailey Circus was coming to Saint Paul. I really wanted to go. My parents frowned on the idea. My mother was worried about fire. In the late 1940s, several people had been killed in a circus tent fire. My father was less concerned, but said he couldn't get off work to take me. The circus usually set up behind the old Prom Ballroom off University Avenue next to Lexington Park, home of the American Association Saint Paul Saints baseball team. We lived on Lincoln and Syndicate, only a mile from the site. I told my parents I could ride my bike. They agreed, but I had to find a friend to go along. And, we had to attend the daytime matinee performance.

I recruited Larry Marofsky. On the big day, mother packed lunches and off we went. We pedaled past the fortress of old Central High School to the circus site, where we expected to see tents, booths, and lots of people. Instead, there were just some kids milling about and a few old guys smoking cigars and scratching their heads. The circus was late. As this news soaked in, the circus train was slowly backing down the rail spur that ran through the midway from the Milwaukee Road mainline. Word spread that the matinee performance, scheduled for one o'clock, would be cancelled. The circus people hoped they could set up in time for the evening show.

Suddenly there was a big commotion. All the kids began running. Larry and I dropped our bikes (no locks needed) and our lunches and ran after them. We found ourselves in a line of pushing-and-shoving kids. They said we could get a free ticket to that night's performance if we helped set up the circus. Help? This was a boy's dream come true! Soon we were pulling on ropes, opening boxcar doors, and unloading wagons. We stretched canvas as small tractors buzzed back and forth. Just like in the movies, elephants pulled ropes to raise the big top. It was dusty. I remember sweat stinging my eyes and running down my back. Larry and I were assigned to a crew setting up benches on the bleachers that were rolled in under the big top. Row after row, section after section. Some guy was yelling at us. At one point a water wagon circled the three circus rings and sprayed water to wet down the dust. We were in the way and got a good soaking. After several hours and a few more jobs, including setting up animal pens, the circus was ready. We were ushered into another line and given our general admission tickets. Show time!

They said we could get a free ticket to that night's performance if we helped set up the circus. Help? This was a boy's dream come true! Soon we were pulling on ropes, opening boxcar doors, and unloading wagons.

After all that work, and having lost our lunch bags, we were starved. We bought hot dogs, pop, and candy with the admission money our parents had given us. It was an exciting, well-choreographed set of performances mostly happening all at once in all three rings. Clowns, contortionists, acrobats, and animal acts. Lions, a bear that danced on a ball, and horses circling a ring while beautiful almost naked girls stood on their backs.

When we left the big top, filthy and enthralled, we realized it was dark. Only then did we remember that our parents had sent us to the matinee performance. They had probably expected us for dinner. We found our bikes and pedaled quickly home to the punishment that surely awaited us.

By the time we got home my mother was hysterical. My dad was just plain mad. I got the strap that night, but it was definitely worth it. Especially when it was announced that from now on, Barnum and Bailey would no longer perform under canvas tents, but only in indoor arenas. I knew then that Larry and I had taken part in history.

⇨ "The artistic self is experiencing serious neglect in today's society and economy, which necessitates an elevation of our work and focus. I hope to remain a part of that movement."— Khary Jackson, performance poet and playwright

JULY

S	M	T	W	T	F	S
1	2	3	4	5	6	7
8	9	10	11	12	13	14
15	16	17	18	19	20	21
22	23	24	25	26	27	28
29	30	31				

9 Monday

Dragon Festival and Dragon Boat Race

Saint Paul Almanac Lowertown Reading Jam

10 Tuesday

Saint Paul (Seventh Place) Farmers' Market

Nine Nights of Music Series

Dragon Festival and Dragon Boat Race

🐾 July 10: Edward William Lowe, inventor of Kitty Litter, was born today in 1920.

11 Wednesday

World Population Day

12 Thursday

Saint Paul (Seventh Place) Farmers' Market

Music and Movies

Music in Mears Park

🐾 July 12: William Wallis Erwin, nationally known labor attorney, was born today in 1842.

Photo © Tom Reynen

Saint Paul Cathedral at night

13 Friday

14 Saturday   Saint Paul Farmers' Market

15 Sunday   Saint Paul Farmers' Market

Phoebe Fairgrave, a 19-year-old living in Saint Paul, set a women's world record for a high-altitude parachute jump, at 15,200 feet, in 1922.

Booker T. Café and Tavern, 381–383 Rondo

Summertime Down on Rondo

Bertha Givins

The long, dark days of winter have finally come and gone, and the long, hot days of summer have returned to claim the throne. It's Saturday night in the city, and we are strolling down Rondo Street. Sweet aromas tease our nostrils 'til they make our stomachs leap. We smell fried chicken, fish, collard greens, ham and black-eyed peas, and the familiar scent of Bar-B-Q coming out of old Mr. Booker T's.

The blinking light of the taverns seem to light up the evening sky like the glowing fireflies that came out every night. As we pass the many houses up and down the street, we can tell from the activity that the people had things to do. We can hear the sound of laughter as they go about their chores, and smell the scent of pressed hair coming through the open doors. A lady snaps her fingers to the tune of "Moody's Blues" as she stands there by the window tryin' to see which dress she'd choose.

Farther down we help a couple tryin' to get inside their door, 'cause they got cleanin' bags and groceries, and beer from the liquor store. We help them take the stuff inside, and imagine in our hearts: "They either playin' cards tonight, or they havin' a chitlin strut." And then we go down past the old folks; they out sittin' on their porch, exchanging all the news they'd heard all week about the other folks. They have their Sunday best laid out, and picked and washed the greens. Now they waitin' for the happenings while they enjoy the summer breeze.

Well by the time we make it home that night, curfew time has come and gone. And we know that we in trouble for being gone so long. So, right after supper, we got to lay it down to sleep, and we can't even mumble a single word, not even just a peep. I'd say it had to be about midnight when we heard the commotion going on. And we wake to John the Concord, beltin' out his favorite song. And folks come from everywhere just to take a peek. But by the time we hit the sidewalk, Old John lays helpless in the street.

We can hear the sound of laughter as they go about their chores, and smell the scent of pressed hair coming through the open doors. A lady snaps her fingers to the tune of "Moody's Blues" as she stands there by the window tryin' to see which dress she'd choose.

"Somebody better call the law!" the neighbor lady says.

"No! Call Brooks the undertaker, 'cause I think this old man's dead."

"I just seen him staggerin' down the street just a little bit ago."

"Lord! If he lives to tell this, I bet he won't drink wine no mo.'"

And just that quick Old John stood up and smiled a toothless grin. "My name is John the Concord. Yes it's me, and I'm drunk again."

Just a little humor from old Rondo Street.

Dedicated to my sister, who passed away many years ago. My folks got her piano lessons, but she wouldn't have it. She played by ear and taught me to play "Chopsticks." She also wrote a song called "Down on Rondo."

⇨ "My life purpose is to help younger generations spread their wings and soar. For that end, I seek any opportunities to continue to develop myself and help others do the same."—Marcella de la Torre, co-founder of the Association of Latina Women of Minnesota

JULY

S	M	T	W	T	F	S
1	2	3	4	5	6	7
8	9	10	11	12	13	14
15	16	17	18	19	20	21
22	23	24	25	26	27	28
29	30	31				

16 Monday

17 Tuesday

Saint Paul (Seventh Place) Farmers' Market

Nine Nights of Music Series

🕏 July 17: Vetal Guerin, French-Canadian pioneer, was born today in 1812.

18 Wednesday

19 Thursday

Saint Paul (Seventh Place) Farmers' Market

Music and Movies

Music in Mears Park

Sunset Affair

Photo © Patricia Bour-Schilla

Como Park flowers

20 Friday   Highland Fest

Ramadan Begins

July 20: Mike Gibbons, famous Saint Paul boxer, was born today in 1887.

21 Saturday   Saint Paul Farmers' Market
                                                    Highland Fest
                                                    Rondo Days

22 Sunday   Saint Paul Farmers' Market
                                                    Highland Fest

Bob Dylan and Willie Nelson performed at
Saint Paul's Midway Stadium in 2005.

Summer: 1976

Julia Klatt Singer

The summer before my father died
he sat at the kitchen table, the windows open,
the night air thick with tar and cricket song,
writing the cheerless history of the Cubs
in a yellow legal pad. His block printing
sharp and angular pressed through
to the sheet below.

The words were all that mattered. He earned them
the same way I earned my name, the one
he called me late at night, when the lamps had halos,
when the trees were lost in shadows.

The slant and sway of his lines I loved
their three-four time, the way they took
the rug out and shook it, danced
barefoot on the wooden floor,

and the dimple in his cheek, there for me
as I entered the room. The overhead light
made his hands glow, made each bead of sweat
a jewel on the amber-glass bottle of beer.

If we had known that winter
would find him buried in the ground—
would we have sat in the garden
wished otherwise on every singular star?
Would we have packed the tent and
cooler, the records and baseballs
the tackle and dog, kept moving?
Would I have asked the questions
I am left with now?

He knew what it meant to be fatherless, how many
pounds of newspapers it took to get
a buck. Knew the smell of shoe polish,
how to make things shine. And to marvel
over the wonders of this world—
the slim lead of his mechanical pencil
its soft pink eraser cradled in a crown.

And he left me space
between every line.

Hazainyankwin

Sharon M. Day

She was a woman
A Dakota woman
Who the white folks called
Old Betsy
Well, the white folks thought her kinda crazy
But old Betz was kinda cagey

She owned a ferry
And for two bits
Ferried them across the river
She took their money
Gave it to Dakota children
Who were starving
In the mission schools

Well, the white folks
Kept a'coming
Took all the land
Poisoned the river

But we are
We are still here
And we say "thank you"
Pidamaya

To old Betsy
You are our hero
You know we love
And we say "thank you"
Pidamaya

Berry Pickin Woman
Hazainyankwin

Painting © Andrew Falkenshield

Old Betsy

▷ On July 24 in 1912, officers were elected for the newly formed International Brotherhood of Electrical Workers (IBEW) Local 110. Members also voted to affiliate with the St. Paul Building Trades Council.

			JULY			
S	M	T	W	T	F	S
1	2	3	4	5	6	7
8	9	10	11	12	13	14
15	16	17	18	19	20	21
22	23	24	25	26	27	28
29	30	31				

23 Monday

24 Tuesday

Saint Paul (Seventh Place) Farmers' Market

Nine Nights of Music Series

Lake Phalen
in the boat I drive fast,
get up to fifty in no time,
turn quickly, water spills aboard
sloppy minnows
lie next to lines and sinkers.
there are fish in the bucket,
snagged, poked out eyes,
guts emerging.
my little boy cries.
we stall in the center of the lake
i tell him, look no farther, eyes cast out.
depths unrecorded
the anchor is lifted
and boy! ain't that heavy.
got to have hunger to be a fisher,
courage to float.
Sandra Erskine

25 Wednesday

26 Thursday

Saint Paul (Seventh Place) Farmers' Market

Music and Movies

Music in Mears Park

Rice Street Festival

Young photographers in front of the Landmark Center

Photo © Tobechi Tobechukwu

27 Friday

Rice Street Festival

Car Craft Summer Nationals

Fourth Friday at the Movies

🎭 July 27: Jerry Juhl, television and movie writer, best known for his work on the Muppet Show, was born today in 1938.

28 Saturday

Saint Paul Farmers' Market

Rice Street Festival

Car Craft Summer Nationals

29 Sunday

Saint Paul Farmers' Market

Car Craft Summer Nationals

Ole Bull, a famous Norwegian violinist, gave a concert at the Capitol building in Saint Paul in 1856.

Acknowledgments

Linda Back McKay

I'd like to thank the clouds for last night,
and the rain and eager ripeness
straining against the garden fence.

I would just like to say thank you
for the hopeful quality of this sunset,
how it hints pink for tomorrow,

and to my shovel and the tools
that build my moraine of
a brain and dear Mrs. Sullivan,

lay teacher at St. Joseph's Catholic
School on Butler Avenue,
land of the faithful and sure,

thank you for teaching me how
to diagram a sentence.
My hat's off to black dirt, earth

worms, my mother and father
for getting me here. For the pleated
skirt, the Peter Pan collar and barely

nothing of a breeze, the rustling paper
leaves, the visiting monarchs, like
paper themselves as they float

among raggedy roses, burr-faced
coneflowers, benign bumble bees,
river and land mass and this is just the short list.

And finally, thank you, veins and sinew, delicate
orbs, newest of fruits and the juices within.
None of this could have been possible without you.

Painting the Town

James McKenzie

From the iconic animal forms on the cave walls of Lascaux, France, through centuries of murals in cathedrals and castles, to the vineyards and grapes gracing the side of Thomas Liquors on Saint Paul's Grand Avenue, colorful wall paintings have drawn the human eye. What is it these murals offer our eyes and spirits? What do they give to you?

The 2012 *Saint Paul Almanac* celebrates four of the city's many dozens of such art works (no one has even counted them all), and invites readers to become writers for future editions, telling others about your favorite Saint Paul mural, just as we've done last year and this year. Many murals await your investigation and imagination.

To contribute to this project, email stories@saintpaulalmanac.com with your favorite mural's location, and a description in 200 words or less.

Photo © Patricia Bour-Schilla

Untitled (Java Train) by various artists
1341 Pascal Street

Graffiti-like in appearance (it was spray painted) this mural grew and changed as graffiti often does, with several additions by different hands over its six-year life. Its most recent addition, a water tower by barista Brian Johnston, covers an alien whose claw hands and other features were too scary for neighborhood children, though Brian showed me where a bit of the underlying alien remains.

Photo © Patricia Bour-Schilla

Untitled (planets) by Armando Gutierrez
1459 St. Clair Avenue

Because of their large scale, murals often involve several, sometimes many, sets of hands besides those of the commissioned artist. Armando Gutierrez's striking planetary scene on the side of ArtSpace's ArtScraps building employed more than a dozen teenage artists in the summer of 2009, the culmination of an ArtStart project that had them also making art kits, working in the store, researching the planets, and engaged in other tasks in its arts mentorship program, called Signature.

A mural in a neighborhood such as this one engages neighbors as well. Russell Rosen, whose house nearly touches the north end of it, near the mural's green profile of North America on Planet Earth, watched its daily progress with interest, was there for its dedication, and likes being in its colorful, inspiring proximity. "I hope it helps attract people to the store," he adds. "Murals do that."

For all the stark, deep-space, static beauty of this piece, Gutierrez's mural pulses with life, an effect of the broad, undulating waves that coil out from Earth across the whole wall to the St. Clair end of the painting: a big, glowing moon, where the wave's teal, aquamarine, and white bands wind up in a nautilus spiral under that image of our nearest celestial companion. All the planets are there, and some white stars too, vivid against the inky, cobalt blue background; but the eye is quickly drawn to a mysterious sprocket, suspended halfway between Earth and its moon, like a hub for the whole machinery of space—a satellite, something besides the imagination of the work itself, that reminds us of human presence, of technology.

Photo © Patricia Bour-Schilla

Art Lesson by Caprice Kueffner Glaser
Sibley and Fourth Streets

Like several other muralists featured in this year's *Saint Paul Almanac*, Caprice Glaser's studio and work is an anchor in our city's burgeoning Lowertown arts scene. But even though it's a short walk from Glaser's Jax Building studio to her most visible work, none of that mural's many admirers at TPT, where the mural is located, could tell the *Almanac* who made it, nor could anyone at City Hall, where we were referred for further information. A paradox of public art: seen by thousands every day, appreciated by many, yet familiar, part of the scenery, almost anonymous.

"It's a sculpture," Caprice explained the day the *Almanac* visited it with her. I'd been delighted by the whimsy of a powder-blue, plastic stream of water pouring out of a window and down the flat side of the mural, but had not noticed how it continued into the children's park, which is an integral part of the piece. Glaser's waterfall turns into a blue stream on the floor of the park, winding past its climbing structures, slides, steamboat, train, rocks, and benches.

"When are you going to finish it?" someone had called up to her when she was working on it, referring to the outlines formed by the image of a pencil that is part of the mural, and the irregular swath of blue seemingly coming from a brush at the other end. Maybe it's we, its viewers, who complete it. And that's part of the lesson.

Photo © Bjorn Christianson/bjornery.com

Hamline-Midway Coalition building designed by Clarence Wigington

Two Men Sharing a Common Cultural Legacy:
Clarence Wigington and David Vassar Taylor

Anura Si-Asar

While selecting this excerpt from a book about Saint Paul architect Cap Wigington, a giant within the African American community, I thought about Dr. David Vassar Taylor, the author of *Cap Wigington: An Architectural Legacy in Ice and Stone,* another major influence within the Rondo African American community for his research into the struggles and major personalities shaping the political and social landscape of Minnesota. These men represent two generations and I a third that are all attempting to share a mosaic of legacies and contributions that have improved African Americans' way of life in Saint Paul. I was enamored with the power of such stories, values, and work that are being passed down from one generation to the other.

I, too, was born and raised in Saint Paul, like Dr. Taylor, and went to Saint Paul Central and the University of Minnesota, as he did. I even took a graduate school prep writing course from him while at the U. My son, a student at St. Anthony Park Elementary School, and destined to attend Saint Paul Central, is a fourth-generation African American young man, who wants to be an architect. When I took him to visit some of Mr. Wigington's work around the city, my son stated with amazement while looking at Wilson Junior High School, "One of our ancestors built that! I want to do that too!"

Dr. Taylor's characterization of Mr. Wigington's "architectural legacy in ice and stone" is simply a capstone to the great heritage emanating from the African American community. This legacy, however, is often muted by the inefficient transfer of this knowledge to younger generations by our institutions—such as our families and schools.

Dr. Taylor researched and wrote a story hidden to most of us, about the state's first registered African American architect, Clarence "Cap" Wigington. Dr. Taylor, a native Minnesotan and Saint Paulite, pleasured himself with the documented discoveries of one of the most ambitious architects of the time and a renowned leader in the historic African American Rondo Community.

David Vassar Taylor with Paul Clifford Larson, *Cap Wigington: An Architectural Legacy in Ice and Stone* (Minnesota Historical Society Press, 2001): preface, 4–5, 53

My research on the life of Clarence Wigington has filled me with the same awe [as the life example of Dr. Benjamin Mays, the legendary educator, scholar, and former president of Morehouse College]. During a period of great social change in American history, he labored, as both a professional and a private citizen, to build bridges across the divide that separated races. He was a practical man, conservative at his core, but principled. The buildings he designed were built to serve. The leadership he provided in St. Paul's African American community was an extension of his belief in returning the benefits of blessings bestowed on him. ...

Wigington's move to St. Paul coincided with the "Great Migration" of African Americans in the early years of the twentieth century. In search of better employment opportunities and housing, they came by the thousands from the rural South to industrial cities in the North. ... [Between 1910 and 1920,] the black population in Minneapolis grew by only 5.1 percent and St. Paul registered a modest increase of just 7.4 percent. By war's end, however, 49.1 percent of Minnesota's black population had come from the South. ...

Wigington's decision to move to St. Paul in 1914 brought him to the right place at the right time. There he found a cadre of African American leaders who not only welcomed him into the community's social order but also began grooming him for leadership. Among his new mentors were the editor of *The Appeal*, John Quincy Adams; attorneys William R. Morris and William T. Francis; Doctors Val Do Turner and James H. Redd; the Reverends A.H. Lealtad and Stephen L. Theobald, clergymen of St. Philip's Episcopal Church and St. Peter Claver Catholic Church, respectively; and community activists Mrs. Nellie Francis, Mrs. T.H. Lyles, and Orrington C. Hall. It did not take long for Wigington to demonstrate his own capacity for leadership.

July

Diego Vázquez Jr.

face the heat
wear as little
as necessary
drink all things
cold, delicately
collect sunlight
on winter skin
adapt
to anything
harmful,
run fast to see
games played
outside all day
all night if possible
sleep fast
ready to introduce
days of this month
to sunlight and
desire, to involve
yourself as expert
on how good it feels
to have warm bones.

August

Photo © Patricia Bour-Schilla

Bake-Off Queen

It's Marjorie Johnson! Munchkin grandma, four-foot-eight
State Fair celebrity, famous for doing what she loves best,
won 19 baking ribbons this year—7 blue and 2 sweepstakes—
one for her apple pie, adding up to 2500 ribbons during
her 32-year Fair career, started baking at 8 and she's
never stopped, *Oh brother!* how fast she talks, takes
notes on everything she bakes just like an experiment,
makes a chart, always tries to improve, *Oh my gosh!* she's
been on Jay Leno with uploads to YouTube, for years she
entered the fair in 70 categories, didn't enter cookies
this year—only 25 categories allowed now—Oh brother!
a hard choice, always wears a red dress, drip dry, shows
up well on TV, rinses it out at night, hangs it over the
tub to dry, *Oh my gosh!* she's one of a kind! Best of show!

Jill Breckenridge

169

S	M	T	W	T	F	S
			1	2	3	4
5	6	7	8	9	10	11
12	13	14	15	16	17	18
19	20	21	22	23	24	25
26	27	28	29	30	31	

⇨ The Saint Paul Yacht Club, originally called the Saint Paul Motor Boat Club, was founded in 1912 to promote boating on the Mississippi River.

August

30 Monday

31 Tuesday

Saint Paul (Seventh Place) Farmers' Market

Nine Nights of Music Series

1 Wednesday

🏵 August 1: Clara Kellogg, teacher and settlement house worker, was born today in 1870.

2 Thursday

Saint Paul (Seventh Place) Farmers' Market

Circus Juventas

Music in Mears Park

More than 90,000 people witnessed team Major Trouble and the Dirty Dixies soar into victory when they flew 207 feet at the Red Bull Flugtag at Harriet Island in 2010

3 Friday	Circus Juventas

Can Be Good
I know this lady who has a houseful of cuckoo clocks.
Her husband only lets her run them once a month.
Whereas all the cuckoo birds get to sing together.
Orchestrated songs can be heard in every room.
On that day, her rotten teeth are seen in lips with smiles.
Thanking her husband, she sings like her cuckoos.
Sandra Erskine

4 Saturday	Saint Paul Farmers' Market
	Circus Juventas

5 Sunday	Saint Paul Farmers' Market
	Circus Juventas

Sparky V, a seal who lived and performed at Saint Paul's Como Zoo, passed away peacefully in 2009.

Grandfather, Robert Goff, and Carrie Gagne

Lefse at the Fair

Carrie Gagne

In all of his years as a Minnesotan, my grandfather has never once missed so much as a Pronto Pup or a Tom Thumb donut on our annual trek to the State Fair. And even though he hates crowds, he picks the busiest day of the year to go: the Saturday of Labor Day weekend. He fearlessly forges through the crowds, and if you should fall behind, you could be left among the chewed gum stuck to the sidewalk and the drifting French fry wrappers.

He shares scotch eggs with my mother and haunts the Grandstand, undeterred by the 108-degree heat, to find that one, innovative product that will reinvent the world.

"This is great, you'll need this," he says, thrusting a petrified bonsai tree into my brother's hands.

But it's the Food Building that holds the greatest allure for him, where the nations of the world are waiting to be tasted by Grandfather's seasoned pallet. Ordinary cuisine doesn't stand a chance against the old man's salty tongue. It's there that I once confounded my grandfather by choosing the wrong food to begin our day at the fair.

"What the heck is *that?*" he challenged, pointing to my confection.

I chewed and swallowed, chewed and swallowed, wondering if his tone was as teasing as I hoped. Mom had selected her usual standby, a meatball from the Sausage Sisters. My brother took it slow with a root beer. It was 10:30 in the morning, and I had the audacity to buy a roll of sweetened lefse, a flat Norwegian pancake.

"What the heck are you doing with that Scandinavian stuff?" Grandpa probed.

In another ten minutes or so, my grandfather would lead us to a French kiosk, to buy the biggest strawberry-and-cream-cheese scones I had ever seen. And here I was, a veteran in my own right of the Great Minnesota Get-Together, with a wad of shapeless, colorless dough clutched in my hand.

"What the heck are you doing with that Scandinavian stuff?" Grandpa probed.

While my grandfather has no particular issues with Scandinavians in general (or Norwegians in particular, for that matter), anyone who didn't know him would think he was seriously outraged by my choice. Eating drab dough when there was an acre of colorful food to choose from was like eating a fudge puppy without the chocolate, like filling up on bread before the steak arrived.

I swallowed and looked at the lefse in my hand, a pale comparison to the strawberry-and-cream-cheese scones we would soon be indulging in. I took another bite and smiled at Grandfather, then watched a broad grin spread across his face. He laughed and ushered us along. For a brief, handsome moment my lefse had out-shined the competition at the fair. My defiant smile was enough to place the Norwegian pancake on a par with the likes of a Pronto Pup or even Sweet Martha's Cookies. Maybe next year it'll be something more than just a wad of dough with sugar. Maybe next year my grandfather will greet the lefse booth with the same childlike enthusiasm he shows for Tom Thumb donuts.

AUGUST

S	M	T	W	T	F	S
			1	2	3	4
5	6	7	8	9	10	11
12	13	14	15	16	17	18
19	20	21	22	23	24	25
26	27	28	29	30	31	

▷ "An object that is usually decorative, like a wall hanging, can challenge our assumption and even keep us warm in a pinch."—Sara Langworthy, Saint Paul fiber artist

6 Monday
Circus Juventas

Hiroshima/Nagasaki Remembrance Day

7 Tuesday
Saint Paul (Seventh Place) Farmers' Market

Circus Juventas

Nine Nights of Music Series

🐞 August 7: Garrison Keillor, writer and radio programmer, was born today in 1942.

8 Wednesday
Circus Juventas

9 Thursday
Saint Paul (Seventh Place) Farmers' Market

International Day of the World's Indigenous People

Circus Juventas

Music in Mears Park

🐞 August 9: David Ramaley, early Saint Paul printer, was born today in 1828.

Saint Paul skyline as seen from the eastern bluffs

Photo © Tom Reynen

10 Friday	Circus Juventas
	Irish Fair

11 Saturday	Saint Paul Farmers' Market
	Circus Juventas
	Irish Fair

12 Sunday	Saint Paul Farmers' Market
International Youth Day	Circus Juventas
	Irish Fair

Theodore Hamm and his bride, Louisa Bucholtz Hamm, arrived in
Saint Paul in 1856; they opened Hamm's Brewery in 1865.

August Storm in St. Paul
for Pat Tromp
Ethna McKiernan

Now that Marv was gone,
her house was big.
Lightning at my windows
had kept me from sleep,
and I thought of Pat miles from here
in Burnsville, alone.
Thunder cracks
made me jump as I got up,
and wind whipped the rain
against glass.

At 79 she had grown
suddenly small, and
because she couldn't find
her car the other night
after the poetry reading,
and because I was worried
about us both, I picked up
the phone and called her.

Are you watching the storm
dear? she answered
after two rings.

I could see her as we spoke—
the lance of lightning
fierce as it pierced
falling rain once more—
her small knees tucked
beneath her arms
as she serenely welcomed
thunder, listening
through the long night
for birdsong, which comes
faithfully as she knew
it would
each blessed morning.

Riverview Cemetery

Patricia Cummings

The cemetery keeper told us how to
Find Augusta, our Swedish grandmother...

Come in the filigreed gate
Turn right at the sign with the Cemetery Rules
Go down the hill, round the circle
Start up again to the cedar tree
That stands alone by the road,
Look for the pointed stone
The Indian marker with the primordial symbols
Scratched into its surface and its memory
Of a Potowatomie woman,
Just past her, look for the Bengel family monument
Tall, extravagant, expensive,
Walk to the south, to the two headstones
Flanked by golden chrysanthemums.

Behind them you'll find two flat grave markers,
Two?
Yes, two—Augusta and Ruth.

We followed his guidance and found
The two modest markers
Tucked in behind the strangers' headstones
Easy to pass over, but
Carefully brushed off
Grass trimmed to form perfect rectangles.

Ruth, the daughter, taken by
Tuberculosis at age 12
Augusta, the mother, taken by
Her own hand just ten days later,
Left side-by-side, almost touching.

Lost for eight decades
Found by two granddaughters.

Riverview Cemetery is located at 340 East Annapolis Street.

S	M	T	W	T	F	S
			1	2	3	4
5	6	7	8	9	10	11
12	13	14	15	16	17	18
19	20	21	22	23	24	25
26	27	28	29	30	31	

↪ Saint Paul's school board was abolished in favor of a commissioner of education a century ago, as part of the city's newly established commission form of government.

August

13 Monday

Circus Juventas

14 Tuesday

Saint Paul (Seventh Place) Farmers' Market

Circus Juventas

Nine Nights of Music Series

15 Wednesday

Sky Note #1
What trees do for sky:
bone work.
Holding upright
the onrushing
blue body
of heaven.
Susan Steger Welsh

16 Thursday

Saint Paul (Seventh Place) Farmers' Market

Music in Mears Park

🎯 August 16: Ker Dunlop, famed participant in the sport of curling, was born today in 1859.

Coneflowers

17 Friday

18 Saturday   Saint Paul Farmers' Market

🐞 August 18: Dr. Charles M. Cannon, St. Anthony Park surgeon, was born today in 1861.

19 Sunday   Saint Paul Farmers' Market
Eid al-Fitr   Japanese Lantern Lighting Festival

The Sam S. Shubert Theater opened in 1910 at 10 East Exchange Street. It was renamed the Fitzgerald in 1994.

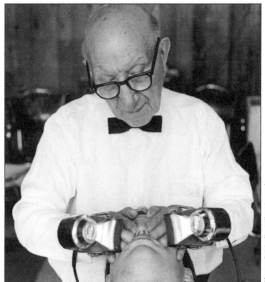

Photo © Media Mike Hazard

Nick with Bob

Nick the Barber

Media Mike Hazard

At 88 in this shot, Nick Delmont was a living museum piece in his knotty pine barbershop in South St. Anthony Park. The fellow in the chair, Bob Rucker, and I were CETA (Comprehensive Employment and Training Act) artists in the late seventies, assigned to the neighborhood like artists of the WPA were assigned to various places in America in the thirties.

This was our tax money at work.

The year changed my life. I went from being an artist trained in the ivory tower who cut his eye teeth on abstract expressionism to being a human being looking for the good life within community.

Rucker now earns a living as a writer and I as an artist.

CETA worked. The WPA worked. Let's put artists to work.

The Ferris wheel at night

The Minnesota State Fair

Gayathri Dileepan

Have you been to the Minnesota State Fair? It is one of my favorite places. In the barns, the animals moo, honk, snort, or neigh a greeting to you. The goats nod their heads as you pass by. The cows moo as if to say "welcome." The horses wave their tails to say "hello!" The birds honk, tweet, or chirp, all saying different things at once.

The rides are wonderful, too; they are pretty at night. They shine as bright as stars far away in the distance. They hold people, fun, and laughter, as they spin, rush, or rise. The ferris wheel is exciting, as you soar high into the sky. Up, up, up you go, until people are just pinpoints. At the upmost point, you can almost touch the clouds.

The roller coaster—a thrilling ride—is what, I must admit, I'm scared of. It starts out at a slow speed, then it bursts with energy, rushing faster and faster, like an airplane! I wonder how people enjoy it, screaming with joy. I scream as well, but I scream of fright. But that is just my opinion; to others, it might be simply fantastic.

The best part of the State Fair, for me, is the parade. I know it's coming when I see people crowding the sides of the streets. I watch and see magnificent horses trotting down the street proudly. I see art cars moving past me, decorated in costumes of different kinds. Clowns on stilts, graceful dancers, statues, floats—people wave merrily as they pass by. My favorite thing is the band! All of those people marching in the same rhythm, creating music that fills your ears, is amazing. If you listen carefully, you can hear each instrument individually. When the parade is done, I always wish for more, sometimes following them, mesmerized by the sounds and sights. There are many more things about the State Fair, all unqiue in their own way, but to list them all would take a lifetime. The State Fair is the funnest place ever!

S	M	T	W	T	F	S
			1	2	3	4
5	6	7	8	9	10	11
12	13	14	15	16	17	18
19	20	21	22	23	24	25
26	27	28	29	30	31	

☼ "Don't question why the birds sing, just enjoy the song."—Alvin Carter, African American artist, muralist

August

20 Monday

University Avenue Community Parade

Hmong Arts and Music Festival

21 Tuesday

Saint Paul (Seventh Place) Farmers' Market

Nine Nights of Music Series

22 Wednesday

🏵 August 22: Rozanne I. Ridgeway, respected diplomat, was born today in 1935.

23 Thursday

Saint Paul (Seventh Place) Farmers' Market

International Day for the Remembrance of the Slave Trade and Its Abolition

Music in Mears Park

Minnesota State Fair

🏵 Aug 23: Lettisha Henderson, teachers' union leader, was born today in 1902.

Woodstock and Marcy with Peppermint Patty in Rice Park

24 Friday

Minnesota State Fair

Fourth Friday at the Movies

25 Saturday

Saint Paul Farmers' Market

Music in Mears Park

Minnesota State Fair

26 Sunday

Saint Paul Farmers' Market

Minnesota State Fair

🐾 August 26: Gilbert De la O, Latino activist and community leader, was born today in 1945.

Washington School, the first public education building in Saint Paul, was dedicated in 1857.

Elm trees in Saint Paul

Photo © Patricia Bour-Schilla

Viva, Mrs. Luther

Janet Lunder Hanafin

I remember the inchworms. At night, my new neighbor said, if you come outside you can hear them munching, millions and millions of tiny mouths devouring the leaves of the elm trees that laced their top branches together over our street. In the mornings the sidewalks were, well, littered, let's say, with the results of all that munching. We had to hose down the concrete before our children went out with their big wheels and tyke bikes. In a matter of days the elm branches held only lacy remnants of their green leaves.

The adjective that described the way those elegant elms interlaced their branches, I learned from my uncle, a purveyor of words who edited dictionaries for a living, was "pleached." With the elms pleaching over our streets, the neighborhood was settled, established, permanent, shaded. We didn't know that in only a few years another minuscule critter would take on the elms and destroy them.

Mrs. Luther lived next door. She drove a '59 Chevy. When she pulled into her garage and the back wall bulged out, she knew she was in far enough to close the garage door. She kept her eyes open, watching our children and taking them as well as us young mothers to task for unruly behavior, most of which involved games of tag or kick the can across her lawn. She knew which of the local merchants offered good deals and which we should avoid; how to get spots out of the laundry we hung on our clothes lines; who lived in the second house down before "what's-their-names" moved in; what color my kitchen used to be; and that the former resident of our house had died in bed, listening to his radio with headphones on.

"Just think," she said. "There he was, dead all night long and listening to the radio."

Mrs. Luther lived next door. She drove a '59 Chevy. When she pulled into her garage and the back wall bulged out, she knew she was in far enough to close the garage door.

Two of the neighborhood four-year-olds decided they would get married when they grew up. There was only one problem. They couldn't decide which of their mothers they should live with. An older friend told them they would probably want their own house, so they talked it over and then announced that they would live in Mrs. Luther's house, "Because she's so old she'll probably be dead by then."

One by one the elms fell to the whine of high-powered saws. One by one the elderly neighbors, Mrs. Luther's contemporaries, moved away to senior housing, or nearer their children, or to the cemetery. But the elm tree in front of our house hung on for dear life, and so did Mrs. Luther. Who knows how old the elm tree was, but Mrs. Luther was, she said coyly, "more than 90."

In the spring, our elm tree had been given the red ring, the kiss of death. We went away for a week in July and when we returned home we saw the drift of sawdust and the wheel of raw wood left as its only memorial.

That night, Mrs. Luther's lights didn't go on, and in the morning no one answered when I rang the doorbell.

"She moved," the neighbor kid yelled from across the street.

The world shuddered.

Some months later a young couple, the world's best neighbors, moved into Mrs. Luther's house. Hackberry trees have replaced the elms. They have grown tall and full, and inchworms don't seem to like their leaves, so the neighborhood is shady once more.

We have lived here a long time. I know which of the girls at the local salon gives the best pedicure, who always wins the alley garden award, what time the school bus comes, and who moved into what's-their-name's house.

I've become Mrs. Luther.

Photo © Gordon Parks/Getty Images

Photo by Gordon Parks of two boys fishing

This Is My Life

Lawrence Daniels

I hit my first baseball in 1963; it was one of my great moments. At that second I knew this was what I wanted to do with my life. I would start modeling my game after the great "Say Hey Kid," Willie Mays. So 1971 became a major year for me—my daddy signed me up for the little league. I always wanted to be a pitcher, so I talked with my daddy about the chance to become the first pitcher in our family history. My daddy played catcher, Uncle Toe-Toe played first base, and Uncle Bobby played right field. So with my Pops being a catcher in his playing days, it gave me the advantage over the other kids!

He showed me how to hold the baseball on different pitches, like the screwball, curve ball, and fastball. The year I turned fifteen, I was throwing the ball about eighty-three to ninety-one miles an hour. That was without a radar gun, but Pops said it was smokin'. That same year my team won the city championship game and I took the MVP. There was a parade and I rode on a float shaped like a baseball, the next greatest moment in my young life.

"Good morning, get up! Time to get the earlier bird, son! You can throw a ball straight, let's see how you can shoot!" Here it is 4:30 a.m. in the morning—I am half-asleep wiping mess out of my eyes. I had never been hunting in my life.

It seemed like we were in the car for days, and then there I was out in the middle of the sticks with no direction, with guns as big as I am standing on a step stool. So my pop hands me the 12 gauge and tells me to put the butt of the gun against my shoulder, put my feet apart, aim, and squeeze the trigger slowly.

one of the fishing poles started bending like there was a whale on the other end

That was the biggest kick I had ever felt, and I wanted to do it again, but first I had to learn about the gun and some safety rules. So I sat while my dad and uncles shot birds, and learned how to be still and quiet at the same time; not easy for a 15-year-old kid that had just been exposed to the rush of shooting a big safari gun. Little did I know that my father was teaching me life skills and shooting a gun was no different, because the first thing he told me was that it wasn't a toy.

One day, my friend and I were going fishing down by the Big River. There have been stories about Big River—the Mississippi is one of the widest and deepest running waters in the country. They say that the flathead catfish could swallow a man whole. So Jimmy started walking the bank to find a good bend in the water where trees had fallen and gotten mashed together, making a great spot for big fish to hide on the bottom while bait fish swim by. We baited our hooks with chicken meat and some of my great-great-grandpa's "smell good." As we were launching our poles in the water, Jimmy saw a couple of cottontails, and he always brought his BB gun.

About the time that Jimmy retrieved the rabbits, one of the fishing poles started bending like there was a whale on the other end, so I let it run for a while, then I set the hook and I started digging in and pulling back, turning the reel like my life depended on it. There was this flow running through my body that told me it was going to be an all-night party and I would be the guest of honor.

My arms were burning like fire, and my legs were about to give out, and then there it was: a big flathead channel cat. As I started backing up, Jimmy grabbed the fish by the mouth and pulled it onto the bank. It was as long as a shark and as wide as Jimmy and me put together! Jimmy and I were so tired. We took a tape measure—it was seventy-eight inches long. There is a picture on my grandma's wall of a catfish that my grandpa caught in the Mississippi near Tennessee that weighed seventy-six pounds. My daddy said he landed it with a cane pole. So here were Jimmy and me, with this big fish to drag back home on some gunnysack. I couldn't wait to show it to my Pops.

Photo courtesy Kate Cavett

Lucia Theresa Wroblewski

Oral History

Oral histories are personal memories shared from the perspective of the narrator. Transcribed interviews are not edited to follow the standard language usage of the written word; they are lightly edited only for clarity and understanding. Reading a print oral history aloud enhances its appreciation. Oral histories complement other forms of historic text while capturing the flavor of the narrator's speech and convey the narrator's feelings through the timbre and tempo in their speech patterns. Oral history recognizes that memories often become polished as they sift through time, possibly taking on new meaning or reshaping the essence of an event. Memories shared create a picture of the narrator's life—the culture, food, eccentricities, opinions, thoughts, idiosyncrasies, joys, sorrows, and passions—the rich substance that gives color and texture to this individual life. This oral history was documented by

Oral Historian Kate Cavett · HAND in HAND Productions · Saint Paul, Minnesota · 651-227-5987 · www.oralhistorian.org

Lucia Theresa Wroblewski

I was born in Saint Paul and named Lucia Theresa Wroblewski. I was raised on the East Side of Saint Paul at 1163 East Magnolia, then at 947 East Jessamine. My dad, Boleslaw "Bill" Wroblewski, was a fabulous athlete. He came from Poland and he was actually offered a semi-professional soccer contract to play in Chicago, but chose to stay in Saint Paul with his dad, Jozef, as he was his only family survivor from World War II. During the war, his family was forcibly taken to the Russian Gulag. When the Germans invaded Russia, they were separated—his dad went to fight for the free Polish 2nd Corps and his mother died of dysentery in Tehran just before being reunited with her young son. My mom—Alicja "Alice" [nee Rowinski's] family was forcibly taken to Dachau concentration camp. They were then farmed out by the Germans as forced laborers. They spent five years in a displaced person camp in Inglestadt Germany before being approved to move to the U.S.

I'm first generation Polish American, and what they suffered through has given me a huge sense of justice—it's really intense wanting justice for all people. My parents, they're survivors and, I think that it runs through your veins and runs through your blood. I'm very protective of my family and my friends, too. But that survivor mentality, I think, influences how you play sports and live your life.

I remember going to my dad's soccer games at Harriet Island. His teams played World War III, all the nationalities played soccer and would be kicking each other's butts on the field. He got me involved in sports and I played from the first time I could be competitive in junior high, high school at Johnson. I was the captain of the State Championship, Johnson's Class AA, so it was the big school Championship team. Then at Macalester College I played volleyball and soccer, I was a three-sport athlete. I was captain of every team by the time I left, and we went to National's twice with me as a setter on the volleyball team, we were seventh in the Nation one year, we rocked, it was great. Those were some of the best—there's nothing like it, if you've ever been on a team like that. I went from a team like that at Johnson, luckily, to a team like that at Mac. I'm not bragging, it takes the whole team, but being the setter, you're kind of the quarterback and I was always kind of a leader in that regard, and the whole team just meshed. We were all there for each other, it was fabulous.

The way we played volleyball, it was a contact sport. We would dive into chairs over people's legs completely scraped up. I had my nose broken in college, going up for a header and you have three people going up at the same time, hitting your nose so hard that it hairline fractures and blood all over my uniform. I was always a physical player. I know it sounds crazy, volleyball, some people consider a sissy sport. We would do anything to not let that ball hit the floor, I mean, you're sacrificing your body, you will dive ten feet to stop that from happening, do everything you can. The big thing is try not to make any mistakes and even if you do make a mistake, you want to work your way through it. We worked so hard and we always achieved our goals. We said, "We're gonna win the State Championship" and, by golly, we did it, and it's because of that never give up, that survivor mentality. I think I had an edge, learning from my parents how to be physical, and mentally, a survivor. And that's that same mentality that serves me well, wanting justice for the citizens I serve as a Saint Paul Police Officer. I have an honorable profession.

Illustration © Roberta Avidor

Seaside, Midway Shopping Center

Jeri Reilly

Sunday afternoon, big box parking lot
(some need I think, has brought me here)
But what's this ruckus?
Sea gulls in St. Paul?—nose diving
cars and shopping carts?—careening
round light poles and security cams—

these are not city pigeons, flouncing in the park

They are squawking sea talk, pulling up the tide—

they are not shy of shoppers crossing this hard pressed strand.

Here now comes one, her walk stuttered
by the heft of a polythene bag, swishing from side to side.
She does not look up.

A few cars away a man shifts fertilizer bale from cart to trunk.
In backward cap and sunglasses he does not seem to see
the sea gulls tearing up the air,
their hooked beaks polished and sharp.

He drives off, new car pulls in, door flies open—

Out hops a small ballerina dressed in pink.

She spreads her arms to the sky and calls

    HELLO SEA GULLS!

Her mother gets out of the car, locks the door, checks the time

the girl jiggles on tiptoes between the cars—

    LOOK MOMMY, SEA GULLS, SEA GULLS, SEA GULLS.

The mother proceeds toward the big box doors while the girl beside her
    shrieks and whirls and flaps her wings

September

Photo © Tobechi Tobechukwu

O Minnesota, your weather!
A person requires skin of leather.
Like the Fair roller coaster,
From freezer to toaster—
Thank God we're all in this together.

Garrison Keillor

⇨ Harry Blackmun met Warren Burger in kindergarten in Saint Paul's Dayton's Bluff neighborhood in 1912. Nearly 60 years later, they were both serving on the U.S. Supreme Court.

S	M	T	W	T	F	S
						1
2	3	4	5	6	7	8
9	10	11	12	13	14	15
16	17	18	19	20	21	22
23	24	25	26	27	28	29
30						

27 Monday   Minnesota State Fair

28 Tuesday   Saint Paul (Seventh Place) Farmers' Market

Nine Nights of Music Series

Minnesota State Fair

29 Wednesday   Minnesota State Fair

30 Thursday   Saint Paul (Seventh Place) Farmers' Market

Minnesota State Fair

September

Sunflower

September

---

31 Friday   Minnesota State Fair

---

1 Saturday   Saint Paul Farmers' Market
                                                 Minnesota State Fair

🐞 September 1: Emily Borth, longtime girl scout leader, was born today in 1904.

---

2 Sunday   Saint Paul Farmers' Market
                                                 Minnesota State Fair

🐞 September 2: Leigh Kamman, jazz musician and radio host, was born today in 1922.

The Neighborhood House Association took possession of a small two-story structure on Saint Paul's West Side in 1900.

September 193

Gangsterland *movie poster*

On the Set in Saint Paul

Bick Smith

"What do you mean you can't make it by seven? I've got the band and dancers and extras here waiting! There are hundreds of people here and we have only so much time in the caves!" I said.

"I know. I got delayed at work. I'll get there as soon as I can."

This was my phone conversation with "John Dillinger" that warm summer night in 2010. Dillinger was being portrayed by one of many actors who were working basically for free in our movie about 1930s gangsters in Minnesota. I hung up the cell and looked over at the actor playing his partner in crime, Homer Van Meter.

"Want me to do that scene down by the river while we're waiting, Bick?"

"Sure, great idea."

This was one of the relatively few hurdles we encountered during a magical late summer, shooting the bulk of *Gangsterland*. There was no budget to work with and every scene involved a great deal of resourceful-ness. I asked my wife and co-producer, a native East Sider, if Saint Paul had enough history left standing to get the job done. She told me that would certainly not be an issue.

Almost all the big-city scenes in "Gangsterland" were shot around downtown Saint Paul. Alvin "Creepy" Karpis got a shave while telling how the city put out the welcome mat for criminals like himself, thanks to an arrangement between them, business owners, and some of the police. We set up in the Hamm Building to speak with a local "beer brewer" about the kidnapping of his company's president. We went out to Lilydale Road to hear from Van Meter about how gangsters "did away" with snitches who broke the criminal rules of conduct.

Almost all the big city scenes in "Gangsterland" were shot around downtown Saint Paul. Alvin "Creepy" Karpis got a shave while telling how the city put out the welcome mat for criminals like himself, thanks to an arrangement between them, business owners, and some of the police.

Some of the most important shots in *Gangsterland* came from picturesque spots along the Mississippi River, up at Mounds Park, and on the downtown streets. Historic buildings like the Cathedral of Saint Paul, the Capitol, the First Bank Building, and the Landmark Center came into focus just as they were in the early 1930s.

The most challenging scenes came in the dimly lit Wabasha Street Caves, which originally opened as the Castle Royal nightclub during the fall of 1933. In one of them, we see a woman dancing with a charismatic man during the final days of Prohibition. She finds out later from the bartender that her dance partner was John Dillinger.

During the shooting process, I drove the back roads and streets throughout Saint Paul, getting a shot here of a railroad track or a shot there of an old bridge. Since moving to Minnesota in the 1990s, I'd driven around the city plenty of times, but it took making a movie to realize how historically well-kept Saint Paul is. I was amazed at how each street seemed to bring another vintage look for the camera lense. It was exciting, and for those who have criticized getting around Saint Paul, citing its street layout, all I can say is: It's not a big deal.

The city that had one of the country's darkest secrets during the Depression has evolved into a crown jewel as a venue for telling its story nearly eighty years later. Police, City Hall, and business owners operate a lot differently now in Saint Paul, but there are still plenty of glimpses of its history around every turn.

⇨ The cornerstone of the new Central High School at Marshall and Lexington avenues, designed by architect Clarence H. Johnston Sr., was laid this month in 1912.

SEPTEMBER

S	M	T	W	T	F	S
						1
2	3	4	5	6	7	8
9	10	11	12	13	14	15
16	17	18	19	20	21	22
23	24	25	26	27	28	29
30						

3 Monday

Minnesota State Fair

Labor Day

4 Tuesday

Saint Paul (Seventh Place) Farmers' Market

Evening Chores
When the door claps its frame
  the goat runs as if I were
    bringing the world instead
of rotting squash. His
  strong teeth search
    me for more—gently
as if he couldn't bear to know
  that one world is all I have
    to feed him—
      and one is not enough.

Sarah Clark

5 Wednesday

🐾 September 5: Lee Pao Xiong, Hmong activist and educator, was born today in 1966.

6 Thursday

Saint Paul (Seventh Place) Farmers' Market

Photo © Camille Washington

Little Grocery at 1724 University Avenue

7 Friday	Concrete and Grass

8 Saturday International Literacy Day	Saint Paul Farmers' Market Concrete and Grass Selby Avenue JazzFest

9 Sunday	Saint Paul Farmers' Market

Minnesota's first Labor Day celebration was held at Cottage Park in White Bear Lake in 1885.

Dangers on the West Side for a parakeet

West Side Wildlife

David Mather

This is an exotic bird, and the others don't like it. We often eat on the patio, weather permitting, and we're accustomed to feathered traffic nearby at the bird feeder. But this visitor brings enough commotion that we leave our plates unattended. Blue, white, and green, this is a parakeet, someone's lost pet. It is a bit unsettling to see the viciousness of the other birds. They seem to sense that it doesn't belong here. They dive and peck, seeking to drive it off, but hunger keeps it near the feeder.

Back yard wildlife is part of our world here. Some are residents, like the robins who defend their nest from squirrels in the maple branches overhead. Others are frequent visitors. Nuthatches often spiral around the tree trunks. Downy and hairy woodpeckers peck into the bark. Mourning doves are frequent guests, alone or in several pairs. Goldfinches change color with the seasons. And there are the crows, starlings, grackles, and brown-headed cowbirds, arriving in bursts of dark plumage.

The unusual visitors easily capture our attention. One day a flock of wild turkeys struts through the yard. A Cooper's hawk terrorizes the flocks of sparrows in the hedge, and the neighbor's cats, and over time comes back for more. A red-tailed hawk watches from the branches over the patio for the better part of one late-winter day, but the other animals quickly disappear. On a different summer evening, our young daughter gains a lifelong affection for great blue herons as one drifts down and slowly lands on the roof next door. She sees it first—"Look! Mama,

September

Daddy, look!" An impromptu block party soon forms on the sidewalk to stare up at the giant bird.

Herons with their crooked necks are a frequent sight high overhead, their broad wings beating in an effortless trajectory to the horizon. Bald eagles follow the arc of the nearby bluff, particularly when the ice opens on the river below. Turkey vultures follow this route in the warmer months, sometimes so low that their bald red heads stand out. Seasonal migrations fill the sky. There are the expected *V*s of Canada geese, but also cormorants, ducks, and gulls.

White-tailed deer are followed by coyotes. The neighborhood raccoons have a regular patrol at dusk. On more than one day I follow a skunk up the driveway on my way home from work, careful to keep a respectful distance.

The river is a constant presence here near the top of the High Bridge, although it is out of sight from our yard. The downtown skyline and the Cathedral and Capitol domes are visible through the trees, across the chasm of the ancient river valley. That greenway is the source of some of our birds, but also other animals. White-tailed deer are followed by coyotes. The neighborhood raccoons have a regular patrol at dusk. On more than one day I follow a skunk up the driveway on my way home from work, careful to keep a respectful distance. Bats circle the big oak tree at dusk. And on one autumn day, a treefrog moves into the house with the plants from the porch.

My father-in-law teaches English. On a weekend visit, he tells us how his Russian students marvel at the diversity of urban wildlife here in the Midwest. America is a rich country, they say, because we do not eat the animals all around us.

Tonight, I fear for the parakeet. It clearly won't last long out here. I'm skeptical as my wife crouches nearby with her finger out (not that I have any ideas). The bird moves across the yard and she gently follows. This happens several times before the parakeet makes a quick decision. It flies to her finger, coming in from the wild West Side.

SEPTEMBER

S	M	T	W	T	F	S
						1
2	3	4	5	6	7	8
9	10	11	12	13	14	15
16	17	18	19	20	21	22
23	24	25	26	27	28	29
30						

⇨ The large IOOF lodge monument in Oakland Cemetery was erected by the Saint Paul fraternal organization in 1912.

September

10 Monday

September 10: Emmanuel Masqueray, architect of the Saint Paul Cathedral, was born today in 1860.

11 Tuesday   Saint Paul (Seventh Place) Farmers' Market

September 11: John Ireland, archbishop and writer, was born today in 1838.

12 Wednesday

September 12: Sarah Colvin—nurse, author, and activist for women's rights— was born today in 1865.

13 Thursday   Saint Paul (Seventh Place) Farmers' Market
Saint Paul Almanac Book Release Party

Harvesting red potatoes at Gordon Parks High School

September

14 Friday

---

15 Saturday   Saint Paul Farmers' Market

International Day of Democracy

---

16 Sunday   Saint Paul Farmers' Market

International Day for the
   Preservation of the Ozone Layer

September 16: Thomas Frankson, successful politician and real estate developer, was born today in 1869.

The newly formed Olympic Club, a Saint Paul baseball
organization, played one of the city's earliest games in 1860.

September 201

A Childhood Memory
of Downtown Saint Paul

Lenore Gollop

Most children don't have glorious memories of visits to the dentist; my childhood dental experiences held wonder and excitement for me.

My parents instructed me to take the bus from school to downtown Saint Paul, and when I didn't stand on the wrong corner or take the wrong bus, the trip was fascinating, because there was so much to look at along the way. When I arrived at the Lowry Medical Arts Building and entered the dentist's office, I can't deny that the smell of the Bunsen burner made me a little queasy, but the feeling dissipated as I watched the dentist melt wax and sterilize instruments in his laboratory. I felt as if I were watching a magician prepare his tricks for the audience, and I knew that most patients were too nervous to be as curious as I was, so I was doubly fascinated.

After my appointment, I frequently walked to the Central Library to read and check out a few of the many books I read each week. I would then windowshop at some of the downtown department stores: Schuneman's, The Golden Rule, Maurice L. Rothschild, and my two favorites, Field Schlick and Frank Murphy's.

My excursion ended at Daniels Liquor Store at Fourth and Robert streets, where my father worked as a salesman for my uncle. I loved memorizing the names of the bottles on the shelves—Four Roses, Old Granddad, and Black & White Scotch. When I tired of studying bottles, I went to the back room to sit on whiskey kegs that had been made into comfortable seats. There I sat and read my books while I waited for my father to finish his day's work and drive me home.

Photo © Minnesota Historical Society

Lowry Building, 358 St. Peter Street

Railroads

Evelyn D. Klein

That distant whistle

pierces fog of dreams
as if summoning to some faraway place
day and night

"You can't miss them"
the railroad man said
"trains are everywhere in St. Paul"

and I listen
time and again
as if to some secret message

thoughts stow away
vagrants that sleep
in railroad cars or under bridges
crisscross on tracks too numerous to mention

freight trains gather
in railroad yards like thoughts
racing the Mississippi carrying barges like stories
by day we watch with fascination
as goods and raw materials of imagination travel
the network of our existence

unloaded
railroad cars stand in lifeless silence
while workers check engines and repair brakes
at last breathing life into them with new loads
trains are switched and released to new destinations
of our needs and wishes

the whistle screams
time and again
soon daylight will obliterate vision

train whistles
that sweet longing
of compressed days and solitary nights
call us to move on

From *Once upon a Neighborhood* by Evelyn D. Klein

S	M	T	W	T	F	S
						1
2	3	4	5	6	7	8
9	10	11	12	13	14	15
16	17	18	19	20	21	22
23	24	25	26	27	28	29
30						

⇨ The Women's Institute drew 12,000 women to the Saint Paul Auditorium in 1939 to see June Hamilton, a style impressario, and Eleanor Roosevelt.

September

17 Monday

Rosh Hashana

September 17: Warren Burger, Chief Justice of U.S. Supreme Court, was born today in 1907.

18 Tuesday   Saint Paul (Seventh Place) Farmers' Market

19 Wednesday

20 Thursday   Saint Paul (Seventh Place) Farmers' Market

The day seems tired,
it hasn't made
a single
cloud.
Charles Matson Lume

My Milton dapperly dressed in Saint Paul

21 Friday
International Day of Peace

22 Saturday   Saint Paul Farmers' Market
Autumn Equinox

23 Sunday   Saint Paul Farmers' Market

Saint Paul's first McDonald's opened on West Seventh Street in 1964, selling burgers for 15 cents.

I See Black People in Saint Paul

Nneka Onyilofor

It is true that in some parts of the country, people are surprised when they hear that there are Black people in Minnesota. Despite the vitamin D deficiency that often plagues some Black people in this state due to the lack of sunlight for most of the year, Minnesota, particularly Saint Paul, has been a microcosm of diversity; with Black communities of different ethnic groups, from East African to African American.

I arrived on the University of Minnesota's Saint Paul campus eleven years ago. My freshman year of college, I remember staying up late watching all-time Black movie favorites such as *Love Jones* and *The Best Man* with other Black students in my residence hall. I also remember getting my hair braided by other African American students who offered this service to many of us sistas on campus. I attended Black fraternity and sorority parties, along with African Night at the Saint Paul Student Center. All of these events diversified my experience at one of the largest predominantly white schools in the country. I discovered that the myth was not true . . . there are Black people in Minnesota!

Granted, Saint Paul is definitely not "chocolate city," but I lived in Frogtown for seven years, right next to the Martin Luther King (MLK) Center, Penumbra Theatre, and various African American churches and funeral homes.

After almost two years living on the Saint Paul U of M campus, I moved off campus to the thriving Rondo community, right off of University and Dale Street. I then began to explore the Black experience outside the parameters of college. Granted, Saint Paul is definitely not "chocolate city," but I lived in Frogtown for seven years, right next to the Martin Luther King (MLK) Center, Penumbra Theatre, and various African American churches and funeral homes. I frequented a Black-owned spot called Golden Thyme Café, right on Selby Avenue. Golden Thyme Café hosts an annual jazz festival in the heart of the Rondo community, which I attended as well. Then there is "Rondo Days," an annual outdoor summer festival that celebrates this thriving Black community and all the talent that exists within it.

2011 Rondo Celebration at Hallie Q. Brown Community Center grounds

Fresh out of college, my first job was at the Saint Paul location of African American Family Services, where I saw many Black faces for forty hours a week. I was able to network with many prominent African Americans in the state of Minnesota. Years later, during graduate school, I did a lot of travelling all over the U.S. and around the world, but Saint Paul has proven to be one of the most diverse places I have been. In Saint Paul I attended my first Nigerian-Igbo Festival, right on the University of St. Thomas campus! I am half Nigerian, and at this festival I was able to connect with other Nigerians from across the state.

From buying African artifacts at African-owned businesses, to getting my hair done at beauty shops, to dining at soul food and Ethiopian restaurants, I am at home here in Saint Paul, and cannot imagine what my life would be like without the presence of the Saint Paul Black community. Every city has its own flavor and Saint Paul is no different. In Saint Paul I learned much about Black history of all kinds, from the Egyptian Science Museum exhibit, downtown Saint Paul, to the summer Afro-Brazilian music bands that play at the History Center. I see Black people in Saint Paul, Minnesota . . . everywhere!

➪ In 1951, African American bowlers participated for the first time in the American Bowling Congress National competition, held that year in Saint Paul.

SEPTEMBER

S	M	T	W	T	F	S
						1
2	3	4	5	6	7	8
9	10	11	12	13	14	15
16	17	18	19	20	21	22
23	24	25	26	27	28	29
30						

24 Monday

25 Tuesday Saint Paul (Seventh Place) Farmers' Market

26 Wednesday

Yom Kippur

🏵 September 26: Albert Wolff, German American newspaper editor, was born today in 1825.

27 Thursday Saint Paul (Seventh Place) Farmers' Market

Saint Paul Almanac party at Clouds in Water Zen Center, September 2010

28 Friday	Fourth Friday at the Movies

29 Saturday	Saint Paul Farmers' Market

30 Sunday	Saint Paul Farmers' Market

Almost 8 inches of rain fell in a 24-hour period starting in 1892, causing Como Lake to rise 14 inches.

Estate Sale

Martin Devaney

The price tags
are pieces of masking tape
written on
with a marker.

Twenty-five cents
for a paperback.
Three dollars
for the teapot.

I take a green
necktie from the rack
marked
"All ties 50 cents."

The dining room
table has a sign
that reads
"Not for sale."

"It's going to
their daughter,"
someone softly
explains.

Weaving through the rooms
the air is thick
with the musty scent of closets
and basement corners.
The history of this house is put on hold.

I slide two quarters
across the card table
on the porch
to an old woman
with bruises
up and down her arms.

She writes out
a paper receipt
and licks her

thumb
before separating
the carbon copy.

It's September
and I wonder if
there is anything as sad
as a family
selling off
its past.

Joanne biking as a child in the Midway neighborhood

Photo courtesy Joanne A. Englund

Town of Midway

Joanne A. Englund

Growing up in the Midway area was living in the big city and having your own small town all at the same time. We lived at 1431 Edmund Avenue, where the streets and alleys got tarred annually, the milkman put the milk bottles on the top step, the rag collector hollered as he rattled his way down the alley, the mailman (always a man) came twice a day, and the reliable streetcar was only a few blocks away.

There was an empty lot on the north side of the block. A small bungalow was built there around 1940. I was about ten and impressed with this modern upscale to our "old" two-story neighborhood. Corner grocery stores inhabited three corners of our block. My scary job was to carry home the heavy glass bottles of milk when we ran out. Skipping to the corner with fifty cents to buy a pound of meat was more fun. Joe Dolzer, the butcher, had the softest-looking hands and worked with precision as he set down a leg of beef on his chopping table, steeled his knife, and cut off an even pound. We both shared his pride at the scale's exact reading.

Ice was another matter. I took my red wagon a couple of blocks to Hamline and Thomas where the iceman had his cache. He grabbed his huge tongs and lifted a twenty-five pound slab from the sawdust into my wagon. I had to hurry home with this prize before it melted. My dad carried it into the house and chipped with his sharp pick until it fit into the tightly latched, brown, wooden box at the top of the basement stairs. I got some of the watery slivers.

Skipping to the corner with fifty cents to buy a pound of meat was more fun. Joe Dolzer, the butcher, had the softest-looking hands and worked with precision as he set down a leg of beef on his chopping table, steeled his knife, and cut off an even pound.

This same commercial corner also housed a dry goods store that had all sorts of fascinating discoveries. I saved my allowance to buy little hardcover, ten-cent books. I collected a set that I still treasure including birds, insects, rocks, animals, and the special *Seven Wonders of the World*.

Montgomery Ward's, only a few blocks south, was the big shopping center. I loved walking through the store just looking at merchandise, especially way back in the southwest corner of the lower level where the horse saddles and supplies were kept. I absorbed the smell of leather and imagined my very own horse under one of those saddles. The Ward's Catalog was our family reference for anything wanted or needed. When we found what we wanted, someone phoned the store and ordered it. I liked going along to the pick-up counter on the second floor where teens on roller skates wheeled back and forth down the aisles to get our order and bring it to the counter. I wanted that job someday.

I did work at Ward's for a while, but had the dull job of entering patron data on file cards. Never did get to ride those skates. Years earlier, though, I had an astounding surprise when I went to Ward's to buy a flashlight. I had saved my allowance for a long time and finally had what I thought was enough. I got the clerk and the flashlight together only to learn that I was five cents short. I was devastated. Then, to my amazement, the clerk pulled a nickel out of his pocket and added it to my handful of coins. I went home happy with my prized new possession and humbled that anyone was so generous.

In my Saint Paul, my feet, wagon, roller skates, bicycle, and a few streetcar tokens got me safely anywhere I wanted to go.

Brittany Delaney reading at the 2011 Saint Paul Foundation Facing Race Celebration

Where We Left Off

Brittany Delaney

We were friends before our minds developed pigment
Joint at our hip bones the perfect mixture of sisterhood and innocence
Our relationship from day one was innate
Packed full of tea parties, dress up days and overnights our parents
   scheduled when we begged
It wasn't until one day I imitated your actions in the presence of my fam-
   ily that I was made aware that you were my "WHITE" friend
And racial constructs rose from the cement grabbing hold of eyelids
There were no more gray areas
Just black and white

I knew you knew the difference long before I did
Your family had told you a million times over not to pick up any "hab-
   its"
And it was only then that I realized the awkward twist of your mother's
   face every time you asked to stay over
The standoffish behavior of your aunt when I attended your birthday
   party
The snickers and laughs of those around us
And why they said we were day and night
We wanted so badly to be innocent but no history is meaningless enough
   to stay away from the present
It was always lurking at the heels of our multi-colored jellys waiting to
   rear its head at our next playtime
I saw it
In our mannerisms
In our speech

In our homes
In our eyes
I just didn't know that it mattered
Now we are awkward pauses in grocery stores
We are weak embraces followed by frail "good to see you's"
We are strangers who once knew the blue prints of one another

The elephant in this room has grown tired of being our excuse for our
    discomfort
And after 10 years of standing between our arms I think we owe it to
    each other to say the obvious
I'm black
Your white
My eyes are brown
Yours are blue
But tea parties are pink and white
Overnights are orange blankets and green PJ's
Birthday parties are yellow balloons
The gift wrap from the first presents we exchanged was light blue
They are colors
And while they matter
They aren't everything
Friendship is the shade of clear connection
We don't need to be colorblind
But we also don't need to be color blinded

So next week I'm going to call you after work
Schedule time to see you
And when we meet again we will embrace in the skin of our childhood
We will erase the tension in our silence and replace it with memories and
    wholehearted laughter
We will talk about it
And then we will allow it to complement us as it once did
Your eyes the color of the sky
And mine the color of soil
We will face our race
And when that's over we will have tea and pick up right where we left
    off
In the moment we realized our difference
And we will carry on in the moment
Where we realized
That it was okay

Mathal Al-Azawi

My First Week in Saint Paul

Mathal Al-Azawi

My family is the most important thing in my life. My family members include my husband and my daughter. I want to give them a better life and future. When I came to the U.S. I saw everything was different, especially the language. I felt scared for my family, especially for my daughter, because she had to go to school directly and she didn't have any idea how to speak English. When I want to register my daughter, many teachers help me. The next day, my daughter went to her school, and I waited for her in the apartment, but I was very worried. When she came back, I looked in her eyes and I saw a lot of drops, but she never cried. She just said, "Mom, give me a hug."

October

Walking along Summit Avenue, Past Mrs. Porterfield's Boardinghouse

F. Scott Fitzgerald will join me shortly
and we will sit together on the front porch,
sipping gin and tonics, speaking of each other's work.
Mine is coming along, I'll tell him. *And yours?*
Oh, it's progressing. I'm a bit stuck,
you know, sometimes those damn words
just won't come. I nod reassuringly
and slowly drift back to my Summit.
The street is covered in damp, fallen leaves
and instead of meeting F. Scott, I meet a crispness
in the air, telling me, soon man, it will be winter,
and you'll waste all your time in coffee shops
trying to ply your words with caffeine
and stale croissants.

Alexander J. Theoharides

S	M	T	W	T	F	S
	1	2	3	4	5	6
7	8	9	10	11	12	13
14	15	16	17	18	19	20
21	22	23	24	25	26	27
28	29	30	31			

⇨ The Women's City Club held a rally at the Saint Paul Auditorium in 1943, called Miss America Marches, for the women serving in WWII.

1 Monday

International Day for
  Older Persons

2 Tuesday

🐞 October 2: Charlotte Ordway, pioneer in baby welfare work, was born today in 1887.

3 Wednesday

World Habitat Day

4 Thursday

🐞 October 4: Josip Temali, youth leader, founder of Saint Paul Big Brothers Big Sisters program, was born today in 1914.

Darneesha, Jason, and Tanisha at Wing Young Huie's University Avenue Screening

5 Friday

World Teacher's Day

6 Saturday   Saint Paul Farmers' Market

7 Sunday   Saint Paul Farmers' Market

The Thursday club, dedicated to literary study for young women, met in 1894 for the first time.

Mothers of the Mighty Midway

Carrie Pomeroy

My neighbor Jill was up nursing her baby son the October night my daughter was born at our home on West Minnehaha Avenue. Jill said she knew we'd had our baby when she saw my husband in the kitchen making toast at three in the morning.

Even after Jill's son had dozed off in her arms that night, Jill leaned forward in her glider, watching agog as the midwife sat at our kitchen table working on a mysterious pile of capsules, methodically opening each one, dumping its contents in a bowl, then opening another. I solved the mystery for Jill the next day: the midwife was harvesting goldenseal powder to rub on the baby's umbilical cord stump.

A few mornings later, I was up at dawn breastfeeding my daughter when I glanced out the window and saw Jill changing her son's diaper. She was in her pajamas, uncombed brown hair sticking up in funny directions. I watched as she leaned over her son on the changing table. The movements of her shoulders and head told me that she was talking to him, friendly and companionable, even after a night of waking up with him every few hours. I could see him gazing up at her and kicking his bare legs.

Jill said she knew we'd had our baby when she saw my husband in the kitchen making toast at three in the morning.

Jill and I each have two children. Her oldest, a girl, is only a few months older than my oldest, a boy. Her son was born a few months before my daughter. As toddlers and then preschoolers, our older children took turns opening the swinging door in our shared fence to run into each other's yards. I watched Jill's children when she had to attack her flooded basement with a Wet Vac. She watched mine the day a long heat wave broke and I finally had the energy to clean house. On summer nights when the windows were open, she could hear when I was having an especially rough night with a crabby baby. I knew when her husband's cough was acting up. Day after day, as she shepherded her children to her green Chrysler with the orange ECFE sticker in the back window, she waved and smiled at me as I stood chopping onions at my kitchen counter or making PBJs.

Jill with her daughter and Carrie's son in the Midway

When Jill's oldest child was four and mine almost four, Jill's family moved back to their native Ohio. Our family has visited theirs twice in the almost five years since then. It's easy for us to fall back into the old, friendly rhythms, but it's not the same as being neighbors.

Those first years of our children's lives, when we were both so vulnerable and so very, very tired, Jill and I watched each other closely, reassured by the ways our movements mirrored one another, intrigued by the ways our paths differed. I don't think either of us ever minded each other's good-natured spying. For me, it was deeply comforting to know that Jill was across the driveway, the two of us raising our children side by side, witnesses to one another's humble, hidden, necessary work.

The Carondelet Center, a brick Beaux Art landmark designed by architect John W. Wheeler, was built in 1912 at 1890 Randolph Avenue as the novitiate for the Sisters of St. Joseph of Carondelet.

OCTOBER

S	M	T	W	T	F	S
	1	2	3	4	5	6
7	8	9	10	11	12	13
14	15	16	17	18	19	20
21	22	23	24	25	26	27
28	29	30	31			

8 Monday

9 Tuesday

🐞 October 9: Nick Swardson—actor, stand-up comedian, and writer—was born today in 1976.

10 Wednesday

World Mental Health Day

11 Thursday

Indigenous Peoples Day

World Food Day

🐞 October 11: Russell M. Berthel, field biologist and ornithologist, was born today in 1901.

October

Painting with abandoned building in the Bruce Vento Nature Sanctuary

12 Friday
International Day for
  Natural Disaster Reduction

13 Saturday
Saint Paul Farmers' Market

14 Sunday
Saint Paul Farmers' Market

James Melvin Young Sr. riding a camel in Egypt

All Aboard!

Patricia Anita Young

My dad James Melvin Young Sr. became a second generation "Red Cap Porter" when his uncle William A. Young retired circa 1949. Melvin was 23 years old when the Saint Paul Union Depot at 214 Fourth Street in Lowertown was the gateway to the world. Working there was the spark that ignited a love for world travel for my dad.

There were approximately thirty-six Red Cap Porters employed at the Depot, all African American. Their red caps became synonymous with integrity and reliability. Their work was demanding.

"We were never offered a clear job description," Dad says, his voice unsteady. "One minute I was mopping floors (and other housekeeping duties) in the 'head house,' the next minute I was racing up to the concourse to meet passengers, carry their bags, then returning to the head house to trim the hedges, shine patrons' shoes or the brass handles on the entrance doors, wash windows, work the elevator (license required) or park cars."

Dad read the newspapers daily to be prepared to answer the unlimited questions travelers asked: "Where is the Convention Center? Where is an event being held?"

There are some pleasant recollections: "The tile work on the ceiling of the concourse was my favorite part of the depot."

The Depot bar, Sugar's, and Rossini's sold food and filled the building with their unique aromas. "I still have a taste for Rossini's German potato salad," Dad recalls.

The men played checkers in their locker room during their lunch breaks. "The Red Caps sometimes pooled their money to help someone in the Depot out of a bad situation."

My little sister at five years old and I, then eleven, would ride to work with Dad. Before he clocked in, he would buy tickets and put us on the Milwaukee Hiawatha Train, destination: Minneapolis, where we had moved. Riding unescorted made us feel special. We pretended to be movie stars traveling on the "Orient Express" looking for something exciting to happen. Our mom would meet us.

My dad's passion for travel all began at the Saint Paul Union Depot. He aimed beyond what he saw with a child-like anticipation and a determination to make it happen.

There are painful memories too. The Red Caps were not immune from the racial issues of the times. Dad focused on the things he could change. Traveling the world became his "College without Walls."

He fulfilled a personal dream to prove that "No matter what color skin a person happens to have, most people are honorable, empathetic, and deserving." I nicknamed him the "Peacemaker." He rode the rails from Saint Paul to New Jersey, to Washington State, California, to Quebec, through the Deep South and all the states in between, on vacations.

In 1969 he became employed as a skycap at the Minneapolis-Saint Paul Airport and began dreaming globally. He purchased custom shoes in Hong Kong, tailored suits in Korea, lived with new friends in the Fiji Islands, and participated in religious ceremonies in South America. He flew from England to Austria, and walked in wooden shoes in Holland. He rode a camel around the pyramids of Egypt and cruised the Ivory Coast.

My dad's passion for travel all began at the Saint Paul Union Depot. He aimed beyond what he saw with a child-like anticipation and a determination to make it happen.

James J. Hill, railroad builder, and Charles Sumner Frost, the depot's architect, dreamed of connecting Saint Paul to the rest of our nation. Their vision sparked James Melvin Young Sr. to make peace with new friends in every corner of the world.

Dad and Mom (Lois) are now retired and continue to travel.

May the Saint Paul Union Depot nurture dreams that come true for travelers for generations to come. All aboard!

October

⇨ John A. Johnson was the first governor to have a memorial built for him in front of the State Capitol. It was dedicated on October 19, 100 years ago.

S	M	T	W	T	F	S
	1	2	3	4	5	6
7	8	9	10	11	12	13
14	15	16	17	18	19	20
21	22	23	24	25	26	27
28	29	30	31			

15 Monday

16 Tuesday   Minnesota RollerGirls (Bout)

🎂 October 16: Antoinette E. Ford, author and elementary school teacher, was born today in 1876.

17 Wednesday

International Day for the
   Eradication of Poverty

18 Thursday

🎂 October 18: Raeann Ruth, founder of The Portage for Youth, was born today in 1950.

Downtown Saint Paul viewed from the High Bridge

19 Friday

20 Saturday   Saint Paul Farmers' Market

                                    ZooBoo

21 Sunday   Saint Paul Farmers' Market

                                    ZooBoo

The Minnesota Wild played their first home hockey game against
the Philadelphia Flyers and skated to a 3–3 tie in 2000.

The Day My Son Was Born

Kenia Guadarrama

On October 31, 2008, I was seventeen years old and exactly thirty-six weeks pregnant. I had just moved back in with my parents. My baby's father was in jail for burglary, and I had to meet the prosecutor at 9 a.m. that day. I hadn't eaten anything, and on the way home, I wasn't feeling well. I had a doctor appointment at 1 p.m., but I didn't want to go. I wasn't feeling like myself; I felt lightheaded and wanted to sleep.

When I got to the appointment, they hooked me to a machine to see if I was having contractions, and gave me an ultrasound to see if the baby was growing and how much amniotic fluid I had. Since my pregnancy was high risk, they did that all the time and I didn't think anything of it. But I *was* having contractions—it was the start of pre-labor, and I didn't have any amniotic fluid left.

"You're having a baby," the doctor said.

"Yeah, I know," I said.

"In the next twenty-four hours," she said.

Then it hit me. It felt so unreal. She took me to the birth center at United Hospital and I tried to call my mom. She didn't answer. I was freaking out, but when I finally got ahold of her, she seemed more scared than I was.

Since my son had a birth defect known as gastroschisis, which is an opening in his abdomen, I had to have him as soon as possible. The little contractions were more than my son could handle; while a normal baby heart rate is above 120, his heartbeat had dropped to 67. I was told I would have to have a C-section.

At 8:20 that evening, I was wheeled into the operating room. I was scared at the thought of getting cut open. It took twenty minutes to get my son out, and then he was rushed into the neonatal intensive care unit at Children's Hospital. My baby boy weighed six pounds and nine ounces; he looked just like me, and I named him Anthony James Guadarrama.

My mom offered to stay, but I convinced her to go home. That night I couldn't sleep. I had bad dreams. Maybe it was because little Anthony was going to have surgery the next morning to put his intestines back inside again. I didn't get to kiss him and tell him I would be waiting for him, because by the time I woke up, he was already in the operating room.

It took three hours, but the doctor told me the surgery went well. Little Anthony was hooked up to machines to monitor his breathing and heartbeat. By the next day, he was breathing well and the respiratory machine was removed. He still had a needle through his chest, his main way of getting nutrition—he couldn't breastfeed until he could eat and poop. He looked so little and fragile, and for the first two days, I couldn't even hold him.

At 8:20 that evening, I was wheeled into the operating room. I was scared at the thought of getting cut open. It took twenty minutes to get my son out, and then he was rushed into the neonatal intensive care unit at Children's Hospital.

Anthony began eating on November 9. I was happy, because this meant my son would be unhooked from the needles and come home. It took two weeks for him to gain his weight back and be a healthy boy.

On November 23, Anthony came home to me. In three weeks, my son and I had been through a lot; I went through sad times and happy times and the thought of losing my child. Thank God, that didn't happen. My son is now two years old. I'm proud to be a mom, but not just any mom. I'm proud to be Anthony's mom, because he showed his strength. I know my son can go through anything life puts in front of him, because that is what he had to do the moment he was born.

October

↺ The Saint Paul Red Cross opened a Production Corps in the Endicott building today in 1939 to make garments and surgical dressings for European war relief.

OCTOBER

S	M	T	W	T	F	S
	1	2	3	4	5	6
7	8	9	10	11	12	13
14	15	16	17	18	19	20
21	22	23	24	25	26	27
28	29	30	31			

22 Monday

🐝 October 22: Ossian Euclid Dodge, eccentric musician, was born today in 1820.

23 Tuesday

24 Wednesday

United Nations Day

World Development Information Day

25 Thursday

🐝 October 25: Dorothy Franey Langkop, Olympic speed skater, was born today in 1913.

October

Mummy at Lowertown Halloween party

26 Friday

Eid Al-Adha

ZooBoo

Fourth Friday at the Movies

27 Saturday

Saint Paul Farmers' Market

ZooBoo

Dia de los Muertos Family Fiesta

burdened by beauty
mammoth sunflowers bow their
heads, pray for plainness
Megan Marsnik

28 Sunday

Saint Paul Farmers' Market

ZooBoo

Fred Street, only sixteen and a half feet-wide and one block long, is the narrowest street in Saint Paul.

Sharing My House

David Tilsen

I'm sitting on my front step not smoking. Yeah, not smoking. Not trying to quit, that would be a little more proactive, but I am spending a lot of energy not smoking. I haven't smoked in over forty years. But after Silvia died, a cigarette, or sometimes a cigar, really helps me get through the day.

So I'm sitting here watching some neighborhood kids throw a football around in the middle of Ashland Avenue. I hope they don't get hurt: asphalt can be pretty unforgiving on young skin—old skin, too, I have to say. I decide to go into the house to get ready for the kickoff for the Vikings game.

I am thinking that the only thing I hate more than watching football alone is missing the game when a football bounces into my lap. A brown-eyed fourteen-year-old wearing a Peterson jersey runs up to the sidewalk and motions for the ball. As I throw it, I ask his name.

"George!" he yells, as he catches the ball.

"Like your jersey," I respond. "AP's going to be one of the great running backs."

He grins, "What do you mean, 'going to be'?"

"We'll have to see if he can hold on to the ball," I quip, field-stripping my butt and preparing to go into the house. "Catch you after the game."

"I sure want to watch it," he mumbles as he turns to join his three friends in the street.

I think for a minute, then offer, "George, you can watch it with me."

He looks at me for a second and does a head fake toward the others. His meaning is clear. "Sure, invite them in." It begins just like that—an old man who doesn't want to watch a game alone and some kids who don't have a TV.

The following Sunday I make chili with corn bread and bring in some Coke and Mountain Dew. George, along with Alejandro, Xuan, and Alex just sit around enjoying my 40-inch flat screen with surround sound, emptying out a crockpot that has not seen any use since I became a widower. I admit I am a little nervous about letting these kids into my house, but they are great guests and I tell them they have a standing invitation for the rest of the season.

The next Sunday at about 7:30 in the morning, the doorbell wakes me. At the door stand 'Jandro', Xuan, and about four other kids. The

Watching the football game

others get introduced as Isabella, Grace, George, and Sophie. They have several bags of groceries and ask for the run of the kitchen. About three hours later, we are being treated to a feast of empanadas, spring rolls, and some great soup. Kind of eclectic, but I have never had better.

I soon learn that George and Sophie like computers and want to get jobs. I set up my computers in the spare room and start to teach database design, programming, and business-process flow. Before too long, they are posting their first apps for sale on the iTunes store.

Sure, we've had some incidents, but the kids police themselves. I remember my laptop was missing once, and another time there was a fight. When my laptop was returned to me, I was told that the people involved had been banned from the house for six months. See the sign at the door: "No alcohol, drugs, hooking up, guns, or gang colors." I didn't put it there—they did. They want a safe place to be, and I love having them here.

Sure, I spend money on the kids. I buy food and gas, and I've been known to spring for some clothes and other essentials when I see a need, but believe me, I am getting the better part of the bargain. I am no longer lonely, I haven't had a cigarette or a drink in six months, and I'm happier than I have been since my wife died.

These are my friends, I share my house with them, I help them with their lives, and I get back a lot more than I give. So no, officer—I have no knowledge of any crimes, but I do know a few lawyers. I think I will invite them over.

October

Photo © Henry Jackson

Glockenspiel

Lucy Pavlicek

My favorite place in Saint Paul is the Glockenspiel. My mother used to work there up until I was seven. The Glockenspiel is a German restaurant that sells breaded chicken, bratwurst, sauerkraut, polish sausage, and dumplings. In my opinion, the best food is spätzle, a fried macaroni with swiss cheese.

When I was six, I went to gymnastics in the attic above the Glockenspiel. Every night, I would run down the stairs and meet my mom at our favorite table. She would serve me spätzle and a Shirley Temple with exactly three cherries on top—she knew the drill. My momma's boss and the other waiters visited me at my special table and talked to me and helped me practice for future spelling bees that I dreamed about. I got so much attention, and I loved it!

I remember when I was finished with dinner, my mom's boss, Marrissa, would bring me Black Forest cake with extra cherries. I would get a ride home from my friend Alice. At about 12 a.m., Mom would come home and bring my sister dinner. My sister never came with. But when gymnastics was over, and the Glockenspiel got a new boss, my mom didn't have a job there anymore. It wasn't her fault, though—the place had too many workers. We never went back to the Glockenspiel, but I still have the memories, and that's enough for me.

Eleanor

Looking in All Directions

Media Mike Hazard

Eleanor Savage, community-based media artist and program officer at Jerome Foundation, was walking her dog Stella in the park. Stella was in mourning, having lost her sibling, Billie, earlier in the week. Her grief was palpable when I looked down and petted her.

"I love looking up at the trees against the sky," says Eleanor.

We both looked up.

"There's something about looking up."

From Macon, Georgia, Eleanor learned to love the garden that is life from her grandmother. One of fourteen children, Frances Eleanor was a subsistence farmer. "She liked to grow everything. Endless rows of peas, green beans, squash, watermelon, corn. She taught me to can, before the box freezer."

There's something about looking back.

Juke Joint Named JAZZVILLE

J. Otis Powell!

Like Harlem, Birmingham, Atlanta
And DC nights
Chocolate people in vanilla town
Living chocolate
Old school and new school
Bumping up against each other
In a dim lit smoke filled aroma of catfish
Fried okra
Chicken wings
(And in those days) cigarettes
A Saint Paul DJ fired up a turntable with
Marvin "hot like an oven"
Sexually healing the sickness of Adam
Another fragrance thicker than the haze
In the room
Rose above the music
Floated across silhouettes
Like a come-on
Somehow it always comes to this:
Glances shot without words
Carried innuendo
Between us Marvin issued a warning
"And when I get that feeling..."
Then the thing that scares us the most
Jumped out to mug us
In this place that looks the same
All over America
JAZZVILLE—juke joint, like a national chain
With frozen battered artery blockers
From the same distributor
This village called jazz
Where an improvisation can change a life
Where risk reminds me what it means
To be alive
And at risk
Thankfully Marvin released us
To the return of a not so jazz band
Back from break and the ganja filled air outdoors

As the metal detector beeped at the entrance
I remembered why I couldn't do this scene anymore
Bad jazz, open mic, women wrapped in mixed messages
And allure
Feels too much like home
Feels home to think naughty
JAZZVILLE where the no-good blues
Will come looking for you
She came over and said, "I know you
You write long poems"
I said, "Yes, I have a lot to say"
But what I thought was
My poems are long because
Life is complicated
Every layer unpeels
Mysteries – knotted lies
Yesterday I needed this kind of attention
Today it breaks my stride
It's like why I can't look through Window Pane
Or enjoy Orange Sunshine anymore
The vista is too detracting
Now I got a story and I'm sticking to it
So the village erroneously called jazz
Is a place I can only visit
I can't live here anymore
Snapping back into the room I asked,
"And what kind of poems do you write?"
"Skinny poems"
She said
"About love,
Depression
Cruelty
Against those
Who feel only with
Groping hands
Naked poems that expose why
My emotions will not hide"
My ears heard every word she said
While my eyes betrayed me
She stood there round and talking
With every body part at once
Her dance a gesticulation

Of an ancient sign language
I couldn't ignore
Fixing on my admiring eyes she quipped
"Poems about poets," then she spat
"Who want only sex
When there is so much more
I write poems about pricks"
"I'm sorry," I said as she stormed away
Indignant
Imbroglio I sat feeling misunderstood
Victim of another feminist reactionary,
I thought
But it was so much more than that
We yearned that night in downtown Saint Paul
For crisp, clear distinctions:
Light / dark, winner / loser
Saint / sinner—what we had was nuance
Complexity, confusion and shadows in gray
We mark every struggle, judge every choice
By principled polarities, good and evil
She and I tangled before we met
Because our dynamic is perpetual
The drama between us reeks systemic
Type cast by gender lost in masquerade
Juke joint named JAZZVILLE birthplace
Of the blues—home for the helpless
Museum for the misremembered

Half in light half in shadow
My long poem life plays me in public
Like smoky aromatic night spots play
Purple blues in a toxic arena
Brownish jocolatte royal blues
Not only jocolatte—cola,
Java, black tea—dark liquid blues
Even burgundy, two hearted—unfiltered
Dark and sometimes deadly like us
Complicated like dreams suspended in
A welkin full of doubt
Hovering just above our heads
Threatening bad weather
From a gestalt of ominous rain...

November

Photo © Tobechi Tobechukwu

A Letter to St. Paul

Last night, whole towns were swallowed by snow.
Two-lane roads snaked their way back into the earth.
Streetlights bowed, then hissed themselves out, and
all the living and all the dead slumbered, dreamless.
All that was left us,
was the silhouettes of trees reaching for stars,
the tumble and descent of snow, a world made pure
brilliant, right. All that was left us,
was the hush of night and love enough to fill it.

Yours

j

Julia Klatt Singer

⇨ The Virginia Street Church (Swedenborgian), designed by Cass Gilbert, was dedicated in 1887. It is located at the corner of Virginia and Selby.

S	M	T	W	T	F	S
				1	2	3
4	5	6	7	8	9	10
11	12	13	14	15	16	17
18	19	20	21	22	23	24
25	26	27	28	29	30	

29 Monday

Love of Hockey

Life magazines for shin guards.
Skates too big, stick cracked and old,
jacket patched and tattered.
I ignored the smirks and winter's cold,
Love of hockey was all that mattered.

Louis DiSanto

30 Tuesday

31 Wednesday

Halloween

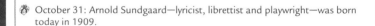 October 31: Arnold Sundgaard—lyricist, librettist and playwright—was born today in 1909.

1 Thursday

All Saints' Day

Day of the Dead

November

Night shot of Saint Paul with Crowne Plaza in the foreground

2 Friday

🎖 November 2: Richard E. Fleming, WWII Medal of Honor recipient, was born today in 1917.

3 Saturday Saint Paul Farmers' Market

4 Sunday Saint Paul Farmers' Market
Daylight Saving Time ends

Choua Lee became the first Hmong elected to public office in the U.S. in 1991 when she won a seat on the Saint Paul School Board.

Life on the River in a Bygone Era

Patrick Coleman

Richard Bissell was a Harvard graduate who plied the Mississippi for eight years in the 1940s, and wrote an autobiographical account of his experiences as an atypical towboat worker, first published in 1950. He impeccably describes the place and the people and a time that is beginning to seem as distant as Mark Twain's.

Richard Bissell, *A Stretch on the River: A Novel of Adventure on A Mississippi River Towboat* (Minnesota Historical Society Press, 1987); pages 24–27.

It was a long trip to St. Paul all the same. I was pretty well worn out and had a smashed-up foot and a couple of smashed fingers. But I thought I would be all right after I could learn to sleep. We worked six hours on and six hours off, week after week. By the time you made the sack and got to sleep you had lost nearly an hour. To eat and make watch time you lost half an hour. That meant that the most sleep you could ever get at one time was four and a half or five hours, but I couldn't get this much.

The deckhands' bunkroom ran athwartships right aft of the engine room. As you lay in your sway-backed bunk plucking the shoddy 12 percent wool blanket, only a three-sixteenths-inch steel bulkhead separated your head from two 800-horsepower Diesel engines. Every so often the whole boat would go into a violent shudder. If through exhaustion I fell asleep in spite of the noise and the vibration, then we would arrive at a lock and the engines would stop, and I would awake from the unusual silence. Then I would toss and listen to the popping of the compressed air as we maneuvered for an hour locking through.

Joe took me uptown in St. Paul while we were waiting for empties. His girl was Irene and she got me a girl and we went out. My girl's name was Merle. I was surprised she was so good looking. But I was so beat up I didn't realize she was actually beautiful until I got to thinking about it later.

"How about a drink?" I said.

"I don't mind," she said.

"Whiskey?" I said.

"Whiskey and sour."

"Want to dance?"

"I s'pose so."

"This your home town?"

"Uh uh."

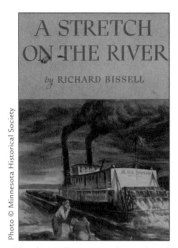

Richard Bissell's A Stretch on the River:
A Novel of Adventure On A Mississippi River Towboat

"Where do you come from?"

"Eveleth."

"That's up in the iron range."

"Uh huh."

"What your folks do up there?"

"My dad's in the mine."

"How come you came to St. Paul?"

"Didn't like it in the sticks."

"Honey, I don't blame you. I hate the sticks too."

"Where d'you get that 'honey' stuff?"

"Want a cigarette?"

"I don't mind."

Well, that went on until around midnight when we took the girls home. We all did a little high school style loving and then Joe and I went back to the boat much refreshed.

That was my first trip to St. Paul on the *Inland Coal* with Joe. I was on her a long time after that.

[Chapter 3]

A long time went by, even a year.

At first I stayed out of stubbornness. Then I began to forget I had ever lived any other way. Then I began to feel sorry for the people on the bank. When I got that far I was a river man.

And there was the girl from the iron range. And there was Joe.

S	M	T	W	T	F	S
				1	2	3
4	5	6	7	8	9	10
11	12	13	14	15	16	17
18	19	20	21	22	23	24
25	26	27	28	29	30	

↪ The toll on the Wabasha Street bridge was removed in 1874 as part of a transfer of the structure from private to public ownership.

5 Monday

6 Tuesday

Election Day

International Day for Preventing
  the Exploitation of the Environment
  in War and Armed Conflict

🐞 November 6: Laurence "Larry Ho" Hodgson—journalist, poet, and Saint Paul
   mayor—was born today in 1874.

7 Wednesday

November

8 Thursday

Fall Flower Show begins

Minnesota State High School
League Girls' Volleyball Tournament

Lady Liberté

9 Friday

Minnesota State High School
League Girls' Volleyball Tournament

Nov. 9: Eyedea (Michael Larsen), hip hop performer, was born today in 1981.

10 Saturday

Saint Paul Farmers' Market
Minnesota State High School
League Girls' Volleyball Tournament

11 Sunday

Saint Paul Farmers' Market

Veterans Day

Oak Hall, once located at 568 Holly Avenue, was the first private girls' school in St. Paul.

Costello's Bar and Grill at 393 Selby Avenue

Drinking in Saint Paul

Matt Ehling

It was fair to say that you enjoyed a drink now and again. Select evenings of your youth were spent passing from bar to bar on Selby Avenue. You would start at either end—Costello's or Cognac McCarthy's—and have a couple until the wallet grew thin. Then, the crew would amble down the street, ending the night at the pub in the old firehouse.

At the time, you lived in the apartment at the end of Dayton Avenue. You met her there on the front step, where she would sit reading her book. She asked you in for a glass of wine. You invited her to dinner.

You went to The Manor on West Seventh Street—half piano lounge and half supper club. It was dumpy and charming in equal measure. You had brought others here in the past, as a kind of hazing ritual. Only she had passed the test.

Fridays would often be spent at The Manor, due to the presence of Jim "Irish" Tolck's Big Band. Syl would bring over the menus, which you didn't really need to look at any more. "The Manor," read the cover page, "Where good food is a traditional." On New Year's Eve, you proposed to each other at the lounge bar.

One afternoon, you sat together above downtown on the gently sloping hill that fades away from the Cathedral, and discussed what was to come. You were young, and the enormity of the future stretched out before you. There was talk of moving east, of new horizons.

Some nights you would go to Mancini's with the priests. Ben knew your wife from school. His colleague appeared to be from Catholic priest

Menu from The Manor on West Seventh Street

central casting—Irish by birth, a ruddy glow about him. "I am in favor of the drink," he would say.

Old man Mancini would dart from table to table, checking on the regulars. On these nights, Ben would make sure to wear the collar. "Hello, father," said Nick. "Everything to your liking?" Later, the management would send a complementary bottle of rosé to the table. "Could you take this back," Ben would ask the waiter, "and bring a red instead?"

Years later, you bought the house off of Snelling. It had been a decade, and you were committed Saint Paulites.

Things rushed ahead now. There were seminars and meetings to attend. Weekend evenings were spent at home, corralling the four-year-old and reading bedtime stories. Once he stopped rustling, you would both open the door to his room, and watch him sleeping in the half-light.

On occasion, you would secure a babysitter, and head out for dinner with friends, to a Chinese restaurant across the river. After two hours she would say, "We really should go. We only have the sitter for a while tonight." This was code for, "Let's have one more, alone."

These nights would end at the Lexington—the old steak house near the site of the Dillinger shoot-out. In the hall by the men's room was a wall of photos akin to the movie star portraits that bedecked New York City diners. Radio personalities and former politicians stared out at you.

You sat at the bar together. Dinner rush for the senior set was just ending. She ordered a zinfandel. You ordered a brandy Manhattan. She leaned against you and closed her eyes for a moment. You were home.

November

NOVEMBER

S	M	T	W	T	F	S
				1	2	3
4	5	6	7	8	9	10
11	12	13	14	15	16	17
18	19	20	21	22	23	24
25	26	27	28	29	30	

➪ Saint Paul celebrated the end of WWI and hope for "peace, prosperity and future world democracy" in 1918 with a big parade downtown.

12 Monday

13 Tuesday

🌑 November 13: Louis Goodkind, an organizer of the Standard Club, a Jewish club in Saint Paul that later merged into the Saint Paul Athletic Club, was born today in 1825.

14 Wednesday
World Diabetes Day

15 Thursday
Muharram begins

🌑 November 15: Professor Emil Anderson, a prominent musician and violin teacher, was born today in 1870.

Sunset

16 Friday
International Day of Tolerance

17 Saturday
Saint Paul Farmers' Market

18 Sunday
Saint Paul Farmers' Market

Ida Maud Cannon was the first visiting nurse for
St. Paul Associated Charities in 1903.

Culture Borderline

Chia Lor

I stand at the borderline,
facing the Mekong.
My spirit calls out to my parents.
I ask myself, "What does it mean to be Hmong?"
In a generation where the young
are losing their native tongue.
I feel the water spinning my body in the melting pot,
along with my Hmong brothers and sisters
that have forgotten the respect for their elders.
From a fading, collective culture that teaches
"blood is thicker than water."
Divisions between the new and old generations;
different values
results from lack of connection.

I was also at the verge of giving up this bond,
only to be so ignorant
so focused on my adolescent needs
I failed to see my parents,
being looked down upon
so low...
by the tall, ignorant whiteness
of Euro-Americans.
But to me, my parents are most intelligent
and the fact that they speak broken English
doesn't make them any more broken in dignity
than the white person they work for.

Last time I saw my mother's hair
I noticed seven more white ones.
Then I asked... "is it because of me?"
White hair caused from mother's overtime hours,
in the late evenings and weekend mornings.
She has one daughter in college
and five other children adventuring life.
White hair from reminding us constantly
to do our homework and be good children.

So hold me, Mother,
brush the hair from my face

with the same gentle hands
that you use for embroideries.
The same hands used to feed me
so your baby girl won't go hungry.

And lift me up, Father,
and place me on your shoulders
that allowed me to see the world.
Have you forgotten
your eldest daughter
who you spent late nights caring for
and taught to be a strong woman?

Chia Lor performing at
Lowertown Reading Jam

I know I was wrong
to be angry when you made me make phone calls;
when I didn't know anything about mortgage or insurance
you yell at me and say "Then why did you go to school for?"
Now I realize that my hurt
can never compare to your hurt of being misunderstood
or the sacrifices you made to bring me here for a brighter future.

So long since I heard you call me "Me Naib."
Despite your conservativeness
I'll cross any culture borderline through sun and rain
Just to have you hold me and call me "Me Naib" again.

My spirit calls out to my parents
Let the tides of our bloodline
Connect us again.

November

⇨ Frank B. Kellogg, Saint Paul attorney and statesman, was named president of the American Bar Association in 1912. He was also a delegate to the Republican Party's national convention that year (as well as in 1904 and 1908).

NOVEMBER

S	M	T	W	T	F	S
				1	2	3
4	5	6	7	8	9	10
11	12	13	14	15	16	17
18	19	20	21	22	23	24
25	26	27	28	29	30	

19 Monday

20 Tuesday

Minnesota RollerGirls (Bout)

Universal Children's Day

World Day of Remembrance
for Road Traffic Victims

21 Wednesday

⚘ November 21: Frederick Weyerhauser, timber mogul, was born today in 1834.

22 Thursday

Thanksgiving Day

Mickey's Diner at Night

23 Friday Fourth Friday at the Movies

Minnesota Hmong New Year

24 Saturday Saint Paul Farmers' Market

Minnesota Hmong New Year

🐞 November 24: Roman Bohnen, stage and screen star, was born today in 1901.

25 Sunday Minnesota Hmong New Year

Buy Nothing Day

International Day for the
   Elimination of Violence
   Against Women

🐞 November 25: Mary Ostergren, Olympic biathlete, was born today in 1960.

Oak Hall, once located at 568 Holly Avenue, was the first
private girls' school in Saint Paul.

Go, Bobby, Go!

Andrea Taylor Langworthy

Whenever Dad yelled up the stairs late on a Sunday afternoon and told us kids to change into our good clothes, we cheered. It always meant the same thing: Dad had called his sisters, Marge and Kaye, and invited them and their families to join us at the Saint Paul Hotel for dinner. An hour later, my family walked through the grand hotel lobby toward the staircase leading to the smorgasbord. I had to stop myself from running and taking the stairs two at a time, which would upset my parents. Being with my cousins was the most fun—especially when it involved the never-ending selection of food known as a smorgasbord. The huge room on the hotel's lower level was filled with tables covered with white cloths, and banquet tables covered with food.

Our group needed two tables. One for the adults and my two little sisters in booster chairs, another for the rest of us kids. As the maître d' showed us to the table for eight, my year-younger sister and I jockeyed for a place near our cousin Bobby. A high school student, he always wore a suit and tie when we went out for dinner. All of the girl cousins agreed that he was really cute. And, boy-oh-boy, could he eat. His capacity to put away food at the smorgasbord is a family legend. It was a thrill just to sit next to him and count how many times he could go back for a new plate piled high with meat and potatoes, corn and carrots, pie à la mode and cake.

But the most fun was keeping count of Bobby's plates. Shamelessly, the rest of us at the table egged him on, and whether he was really that hungry or just responding to our urging, he went back for thirds, fourths, even more.

Once Dad gave us the go-ahead, we would get in line at the salad table, where white plates were stacked at one end. I always took a little of this and a bit of that, because I couldn't decide on just one item. No sooner did I take the last bite of lettuce and set down my fork than the plate was whisked away by a server. That was one of the best parts: always having a clean plate for each course. Our next foray was along a table covered with big silver serving dishes filled with every kind of potato and vegetable you would ever want. The plates were bigger here, and

The Saint Paul Hotel

heavy. At the other end, a man in a white jacket and starched chef's hat sliced turkey, roast beef, and ham. Or all three if we wanted. The person scooping creamy mashed potatoes onto our plates made a gulley on top and poured in smooth-as-silk gravy, asking if we wanted some on our meat, too. Most times I said, "No, thank you."

The dinner was always good. Being dressed up, acting like I was in high school, sitting at a separate table from my parents, all made it special. Laughing and talking with my cousins made it even better. But the most fun was keeping count of Bobby's plates. Shamelessly, the rest of us at the table egged him on, and whether he was really that hungry or just responding to our urging, he went back for thirds, fourths, even more. My little brother and Bobby's, too, looked up at him with awe. Can my memory be right? Does his record really stand at eight? Of course, that counted dessert, too, because Bobby was good at calculating. He always left enough room for one last plate of chocolate éclairs and cream puffs.

November

My Grandma's Green Tomato Mincemeat

Marianne McNamara

Frederika and Karl Mencke began their family in Kiel, Germany, in 1880, with the birth of their daughter Wilhelmina. When little Mina was eighteen months old, the family traveled to America to start a new life. They settled in Saint Paul, where Karl worked as a bricklayer and Frederika raised their five children in the family home on Winifred Street, on the West Side.

I never knew my grandma Minnie—she died five years before I was born. But by all accounts, Minnie was a spunky girl, vivacious and quick to laugh. She was also the first member of her family to speak English. A fast learner at school, she taught her younger brothers and sisters at home.

Minnie graduated from Humboldt High School, a remarkable accomplishment for a girl in those days. After graduation, she worked at the Golden Rule Department Store, at Seventh and Minnesota streets, in the Coat Department. Minnie was popular with customers and employees alike and was moved to Better Dresses. Not long after that, she was promoted to assistant buyer, a wonderful opportunity, and went on buying trips to New York City. In 1916, Minnie was one of the Winter Carnival princesses. That same year, she met and married my grandfather Frank. Minnie and Frank had two children, Frank II and two years later, my mother, Jeanne. Their marriage lasted twenty-six short years, until Minnie's untimely death at age sixty-two in 1942.

Recently I spent an afternoon with my mother, talking about those long-ago days. Mom reminisced about her mother, especially the things she liked to cook, then brought out her mother's well-worn cookbook. Most of the writing is barely legible, but I know there is a story on every tattered, spattered page. Holding my grandmother's cookbook in my hands was a special, almost spiritual, experience. She had held it in her hands many times. It was a link between us, spanning the generations. The cookbook was her collection of the recipes she made for her family's birthdays and holiday celebrations. Inside, there were recipes from her mother, my great-grandmother. There was a recipe for Monkey Faces—wonderful molasses cookies decorated with raisins, Mom's favorite when she was a little girl—Pepper Relish, Ice Box Cookies, Chocolate Angel Food Cake, Sponge Cake, and a recipe for Pecan Cake calling for a cup of whiskey in the batter. I came across Koenigsberger Klops, which I later learned were German meatballs.

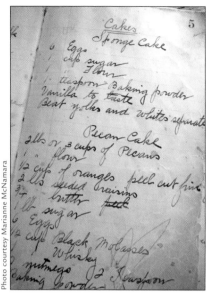

Grandma Minnie's cookbook

I held her memories in my hands and felt a strong connection to a grandmother I never knew. I could tell that being a homemaker had mattered to her. I knew she liked to entertain and serve beautiful food. And I knew she loved her family by the warm way my mother spoke about her.

Mom remembers her mother making Green Tomato Mincemeat for pies. Her brother Frank loved those pies. In my grandmother's day, when they made things like mincemeat, they made large quantities. Then they canned it to use all winter, when fresh fruits and vegetables were not readily available. I don't have any plans to actually make her mincemeat recipe. For now, it is enough to have it and know a little bit more about her, my grandma Minnie.

Grandma Minnie's
Green Tomato Mincemeat Recipe

1 peck green tomatoes
1 peck apples
Grind both.
Add:
1 cup vinegar
6 pounds brown sugar [Imagine: six pounds of sugar!]
2 pounds raisins
2 pounds currants
2 tablespoons ground cinnamon
2 tablespoons ground allspice
2 tablespoons ground cloves
2 tablespoons salt
Cook together for 3 hours. Can. Use for pies.

November

Under the Bridge

Louis Murphy

In the dead hours of a Tuesday night I float down Snelling Avenue in a mixed mania. The trees stare, and a murder of crows haunts me from place to place. Head buried, I slog forward on a path of indifference that eventually leads me to the overpass of Snelling Avenue and Interstate 94. Nearing the north end of the bridge, I see a gate in the fence that separates the frontage road from the freeway. It seems like the only place to hide—down and away from anyone that will think to look for me.

There is no walkway—only snow and footprints; I see another golem passed this way. I step through the opening in the fence, then thrash through drifts, following the footsteps that have gone before. I am crying, but there is no place except here. Perhaps my roommates will figure out that this is where I am, or perhaps I have no friends. I am not sure anymore what to call the people in my life. Even family members seem more distant than Christmas lights glowing in an unknown apartment window.

> **"'Cause if you got friends this is no place to be. See me here? I got nobody. No family; no place— all's I got is them red cars on the freeway. They friends enough for me."**

The deep roar of car engines brings me around again. The concrete under the bridge climbs toward a snowless ledge. This is where he sits— the possible owner of the footprints I followed through the snow. Next to him is an orange, five-gallon Igloo water jug that I can only assume is his. He shuffles down to where I crouch.

"So, what are you doing here, son?" he asks. His unshaven face is frosted by the cold.

"I'm just . . . trying to get away."

The wind burns my face. I stare up at him. He is forty-five or fifty. A grapevine knife scar runs from his left eye to his mouth.

"Son, you got friends?"

Silence, then, "I don't know."

"You got friends out there in the world—people who care where you are?"

His concern stills me.

Under the overpass of Snelling Avenue above I-94

"'Cause if you got friends this is no place to be. See me here? I got nobody. No family; no place—all's I got is them red cars on the freeway. They friends enough for me."

How calm he is. Like a Rodin in the shivering swells of wind.

"Why are you here?" I ask.

"Ain't got no home," he says, patting my shoulder.

I sit on my haunches for five, ten minutes, and stare at the cars that pass. There are red ones—he's got his. What do I have? An apartment with two guys that I have to trust. Paranoia still grips me, but I hold on to the hope that they will forgive me for being who I am—a screwed-up kid who was beaten and taught that you could not rely on others, or even yourself. Now I am afraid to make a move for fear that others will hate me because I am human.

A voice cajoles me: "Now don't you go tryin' to steal my cars. But you can have some of what's in the jug up there if you want."

Slowly, I rise up.

"Thank you" is all that I can mumble.

"You go find your friends," he says finally.

As my feet wind along the trail out of there I see a few things: a place for a small fire; a snow crusted sleeping bag; and, again, the orange cooler. I smell salt misting from the freeway, and hear the rip of water under car tires. I stare back at him and sear the picture into my mind—he sits on his feet and counts red cars.

Poem for Nina Archabal
November 18, 2010

Carol Connolly, Saint Paul Poet Laureate

The leaves on the trees turn to gold,
and before the first snow,
shimmer in the sunlight.
It is harvest time,
and we are thankful
to a wise unflappable woman
who left Massachusetts for Minnesota,
earned a doctorate in music history,
and taught us how to sing
the symphony of our history,
bringing it to new life in lost
languages and resurrected spaces.

This unflappable visionary woman
who never faltered, never stumbled, embraced,
with gusto, the big picture and the smallest detail,
—she can spot a split infinitive a mile away—
gathered what had been scattered
in dark warehouses and small offices,
added the history of ordinary women
and others of the forgotten,
and brought to life, on land abandoned,
a magnificent center and other spaces
that welcome every one of us,
scholars or not.

We muddle through the first snow.
Why is it always a surprise?
We will never forget the brilliant woman
who gave us this living and lasting
gift of passage into a future
that does not forget the past.
We are part of both.

Photo courtesy Carol Connolly

Nina

December

Photo © Pa Yong Xiong

Once, Late on a December Afternoon

on the corner of Thomas and Dale,
a lilac bush hosted a thousand sparrows,
their chatter, a way of keeping warm.
I heard them after a mass for the dead
I lived through by memorizing the altar,
the marble floor's inlaid patterns,
the priest crisscrossing there, his black
polished shoes, the shiny malachite.

On my right stood a wooden creche, that
joy, the mystery of earth's animals
and heaven's angels meeting in a barn;
their hearty singing over the manger,
the priest singing over the casket. Yes.
That is what happened, a way of keeping warm.

Sharon Chmielarz

(venue: St. Agnes Church in Saint Paul)

December

DECEMBER

S	M	T	W	T	F	S
						1
2	3	4	5	6	7	8
9	10	11	12	13	14	15
16	17	18	19	20	21	22
23	24	25	26	27	28	29
30	31					

⇨ The Nushka Toboggan Club was formed in 1885, sponsoring toboggan slides on Crocus Hill, snowshoe hikes to Merriam Park, and parties on Washington's birthday.

26 Monday

27 Tuesday

🐞 November 27: Ethel Hall Stewart, a founder of the Ramsey County Historical Society, was born today in 1879.

28 Wednesday

29 Thursday   Holiday Bazaar

December

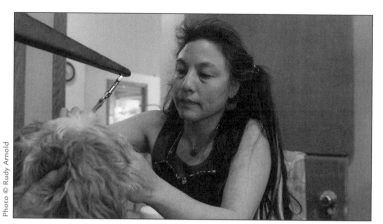

Grand Paws owner Stacy, from series Small Business as Community Catalyst

30 Friday   Holiday Bazaar

🐾 November 30: Mabel Cason, African American educator and activist, was born today in 1918.

1 Saturday   Saint Paul Winter Farmers' Market

World Aids Day

2 Sunday   Holiday Flower Show begins

International Day for the   Grand Meander
   Abolition of Slavery

December

Lessons from Herr Elsing

Dave Healy

Mention the 1960s and most people think of student protest, non-conformity, rebellion. But at Murray High School in Saint Paul, there was little of that. Instead, when the assistant principal said to get a haircut, wear a belt, or lengthen a skirt, we obeyed. Those were days of authoritarian rule. Still, we weren't quite prepared for Herr Elsing.

We first met "the Herr" when he substituted for our first-year German teacher, Frau Hook. Dear, sweet Frau Hook—young, soft-spoken, a bit tentative—just the wrong sort of preparation for Herr Elsing. We were absolutely terrified of him. He strode the aisles like a drill sergeant. Please, God, don't let him call on me. Please, God, heal Frau Hook of her affliction.

Then, toward the end of the year, the rumors began: Frau Hook was leaving, to be replaced permanently by the dreaded Herr. Should we register for second-year German? With great fear and trembling, we signed on for another hitch.

During those first weeks, the Herr was everything we had remembered. "The accusative case is motion *TOWARD*. I *KICK* the wastebasket," he roared, and sent it clattering across the room. We shouted our dative prepositions in unison: *AUS! AUSSER! BEI! MIT! NACH! SEIT! VON! ZU!*

But as the year progressed, another side of Herr Elsing emerged. He was profoundly interested in culture, both his native German and his more recently acquired American. He lectured us on the superiority of European architectural design, on the banality of American television. We memorized Bach's "Herr ich glaube, hilf mir Schwacken" in four-part harmony, each row singing a different part. By the end of the year, there was no question about taking third-year German. We were hooked.

During our senior year, a few of us finally caught up with the '60s zeitgeist by publishing an underground newspaper—the *Senior Satirist.* It was, in retrospect, a rather juvenile effort. But we labored over each issue mightily, honing every word for just the right shade of invective.

We kept our identities a secret until the final issue. No one had suspected us: We were the mild-mannered Clark Kents of our class. But as we gloried in our newfound celebrity status, our euphoria was undercut by a nagging question: What will Herr Elsing think? Herr Elsing—the essence of Old World decorum and propriety. Surely he will not approve of this ill-advised exercise in adolescent bravado.

But the Herr surprised us again. We were invited to his house for tea, an honor heretofore accorded no one in the school. He was gracious, supportive, even friendly. The experience was one the highlights of our high school careers.

I don't remember a lot of my high school German, but I learned more than a language from Herr Elsing. And I can still recite my prepositions.

Photo © Media Mike Hazard

Joe

In Awe

Media Mike Hazard

When he is not hanging out on the streets of Lowertown in awe of the construction, Joe Hang draws.

Trained at Penn as an architect, Joe is now drawing the images that explain what light rail is going to look like. "I make it look pretty."

His sister, Pakou, says, "Joseph is gregarious, artistic, mysterious."

Overhearing her, he says, "I'm an anomaly."

DECEMBER

S	M	T	W	T	F	S
						1
2	3	4	5	6	7	8
9	10	11	12	13	14	15
16	17	18	19	20	21	22
23	24	25	26	27	28	29
30	31					

▷ Tiger Jack Day, in 1978, honored African American shopkeeper "Tiger Jack" Rosenbloom, whose iconic shack sat on Dale Street north of I-94.

3 Monday

International Day of Disabled Persons

🐾 December 3: Janabelle Taylor, African American community leader, was born today in 1920.

4 Tuesday

🐾 December 4: Kenneth Wright, photographer, was born today in 1895.

5 Wednesday

🐾 December 5: John B. Sanborn—lawyer, statesman and Civil War hero—was born today in 1826.

6 Thursday

December

Snow-covered Saint Paul car

Photo © Flickr/Nick Busse

7 Friday

Sky like a mottled-gray egg
Sits low in its nest
Waiting to hatch winter.
Gloria Bengtson

8 Saturday   Saint Paul Winter Farmers' Market

9 Sunday

Hannukah begins

The Saint Paul Police Department graduated its first class of 25
Neighborhood Assistance Officers (NAOs) today in 1977.

City bus

My First Day on the Bus in Saint Paul

Maria Luisa Simon

The first month after I moved to Saint Paul, I made a plan to visit downtown. I got on the bus with my son and daughter.

After ten minutes, the driver asked me, "Where are you going?"

I told him I was going to downtown Saint Paul.

"This bus finished the journey in this area," he said. "In ten minutes, I will take my break for lunch. You sit down inside the bus. I will return in thirty minutes."

My son and my daughter said, "What happened, Mom? I'm scared." But I did not have a problem; I only had to sit for thirty minutes and return with the driver. I was scared, too, but did not tell my children. After, we went downtown.

Saturday, December 12, 2010

Barbara Haselbeck

I looked out the window again. Snow had been falling for sixteen hours, willful winds forming dunes of snow, yet people seemed to feel the need or desire to drive. To get out of the neighborhood, they had to navigate the side streets, which had been plowed on one side only—streets soft with innocent-looking snow, but full of treachery.

The blue Toyota Corolla had been spinning its wheels for one hour, surging forward a few feet, falling back. Now the car had slid sideways, landing with its wheels grooved into the three-foot snowbank on the unplowed side of the road. It had progressed a mere third of a block from the intersection of Cottage and Flandrau.

Another hour passed while the small blue car futilely sought traction, and then three determined souls came to its rescue. Bundled up against the wind and whirling flakes, only one was recognizable: my neighbor Hope, a genuine can-do woman. The three, using shovels, arm signals, and words of encouragement, patiently coaxed the car forward. Once they had freed its wheels from the snowbank, they used someone's overworked snow blower to open a path in front of the car. With each struggle, a few more yards were conquered.

I noted two others—men in snowsuits—standing on the corner with shovels, ready to rescue distressed cars sucked into the snow-covered, icy tracks. They chatted amiably between rescues. I had the urge to bundle up and grab a shovel and join their camaraderie, but some misgivings about the mild pains I had felt earlier while shoveling 16 inches off my own front steps held me back.

By hour three, the car had inched two-thirds of the way up the block. Still shoveling around the wheels while the car accelerated forward and backward, Hope directed and shouted above the gunning of the engine. At one point, a four-wheel-drive SUV, white like the snow, drove up from the opposite direction, its driver intent on chaining the Toyota and pulling it backward from its track. That did not work.

After four hours, the crew had managed to get the car off the road and parked in a neighbor's triple-wide driveway. It hadn't even made it to the end of the block. Now I watched while a father, a mother, and two young children emerged from the car. They were driven away in a Hummer. Phew, I could rest now.

The next morning, when I hung up my car on snow as I backed out of the driveway, I applied the lessons learned watching my determined neighbors: I spent a mere forty minutes freeing my car.

DECEMBER

S	M	T	W	T	F	S
						1
2	3	4	5	6	7	8
9	10	11	12	13	14	15
16	17	18	19	20	21	22
23	24	25	26	27	28	29
30	31					

⇨ The *St. Paul Globe* reported the city's first auto fatality in 1903: 8-year-old Arania Max was run over on Selby Avenue near Dale Street.

10 Monday

International Human Rights Day

11 Tuesday   Minnesota RollerGirls (Bout)

🐝 December 11: Nick Mancini, Italian American restaurateur and founder of Mancini's Char House, was born today in 1926.

12 Wednesday

13 Thursday

🐝 December 13: Olive Foerster Tiller, advocate for deaf education and civil rights activist, was born today in 1920.

December

Taja interviewing Abdisalam Adam at the Sunrise Rotary

14 Friday

Christmas Bird Count begins

15 Saturday   Saint Paul Winter Farmers' Market

16 Sunday

Saint Paul journalist Joe Soucheray began hosting his daily *Garage Logic* drive-time radio show on KSTP in 1993.

Coming Home

Mary Kay Rummel

My father at 90 walked Cathedral Hill
pointing, telling stories of the stones and
buildings within buildings,
as serious as Saint Paul street names,
churches, explorers, saints, and robber barons.
Now you and I, both old-timers and visitors in this city,
linger at the windows of eateries, shops,
barbers, tailors here in the fifties.

That old man rocking over the coffeehouse piano,
fingers blurring,
makes me remember the revolving piano bar
at the top of the downtown Hilton
where we decided one night to get married.
We celebrated by making pilgrimage
and kissing in front of all the places
of our lives spread
on hilltops, in hollows of the old city.

Starting at the marble block of domed cathedral,
we drove Summit Avenue to the Victorian brownstone
owned by the Christian Brothers
who had just released you back into the world,
then further west to Fairview
and the warm sandstone gold of the convent on Randolph
to honor the thick doors I had walked through.

East on Prior to Nativity—your church and school
in groomed gardens,
then down Randolph to St. James,
humble river parish,
where the rag-tag mix of us—Irish, Italian, Hungarian
first generation Americans—learned to read.
Uphill again to our parents' small wood and stucco
houses, one rooted on each side of Snelling,
toward Minneapolis to where the Mississippi curves.
Churches connected the corners of our map
and each churchyard teemed with spirits,
generations of men and women waving us on.

The night ended downtown at an old church
transformed into a theater. The nave was packed
and in the sanctuary, an ensemble—
fiddlers, a hammered dulcimer, a drummer—played.
Under the stained glass saints, music freed itself
from the confines of strings, reed, and hide.
No Jesus, no Guadalupe—
just a church full of strangers who couldn't stop
smiling and tapping their feet.

	S	M	T	W	T	F	S
							1
	2	3	4	5	6	7	8
	9	10	11	12	13	14	15
	16	17	18	19	20	21	22
	23	24	25	26	27	28	29
	30	31					

⇨ A monument honoring Jacob Fahlstrom—fur trader, mail carrier, missionary, and first Swede in Minnesota—was erected near Robert and Kellogg in 1948.

17 Monday

🐾 December 17: Carol Muske-Dukes, writer, was born today in 1945.

18 Tuesday

International Migrants Day

19 Wednesday

20 Thursday

International Human Solidarity Day

🐾 December 20: Mary Livingston Griggs, community activist and philanthropist, was born today in 1876.

December

Ducks on Como Lake in the morning

21 Friday
Winter Solstice

22 Saturday
Saint Paul Winter Farmers' Market

23 Sunday

In 1959, Saint Paul opened a new 10-story apartment in the Mt. Airy project. It contained 174 apartments for low-income families.

The Blue Bicycle

Mike Finley

The snowy woods at Hidden Falls echoed with the crunch of boots and the snapping of dry wood. "How much longer?" my eight-year old son, Jon, asked.

"Not long," I said, huffing frosted steam. "We're almost there."

My twelve-year old daughter, Daniele, was impatient, too. "What did you say we were looking for?"

"Yes," my wife Rachel said, "what is it exactly?"

"Something you'll never see again," I said. I was in heaven, luring my kids out into the cold to see if they could spot the remarkable thing. We finally came to a clearing overlooking a small ravine.

We just stood there for a moment, our breath frosting up before us. "It's right here," I announced. There wasn't a sound except the subtle poof of huge snowflakes landing. Then Jon said, "I see it!"

He pointed up, into the lower reaches of a young cottonwood tree. There, about ten feet from the ground, was a rusted old bicycle. It was not sitting in a branch; rather, the branch had somehow grown around the bicycle. The main bar was entirely enclosed in swarming wood.

"Wow," Daniele said.

I had come across it a few days earlier, when out walking the dog. I had actually passed that spot a hundred times and not noticed. But who ever looks up to see a tree embracing a bicycle? You need luck to see these things. And now I felt like Merlin, letting young Arthur peer into a peculiar mystery.

Based on the bike style, the amount of corrosion, and the absence of tire rubber, I guessed that the bicycle had been in the tree for over forty years. It was entirely rusted except for a narrow path of etched blue enamel just below the handlebars, by the little plate that still said Western Automatic.

The four of us were suddenly giddy with the idea of a bicycle growing in a tree. How did it get there? Did someone lean it against the tree years ago, and the tree slowly reached out and lifted it up, an inch a year, up into the sky?

Or did someone just throw it up there, and the tree held on to it and grew around it?

Whose bike was it, and would its owner remember it?

Was the bike flying? Was the tree riding? Did the wind once blow the wheels around, whispering stories of locomotion?

Everyone agreed, on the way back to the car, that it was a wonderful thing, and we should always keep our eyes keen for other anomalies.

Illustration © Andy Singer

The blue bicycle tree

They must be everywhere, we reasoned. We just have to train ourselves to see them.

But the next time I came to the clearing, in spring, by myself, not only was the bicycle gone, but so was the tree itself. A big wind blowing up the river has no trouble toppling trees rooted in sand. A cottonwood lay on its side like that, head down in the ravine, its roots reaching up like imploring hands.

I looked around for the bicycle. I scouted the area, to no avail. The spring vegetation was already crowding the ground—thick enough to hide a jutting pedal or rusted rim. Over the next couple of years I gently obsessed about finding the bicycle, returning to the spot numerous times, to see if I had merely misplaced it. Occasionally, I thought I glimpsed it. But it was just a curl of riverbank vine, pretending to be a wheel, or the color of rot pretending to be rust.

My heart always quickened when I stood on that spot. A bicycle fashioned of iron from the dirt once roamed this city and raced up and down its hills. Its rider was thrilled to fly through our town. And then the bicycle took up residence, in some unexplained way, high in a tree overlooking the Mississippi, gazing out at the barges and crows. And now it had returned to the earth.

I felt like that archaeologist, Heinrich Schliemann, who found Troy seven cities down, only in reverse. What the earth lifted up, it then took back. Everything combined to make it so. Every falling leaf hid it. Each clump of snow buried it deeper. Every summer hiker's footfall sank it deeper in the wood.

It all goes. My children are grown. But I saw a bicycle ride through the sky, its wheels still turning in the breeze from the river.

December

DECEMBER

S	M	T	W	T	F	S
						1
2	3	4	5	6	7	8
9	10	11	12	13	14	15
16	17	18	19	20	21	22
23	24	25	26	27	28	29
30	31					

▷ James H. Burrell, a 35-year-old former railroad worker, became the first African American member of the Saint Paul police force in 1892.

24 Monday

Christmas Eve

❦ December 24: Charlotte Day, Native American co-founder of Red School House, was born today in 1917.

25 Tuesday

Christmas Day

26 Wednesday

Kwanzaa begins

A Frogtown Christmas
A mountain of small gifts
under a skinny tree
beautiful now
in the solstice dark;
the carols at the piano,
enough voices for soprano,
alto, tenor, and bass;
our father's wine, made
the summer before;
mother, bearing gifts
from the back of the closet
with the dignity
of the magi; midnight mass,
the church candlelit,
a short walk home,
our skinny tree ablaze.

(Published in *Sidewalks #19*)
Norita Dittberner-Jax

27 Thursday

December

Photo © Brenda Manthe

Rocket launch

28 Friday

29 Saturday   Saint Paul Winter Farmers' Market
                     Kwanzaa Family Celebration

December 29: Ta-coumba Aiken, African American artist and muralist, was born today in 1952.

30 Sunday

December

The Yale University Glee, Banjo, and Mandolin clubs gave a concert at the Saint Paul Auditorium on December 26 in 1912.

Illustration © Roberta Avidor

Winter biking

A Winter's Trail

Aleli Balagtas

To bike, or not to bike; that is never a question. It is far nobler to suffer the sting of sleet and numbing cold than to trap one's self within the confines of a motor vehicle. The subzero world's a stage, and all the winter bikers merely actors. Upon this stage I see my friend—in neon vest with taped-on flashing lights, a yellow jacket, yellow pants—atop his pink flamingo beater of a bike ("No, it's salmon," his wife deadpans, as he's already heading out—*clunk-clunk*—on Como, downtown bound); or the sleek Ninja warrior, clad in classic black, messenger bag wrapped across his back, who cuts, insouciant, in front of me, his fluorescent vest a slice of brightness across the bow of winter's somber discontent.

The course of winter biking never does run smooth. Cracked and pitted icy ruts abound, as does peril in the form of drivers, tightly wound. What fools these bikers be! But to their own selves they are true. For us mere mortals, though, there is tomorrow, and tomorrow, and tomorrow.

As I in my minivan creep about the city day to day, at petty pace avoiding potholes, driving roads made narrow by drifts of dirty snow and ice, I sense the end is near, the spring must come.

A bike, a bike. My minivan for a bike.

Wokiksuye

Elena Cisneros

Driving back from the reservation, I cross a small bridge into Saint Paul. I feel the troubled waters. I think of my grandfather's people, the Dakota. I think of how they lived by the water, how they made fire by the water. I think of how my people, the Dakota, my family, were taken to Fort Snelling prison. I think of Many Lightnings and his sons, my family, every time I come back to Saint Paul and see the "Historic Site" sign. I think of how the Thirty-Eight sang their prayer and death songs on the gallows. I think of how my family watched their people hang all together.

I try to see this but the red and green lights distract me. I try to hear them but tires screeching and horns honking distract me. All I have are signs, another "Historic Site Fort Snelling" ahead. All I have is dirty water under a bridge. I don't have their voices. I don't have their words. So I drive into Saint Paul and park my car and walk amongst the cold leaves to my apartment building. I manage a small token of smoke and silence.

⇨ The Saint Paul City Conference was formed in 1898. Soon after, Central High School beat Mechanic Arts in a football game, 25-0.

DECEMBER

S	M	T	W	T	F	S
						1
2	3	4	5	6	7	8
9	10	11	12	13	14	15
16	17	18	19	20	21	22
23	24	25	26	27	28	29
30	31					

31 Monday
New Year's Eve

1 Tuesday
New Year's Day

2 Wednesday

3 Thursday

December

Winter work

Photo © Patricia Bour-Schilla

4 Friday	
5 Saturday	Saint Paul Winter Farmers' Market
6 Sunday	

December

Queries for the Curious:
(From) *The Street Where You Live; A Guide to the Place Names of St. Paul*
Donald Empson

1) Which wetland in the city was used to provide willows for the florist trade?

Willow Reserve: This is a five-and-one-half-acre conservancy district in the North End on the northeast corner of Maryland Avenue and Arundel Street. The former owner brought willow trees from Austria to plant in the wetland; in the spring he cut stems for florists to use in their bouquets. The property was acquired by the sewer department in 1977 after the League of Women Voters (who were doing a water quality study), ornithologists, and the neighbors exerted pressure on the city to buy the land before it was developed. Now used as a detention pond taking the occasional overflow from the storm sewer, the Reserve continues to host a vast array of birds that use the marshy site on their flyway. An adjacent neighborhood is sometimes known by this name as well.

Photo courtesy Donald Empson

Sign at Willow Reserve

2) What is the origin of Monkey Rudder Bend in the Mississippi River?

A monkey beam is a transverse post at the stern of a paddlewheel steamboat. A rudder hung from the monkey beam behind the paddlewheel is called the monkey rudder. In earlier days when the "S" curve in the Mississippi River near Hidden Falls Park was even sharper, the back of a steamboat maneuvering through the curve might brush against one of the banks damaging or destroying the monkey rudder. This curve in the river is known to riverboat pilots as Monkey Rudder Bend.

December

Consuming Desire

Katrina Vandenberg

I'm not making this up. At Cafe Latté's wine bar
one of the lovely coeds at the next table
touched John on the arm as if I wasn't there
and said, *Excuse me, sir, but what*
is that naughty little dessert?
And I knew from the way he glanced
at the frothy neckline of her blouse,
then immediately cast his eyes on his plate
before giving a fatherly answer,
he would have given up dessert three months
for the chance to feed this one to her.
I was stunned; John was hopeful;
but the girl was hitting on his cake.
Though she told her friend until they left
she did not want any. I wish she wanted
something—my husband, his cake, both at once.
I wish she left insisting
on the beauty of his hands, his curls,
the sublimeness of strawberries
and angel food. But she was precocious,
and I fear adulthood is the discipline
of being above desire, cultivated
after years of learning what you want
and where and how, after insisting
that you will one day have it. I don't
ever want to stop noticing a man like the one
at the bar in his loosened tie, reading
the *Star Tribune*. I don't want to eat my cake
with a baby spoon to force small bites,
as women's magazines suggest. And you
don't want to either, do you? You want a big piece
of this world. You would love to have the whole thing.

From *Atlas*, published by Milkweed Editions, 2004.

Architecture and Common Sense

Barbara Davis

My interest in architecture all started with Lincoln Logs. Growing up in a 1950s-built house in Minneapolis, I loved creating everything with my chunky wooden logs—log cabins, modern-Danish-looking houses, lean-tos and castles alike. My mother was sure that, since our family was also full of common sense, this was my future. Architecture and common sense, a good blend.

When I hit college, I moved to Saint Paul, and was enthralled with the grand homes along Summit Avenue, the Victorians on Portland, the houses hidden away on the bluffs overlooking downtown. I dreamed of living in the attic or the carriage house of one of the mansions.

But my main architectural learning experience was about the *lack* of common sense that can sometimes plague a building. I learned this lesson from my Macalester College dormitory's cold floors. I realized that the cold floors were caused by a design flaw: the breezeway underneath half the building allowed cold arctic winds direct access half the year. A paltry baseboard heater did nothing to warm the room.

Never one to let a question lie unanswered, I set up an independent study project and learned about dormitory architecture. My teeth chattered all that winter as I pored over dormitory design books and blueprints, finding out why dormitories were put together the way they were.

I ultimately found out that our dorm in Saint Paul had been designed for a college in Kentucky—common sense undoubtedly on someone's part dictated that they should save money by using the same design. But it had been built without modification, without adaptations; it even lacked such northern essentials as storm windows and insulation.

Decades later, I thought of that dorm when I lay awake, sweating, in the stiflingly hot nights of subtropical Taiwan, in an ill-conceived modern apartment building designed for a temperate climate; a design that did not account for the intense day-and-night heat and humidity. I slept fitfully all year and dreamed of my old dorm's cool floors and crisp north winds.

I never managed to make it to architecture school, but the lessons in common sense that I learned in Saint Paul have stuck with me ever since.

Drums in the front window of the Artists' Quarter

Gary Berg

Daryl C. Jorgenson

A while back I attended a small jazz club in the basement of one of the old buildings downtown. The Historic Hamm Building. Historic buildings always seem to do it for me. Even their basements.

A friendly face met me at the door. Upon paying the two-dollar cover—ridiculously cheap, even in those days—I entered the familiar dark room filled with the light of music. True music. Gary Berg, an old man who had a face like a Muppet, played the saxophone for me and thirteen other guests for over two and a half hours. A man in a white tuxedo with tails accompanied him on a B-3 organ: its speaker whirred behind him and his feet moved smoothly from one pedal to the next, never missing a beat. The rest of the band swayed in waiting as solos were passed around the stage.

The drinks that flowed for me and my fellow listeners that night were strong and easy to come by. A vocalist friend of the band sat in for a few songs and the warm timbre of his southern voice gave us a brief respite from our frigid northern reality.

"The best jazz in North America on a Tuesday night." A hell of a slogan, but not exactly fair. Any night of the week those men could hold their own. I became a regular.

December

Bill Wilson:
A Humble Hero in Saint Paul

Joe Nathan

What makes Bill Wilson keep running? His life is a record of extraordinary achievements. Starting as a young waiter on the Great Northern Railroad, Wilson moved on to become the first executive director of the Inner City Youth League, the first African American elected to the Saint Paul City Council, and the first African American chair of the City Council. But he didn't stop there: he went on to found and become executive director of a nationally known and honored K–12 charter public school. His life has been dedicated to service and a search for justice.

Wilson is a native of Evansville, Indiana, where he remembers being bussed far from home to attend a segregated school. He attended Knoxville College after being awarded a basketball scholarship but was forced to drop out in 1963 when he became ill.

Fortunately for Minnesotans, Wilson then moved to Saint Paul. While working as a waiter on the Great Northern Railroad, he began taking evening classes at the University of Minnesota, where he cofounded Students for Racial Progress, a group working on campus racial issues. The Ford Foundation Fellowship awarded him a scholarship to study at the University of Massachusetts at Amherst, where he earned joint Bachelor's and Master's in Education degrees in 1974. Governor Wendell Anderson appointed Wilson as Commissioner of the Minnesota Department of Human Rights. He served in that position until 1979.

In 1980, Saint Paul reclaimed Wilson when he became the first African American elected to the Saint Paul City Council; he became its president in 1989. Later, he returned to the University of Minnesota and worked as coordinator of Diversity Programs in the College of Education and Human Development.

Though low-key and modest, Wilson has received many awards for his work. In 1994, Governor Arne Carlson proclaimed May 21 as "Bill Wilson Day" in Minnesota. He has received a Certificate of Appreciation from the Saint Paul branch of the NAACP and the William (Bill) Cosby Alumni Award for City Government Service from the University of Massachusetts.

In 1998, Wilson founded Higher Ground Academy, a K–12 charter school located in Saint Paul. *U.S. News and World Report* described the school as one of the best high schools in the United States. The *Star*

Photo courtesy of Joe Nathan

Bill Wilson

Tribune cited its success in helping its students beat the odds; before graduating, Higher Ground students must be accepted into higher-education programs. He has told the Minnesota State Legislature about the difference between the segregated school he was forced to attend and the opportunities families now enjoy to select schools for their children, including Higher Ground.

Thanks to Wilson's vision and energy, Saint Paul is a far different and far better place because he has lived and worked here for more than forty-five years.

Bill has been married for forty-seven years to Willie Mae Wilson, retired president and CEO of the Saint Paul Urban League. He is the father of one son and one daughter, and has a granddaughter.

Thanks to Wilson's vision and energy, Saint Paul is a far different and far better place because he has lived and worked here for more than forty-five years.

December

Benevolence in a Blizzard

Karen Jeffords-Brown

I have many stories about the wonderful people in Saint Paul that I tell friends and family, but by far, this is my favorite.

It was one of those bone-chilling, spirit-freezing mornings in the early 1980s and I was bundled up to the eyeballs (literally) in layers of down and wool, waiting at the bus stop on Cretin Avenue for the MTC express bus. I worked in downtown Minneapolis at the Government Center and enjoyed the convenience of walking four blocks from my duplex on Selby, hopping on the bus, and being dropped off right in front of my building. But on mornings like this when the cold, snow, and wind ground many things to a halt (not to move again until later in the morning when it "warmed up" to zero), the express bus was not only late but appeared to be not running at all.

As I stood shivering and bracing against the wind, I debated my alternatives. I could trudge back home and attempt to start my pickup truck, but it frequently would not start in this weather as I had no garage and had to park outside. I could trudge home and stay there, but that would inconvenience the clients I had scheduled to see that morning. I decided impulsively to hitch a ride with one of the cars crawling down Cretin. I reasoned that serial killers and psychopaths would not be out at this ungodly hour in this ungodly cold, and that I could size up whoever offered me a ride and refuse if he/she looked spooky or deranged.

> I reasoned that serial killers and psychopaths would not be out at this ungodly hour in this ungodly cold, and that I could size up whoever offered me a ride and refuse if he/she looked spooky or deranged.

I stuck out a frozen thumb and gingerly stepped off the curb into the road to underscore my desperation. Eventually a nondescript midsized sedan pulled up and the passenger side window rolled down.

"Are you needing a ride?" An elderly gentleman with wispy white hair and glasses smiled at me, and his equally elderly companion, the driver, leaned over and smiled also. Definitely not the serial killer type, I surmised, and gratefully said, "Yes, I have to get to work by 10 o'clock."

"Hop in," they said.

Snowy highway

They asked me where I was bound and I told them the Government Center in downtown Minneapolis. We crawled up Cretin and crept slowly out onto 94, traveling west. The highway was shrouded in a frozen car exhaust fog that made the urban landscape look like Brigadoon, rising out of the misty hills of Scotland. The windows inside the car were also fogging up as I settled into the backseat and enjoyed the warmth of the heater and their company.

My traveling companions chatted and laughed amiably. I appreciated their ease with each other. Probably old friends having a relaxing morning, they drove slowly and cautiously. We eventually exited 94 and edged into downtown Minneapolis.

As we pulled up in front of the Government Center, I gathered up purse and briefcase and pulled on my gloves. The elderly gent in the passenger seat turned around to wish me well as I started to open the door.

"Thank you so much," I said. "I really appreciate your dropping me off here." They both smiled and said it was "no problem at all ..."

Then I asked where in downtown Minneapolis they were headed on this morning.

"Oh, well," the old gent in the driver seat said. "We weren't actually going to downtown Minneapolis. We were headed for downtown Saint Paul."

Carpenters Local 87

John Sielaff

The union I belong to, Saint Paul Carpenters Local 87, has been in continuous operation since the 1880s. Some of the earliest members were active in The Knights of Labor, the all-encompassing nineteenth-century working people's organization. In the winter of 1885, some of these men decided to form a carpenters local and affiliate with the national union, the United Brotherhood of Carpenters.

In the early years, meetings were held three times a month on Saturday nights and lasted two to three hours, as the men discussed a wide range of labor-related topics. I know this because the meeting notes are preserved at the Minnesota Historical Society in the excellent penmanship of the recording secretary. They supported various labor causes with their meager treasury and brought in outside speakers. In 1886, they paid to have the carpenters union president, Peter McGuire, come and speak at a public meeting. Although the union was not officially recognized by employers, their movement quickly grew so that by 1887 there were three other carpenter union locals in Saint Paul; the German, French, and Scandinavian members wanted to conduct meetings in their own language.

The norm for skilled carpenters at that time was ten hours, six days a week, at twenty-five cents per hour.

In June 1887, frustrated by the contractors' refusal to recognize their union, the Saint Paul carpenters went on strike demanding union recognition and a nine-hour day. The norm for skilled carpenters at that time was ten hours, six days a week, at twenty-five cents per hour. In contrast, the union bricklayers of Saint Paul, who had been officially organized since 1883, got a signed agreement with their contractors in 1886 stipulating a nine-hour day at forty cents an hour. In some eastern cities, construction workers already had the eight-hour day, so the carpenters thought their demands were reasonable.

The Saint Paul newspapers were full of stories about the strike, which was the first of its kind in Minnesota. The union held meetings attended by 3,000 men, according to the *Pioneer Press,* and many special meetings of the four locals were called to swear in new members. Bricklayers and other building trade workers struck in sympathy with the carpenters. This solidarity was met with similar unity by the opposition. The contractors

December

refused to recognize the representatives of the union, and after several weeks, the strikers' resources were exhausted. The other trades went back to work, as did many of the recently recruited members.

Some of the more sympathetic contractors came up with an informal agreement to go to a nine-hour day starting in January 1888, but most of the fruits of this strike were less tangible. Striking carpenters started a co-op grocery store to serve members during the strike and some also incorporated a cooperative construction company. Others went back to work with the Knights of Labor or the newly formed Farmer Labor Party. The president of the German local became editor of *St. Paul Labor,* the local paper of the Socialist Labor Party.

The union went through some tough economic times in the 1890s, with a small core of dedicated members keeping the flame alive. In 1893, when Local 87 had only twenty or thirty members, the *St. Paul Trades and Labor Bulletin* reported that carpenters were working on scaffolding at a new auditorium seventy-five feet off the ground, for twenty cents an hour, for eleven-hour days. It was only with a better employment situation and encouragement from a newly formed union in Minneapolis that Local 87 was to get its first contract in 1897. It was not much—a nine-hour day and wages to "regulate themselves at present"— but they had their foot in the door and an important recruiting tool. By 1900, they had the numbers to successfully demand an eight-hour day at thirty cents an hour. Local 87 still had many struggles ahead, but the nineteenth-century pioneers had built the foundation for the wages and working conditions that we carpenters in Saint Paul enjoy today.

To My Young Hmong Women...

David Vu

To my young Hmong women...
You are much more than your hips and thighs
Speak truth through your lips and eyes
Shake past the pain and lies
Open your heart and realize, when we men bring you down
That only you can stand up and never back down
I'm telling you this from the other side
Cause you are my mother, sisters, aunts, and nieces
Don't let those short skirts and skin be your voice
God gave you a tongue so preach until you're heard
Sing your song, because only you can deliver the melody
Hum your harmony, no matter what your dreams are, let them be forever
Don't let one man make you leave us
Those stories you hear...are stories, there is still good in some of us
You are Queens; don't let any fool be your King
When times get hard don't forget those who were with you from the
    start
And those who broke your heart, don't let them be your light
Many times I have heard your stories
From broken dreams alongside the typical theme
I try to understand the heartache that passes through the soul
But only could hear your words...so here I write to your soul

To my young Hmong women
You are so much more...
Don't let any man tell you you're not beautiful
You are the stars that shine through the darkened skies
There will be times when others leave you dry
Always believe you can fly
Whatever they say, it's your judgment that will lead the way
You are the carrier of our culture, the mother of our seeds
When we men fell, you picked us back up
Your strength powerful beyond measure
Let marriage be for later, for you have not yet explored the world
These are the times when younger yous need you the most
You were meant to play with the boys; they just never expected you to fly

David Vu

What our parents said was the past and your present is your presence

To my Hmong...
We are the change that we seek
It's not that our goals are too high and we will never meet
But that our goals are too low and have already been met
Our fathers told us not to daydream, shook our head, but only pain
    came
There are brothers and sisters that still reside in those refugee camps so
    far away
After so long...half way cross the world, we still seek refuge
Sometimes you have to get off the boat to walk on water

On the Day After

Jim Moore

The old woman who lives across the street
runs her vacuum
on the day after Christmas,
cleaning up after the silence
of the day before.
Two small geraniums in the window
lean into one another
like people whispering at a funeral;
signs of life.

Saint Paul Listings

Events

JANUARY

Rogers and Hammerstein's Cinderella
Dec. 13–Jan.1
Ordway Center for the Performing Arts
651.291.1144

Downtown Saint Paul Winter Farmers' Market
Saturdays, 9 a.m.–1 p.m.
290 East Fifth St.
651.227.8101
www.stpaulfarmersmarket.com
Local growers sell their fresh foods directly to you.

Holiday Flower Show
Through Jan. 22
Marjorie McNeely Conservatory, Como Park
651.487.8200
www.comozooconservatory.org

Shane Hawley at a Saint Paul Almanac Lowertown Reading Jam

Illustration © Lara Hanson

The Saint Paul Chamber Orchestra
Beethoven's Pastoral Symphony
Jan. 6, 10:30 a.m. and 8 p.m
Jan. 7, 8 p.m.
Ordway Center for the Performing Arts
651.291.1144

Land O'Lakes Kennel Club Dog Show
Jan. 6–8
Saint Paul RiverCentre
651.265.4800
www.rivercentre.org
Come watch over 2,000 dogs strut their stuff.

Minnesota Boychoir Winter Concert
Jan. 8, 1–3 p.m.
Landmark Center
651.292.3225
www.landmarkcenter.org
Hear the lovely sounds of over 100 boys aged 7–18.

Saint Paul Almanac Lowertown Reading Jam
Jan. 9, 7–8:30 p.m.
Black Dog Café
651.785.6268
www.saintpaulalmanac.com
Selected writers curate readings around a theme they have chosen and invite other writers and artists to perform with them.

The Saint Paul Chamber Orchestra
Mozart and Liget
Jan. 13, 10:30 a.m. and 8 p.m.

Ordway Center for the
Performing Arts
651.291.1144
www.thespco.org

**The Saint Paul Chamber
Orchestra**
*Christine Brewer Sings Beethoven
and Wagner*
Jan. 20, 8 p.m.
Ordway Center for the
Performing Arts
651.291.1144
www.thespco.org

Minnesota RollerGirls (Bout)
Jan. 22
Roy Wilkins Auditorium
651.265.4800
www.mnrollergirls.com
*The Minnesota RollerGirls are part
of the Women's Flat Track Derby
Association (WFTDA), a national
governing body for female-only, skater-
owned, flat-track roller derby leagues.
The Minnesota RollerGirls league
was founded by the Donnelly sisters in
August 2004, and has grown from six
original members to a current roster of
80 skaters, eight referees and coaches,
and countless volunteers. Great
spectator sport!*

Saint Paul Winter Carnival
Jan. 26–Feb. 5
Downtown Saint Paul
651.223.4700
www.winter-carnival.com
*Lots of winter events: parades, ice
skating, ice sculpture, coronation,
medallion hunt.*

Fourth Friday at the Movies
Hosted by Mahmoud El-Kati

Jan. 27
Golden Thyme Coffee Café
651.645.1340
*Social hour at 6:30 p.m. and film
at 7 p.m.*

**Orchid Society of Minnesota
Winter Carnival Orchid Show**
Jan. 28–29, 10 a.m.–4 p.m.
Conservatory, Como Park
651.487.8200
www.comozooconservatory.org

Global Hot Dish Variety Show
Jan. 28
Minnesota History Center
345 West Kellogg Blvd.
651.259.3000
www.mnhs.org
*A classy, quirky, 90-minute, family-
friendly variety show.*

Saintly City Cat Show
Jan. 28–29
Saint Paul RiverCentre
651.265.4800
www.rivercentre.org
*More than 300 felines compete to be
crowned the Feline King and Queen of
the Saint Paul Winter Carnival.*

Minnesota Opera
Werther by Jules Massenet
Jan. 28, 31, Feb. 2, 4, 5
Ordway Center for the
Performing Arts
612.333.6669
www.mnopera.org
*The passionate James Valenti
returns to star as Werther. Roxana
Constantinescu, who dazzled audiences
in Cinderella, returns as the object of
his obsession.*

FEBRUARY

Downtown Saint Paul Winter Farmers' Market
Saturdays, 9 a.m.–1 p.m.
290 East Fifth St.
651.227.8101
www.stpaulfarmersmarket.com
Local growers sell their fresh foods directly to you.

Saint Paul Chamber Orchestra
Feb. 3, 3 p.m and 8 p.m.
Feb 5, 2 p.m.
Ordway Center for the Performing Arts
651.291.1144
www.thespco.org

Winter Flower Show
Feb. 4–Mar. 18
Conservatory, Como Park
651.487.8200
www.comozooconservatory.org

Minnesota RollerGirls (Bout)
Feb. 5
Roy Wilkins Auditorium
651.265.4800
www.mnrollergirls.com

Saint Paul Almanac Lowertown Reading Jam
Feb.13, 7–8:30 p.m.
Black Dog Café
651.785.6268
www.saintpaulalmanac.com
Selected writers curate readings around a theme they have chosen and invite other writers and artists to perform with them.

Saint Paul Chamber Orchestra
Upshaw Sings Ravel and Debussey
Feb. 16, 7:30 p.m.

Feb. 18, 8 p.m.
Ordway Center for the Performing Arts
651.291.1144
www.thespco.org

Ordway Family: Children's Corner
Feb. 18, 9:30 a.m. and 11 a.m.
Ordway Center for the Performing Arts
651.291.1144
www.thespco.org

A Scottish Ramble
Feb. 18–19
Landmark Center
651.292.3225
www.scottishramble.org
Nothing's cooler than kilts in February!

Vietnamese Tet New Year Festival
Date to be announced
Saint Paul RiverCentre
651.265.4800
www.vietnam-minnesota.org
Vietnamese music, dancing, contests, food, and celebration. Free admission.

Minnesota State High School League Girls' Hockey Tournament
Feb. 22–25
Xcel Energy Center
763.560.2262
www.mshsl.org

Fourth Friday at the Movies
Hosted by Mahmoud El-Kati
Feb. 24
Golden Thyme Coffee Café
651.645.1340
Social hour at 6:30 p.m. and film

*Tou SaiKo Lee at a Saint Paul
Almanac Lowertown Reading Jam*

Saint Paul Chamber Orchestra

Copes Plays Korngold
Feb. 24, 10:30 a.m. and 8 p.m.
Feb. 26, 8 p.m.
Ordway Center for the
Performing Arts
651.291.1144
www.thespco.org

Global Hot Dish Variety Show

Feb. 25
Minnesota History Center
345 West Kellogg Blvd.
651.259.3000
www.mnhs.org
Family-friendly variety show.

Rose Ensemble

Slavic Wonders: Feasts and
Saints from Russia, Poland, and
Bohemia
Feb. 26, 4 p.m.
Landmark Center
651.292.3225
www.roseensemble.org
*Mysterious chants, joyful hymns, and
magnificent choral works mingled
with tales of folk heroes.*

MARCH

Downtown Saint Paul Winter Farmers' Market

Saturdays, 9 a.m.–1 p.m.
290 East Fifth St.
651.227.8101
www.stpaulfarmersmarket.com
*Local growers sell their fresh foods
directly to you.*

Winter Flower Show

Feb. 5–Mar. 20
Conservatory, Como Park
651.487.8200
www.comozooconservatory.org

Minnesota State High School League Boys' Wrestling Tournament

Mar. 1–3
Xcel Energy Center
763.560.2262
www.mshsl.org

Minnesota Opera

Lucia di Lammermoor by Gaetano
Donizetti
Mar. 3, 4, 6, 8, 10, and 11
Ordway Center for the
Performing Arts
612.333.6669
www.mnopera.org
*After winning the hearts of Minnesota
Opera audiences as Eurydice, Susanna
Phillips returns to star as the fragile
heroine of this exhilarating masterpiece of
melodic beauty and psychological depth.*

Minnesota RollerGirls (Bout)

Mar. 5
Roy Wilkins Auditorium
651.265.4800
www.mnrollergirls.com

Minnesota State High School League Boys' Hockey Tournament

Mar. 7–10
Xcel Energy Center
763.560.2262
www.mshsl.org

Saint Paul Chamber Orchestra

Start the Music! A Percussion Family Party
Mar. 10, 9:30 a.m.
Mar. 24, 10:30 a.m.
SPCO Center
651.291.1144
www.thespco.org

Irish Day of Dance

Mar. 11, 10 a.m.–5 p.m.
Landmark Center
651.292.3225
www.irishmusicanddance
association.org

Saint Paul Almanac Lowertown Reading Jam

Mar. 12, 7–8:30 p.m.
Black Dog Café

Khary Jackson at a Saint Paul Almanac Lowertown Reading Jam

651.785.6268
www.saintpaulalmanac.com
Selected writers curate readings around a theme they have chosen and invite other writers and artists to perform with them.

IMDA Saint Patrick's Day Celebration

Mar. 15, 10 a.m.–5 p.m.
Landmark Center
651.292.3225
www.irishmusicanddance
association.org

Saint Patrick's Day Parade

Mar. 17
Downtown Saint Paul
651.256.2155
www.stpatsassoc.org
Once the biggest parade in Saint Paul, and still very big.

Saint Patrick's Day Irish Ceili Dance

Mar. 17, 7–10 p.m.
CSPS Hall, 383 Michigan St.
651.290.0542
www.minnesotafolkfestival.org
Learn the steps of the Irish, because everyone is Irish on St. Paddy's Day.

Saint Paul Chamber Orchestra

Hayden's Drumroll Symphony
Mar. 17, 8 p.m.
Saint Paul's United Church of Christ
651.291.1144
www.thespco.org

Fourth Friday at the Movies

Hosted by Mahmoud El-Kati
Mar. 23
Golden Thyme Coffee Café

Illustration © Lara Hanson

651.645.1340
Social hour at 6:30 p.m. and film at 7 p.m.

Spring Flower Show
Mar. 24–Apr. 29
Marjorie McNeely Conservatory, Como Park
651.487.8200
www.comozooconservatory.org

Global Hot Dish Variety Show
Mar. 31
Minnesota History Center
345 West Kellogg Blvd.
651.259.3000
www.mnhs.org
Family-friendly variety show.

Saint Paul Chamber Orchestra
Schubert's Tragic Symphony
Mar. 31, 8 p.m.
Saint Paul's United Church of Christ
651.291.1144
www.thespco.org

APRIL

Downtown Saint Paul Farmers' Market
Through April 21: Saturdays, 9 a.m.–1 p.m.
Apr. 28–Nov. 18
Saturdays, 6 a.m.–1 p.m.
Sundays, 8 a.m.–1 p.m.
290 East Fifth St.
651.227.8101
www.stpaulfarmersmarket.com
Local growers sell their fresh produce directly to you.

Spring Flower Show
Continues through April 29
Conservatory, Como Park
651.487.8200
www.comozooconservatory.org

Minnesota RollerGirls (Bout)
Apr. 2
Roy Wilkins Auditorium
651.265.4800
www.mnrollergirls.com

Saint Paul Chamber Orchestra
Schubert's Great Symphony
Apr. 6, 10:30 a.m.–8 p.m.
Apr. 7, 8 p.m.
Ordway Center for the Performing Arts
651.291.1144
www.thespco.org

Living Green Expo
Apr. 7–8
State Fairgrounds
651.215.0218
www.livinggreen.org
Environmental fair, workshops, live music, food, and kids' activities.

Saint Paul Almanac Lowertown Reading Jam
Apr. 9, 7–8:30 p.m.
Black Dog Café
651.785.6268
www.saintpaulalmanac.com
Selected writers curate readings around a theme they have chosen and invite other writers and artists to perform with them.

28th Annual Minneapolis–Saint Paul International Film Festival
Apr. 14–30

612.331.7563
www.mspfilmfest.org
The largest film festival in the upper Midwest. Over 150 films from more than 50 countries. Various locations.

Minnesota Book Awards Gala

Apr. 14, 6:30 p.m.
Crowne Plaza Hotel
651.222.3242
www.thefriends.org
Awards presented to best books published in Minnesota the previous year.

Minnesota Opera

Madame Butterfly by Giacomo Puccini
Apr. 14, 15, 17–22
Ordway Center for the Performing Arts
612.333.6669
www.mnopera.org
Kelly Kaduce returns as the tragic heroine, Butterfly. Minnesota Opera's celebrated production evokes the beauty and romance of Puccini's gorgeous, unforgettable classic.

Saint Paul Chamber Orchestra

engine408
Apr. 16, 8 p.m.
SPCO Center
651.291.1144
www.thespco.org

Saint Paul Chamber Orchestra

Schubert's Great Symphony
Apr. 20, 8 p.m.
Apr. 22, 2 p.m.
SPCO
651.291.1144
www.thespco.org

Saint Paul Chamber Orchestra

Mendelssohn's Reformation Symphony
Apr. 26, 7:30 p.m.
Apr. 28, 8 p.m.
Ordway Center for the Performing Arts
651.291.1144
www.thespco.org

Fourth Friday at the Movies

Hosted by Mahmoud El-Kati
Apr. 27
Golden Thyme Coffee Café
651.645.1340
Social hour at 6:30 p.m. and film at 7 p.m.

Saint Paul Art Crawl

Apr. 27–29, May 1
Downtown Saint Paul
651.292.4373
www.stpaulartcrawl.org
More than 200 artists open their studios to the public.

MAY

Downtown Saint Paul Farmers' Market

Apr. 28–Nov. 18
Saturdays, 6 a.m.–1 p.m.
Sundays, 8 a.m.–1 p.m.
290 East Fifth St.
651.227.8101
www.stpaulfarmersmarket.com
Local growers sell their fresh produce directly to you.

Como Memorial Japanese Garden

May 1–Sept. 28
Marjorie McNeely Conservatory, Como Park

Illustration © Lara Hanson

Saymoukda Vongsay at a Saint Paul Almanac Lowertown Reading Jam

651.487.8200
www.comozooconservatory.org
Como opens its beautiful outdoor Japanese garden during these months.

Circus Juventas

May 2–5 and 10–12
651.699.8229
www.circusjuventas.org
Youth performers create a spectacular Cirque du Soleil–style show. Afternoon and evening shows.

Festival of Nations

May 3–6
Saint Paul RiverCentre
651.647.0191
www.festivalofnations.com
Over 90 ethnic groups share the foods, crafts, and traditions that form the mosaic of American culture.

Ballet of the Dolls

May 4, 7:30 p.m.
Ordway Center for the
Performing Arts
www.ordway.org

Cinco de Mayo Festival

May 4–5
District del Sol
651.222.6347
www.districtdelsol.com
Celebrate with live music, food, children's area, community wellness village, parade, and vendors.

Summer Flower Show

May 5–Sept. 30
Marjorie McNeely Conservatory,
Como Park
651.487.8200
www.comozooconservatory.org

Friends School Plant Sale

May 11–13
State Fair Grandstand Building
651.292.3225
www.landmarkcenter.org
The largest fundraising plant sale in Minnesota. Over 2,300 varieties of plants are offered for sale.

Minnesota Bonsai Society Bonsai Show

May 12–13
Marjorie McNeely Conservatory,
Como Park
651.487.8200
www.comozooconservatory.org

Saint Paul Civic Symphony Mother's Day Celebration

May 13
Landmark Center
651.292.3225
saintpaulcivicsymphony.org
Bring your mother to enjoy music at the Landmark.

Saint Paul Almanac Lowertown Reading Jam
May 14, 7–8:30 p.m.
Black Dog Café
651.785.6268
www.saintpaulalmanac.com
Selected writers curate readings around a theme they have chosen and invite other writers and artists to perform with them.

Saint Paul Chamber Orchestra
Xplorchestra! X-plore the String Family
May 19, 9:30 a.m.–11 a.m..
Saint Paul Chamber Orchestra Center
651.291.1144
www.thespco.org
A family concert especially suited to younger audiences.

Fourth Friday at the Movies
Hosted by Mahmoud El-Kati
May 25
Golden Thyme Coffee Café
651.645.1340
Social hour at 6:30 p.m., film at 7 p.m.

JUNE

Downtown Saint Paul Farmers' Market
Apr. 28–Nov. 22
Saturdays, 6 a.m.–1 p.m.
Sundays, 8 a.m.–1 p.m.
290 East Fifth St.
651.227.8101
www.stpaulfarmersmarket.com
Local growers sell their fresh produce directly to you.

Saint Paul (Seventh Place) Farmers' Market
June–Sept.
Tuesdays and Thursdays, 10–2 p.m.
Seventh Place
651.227.8101
www.stpaulfarmersmarket.com
Local growers sell their fresh produce directly to you.

Summer Flower Show
Continues through Sept. 30
Conservatory, Como Park
651.487.8200
www.comozooconservatory.org
Roses, statice, geraniums, Asiatic lilies, heliotrope, New Guinea impatiens, petunias, and caladiums bloom throughout the season.

St. Anthony Park Art Festival
June 2, 9:30 a.m.–5:30 p.m.
On Como Ave. surrounding the St. Anthony Park Library
www.stanthonyparkartsfestival.org
This popular annual event features a juried art show and benefits the St. Anthony Park Library.

Flint Hills International Children's Festival
June 2–3
Ordway Center for the Performing Arts and Rice Park
651.224.4222
www.ordway.org
Parade, performances, dancing, international foods, and hands-on workshops for children.

Ellen Marie Hinchcliffe at a Saint Paul Almanac Lowertown Reading Jam

Grand Old Day

June 3
Grand Ave., Dale to Fairview
651.699.0029
www.grandave.com
Sporting events, parade, family fun area, teen battle of the bands, live music, festival gardens, and over 140 outdoor food and merchandise vendors.

Music in Mears Park

Thursdays, June 7, 14, 21, and 28, 6–9 p.m.
Mears Park
221 East Fifth St.
651.291.9128
www.musicinmears.com
Enjoy the sounds of summer in the beautiful outdoors.

Saint Paul Chamber Orchestra

Haydn's The Seasons
June 8, 8 p.m.
June 9, 8 p.m.
Ordway Center for the Performing Arts
651.291.1144
www.thespco.org

Saint Paul Almanac Lowertown Reading Jam

June 11, 7–8:30 p.m.
Black Dog Café
651.785.6268
www.saintpaulalmanac.com
Selected writers curate readings around a theme they have chosen and invite other writers and artists to perform with them.

Back to the '50s Car Show

June 14–16
Minnesota State Fairgrounds
651.641.1992
www.msra.com
Over 10,000 cars registered last year, over 300 vendors and crafters, over 350 swappers, plus '50s dances Friday and Saturday nights.

Twin Cities Jazz Festival

June 14–16
Mears Park
www.hotsummerjazz.com
One of the best outdoor concerts of the year. Bring your lawn chair.

West End Neighbors' Garden Tour

June 16, 10–4 p.m.
West End Neighborhood
651.222.5536
www.fortroadfederation.org/garden

Accessible tour of private gardens in the West End plus a plant sale.

Fourth Friday at the Movies

Hosted by Mahmoud El-Kati
June 22
Golden Thyme Coffee Café
651.645.1340
Social hour at 6:30 p.m. and film at 7 p.m.

JULY

Downtown Saint Paul Farmers' Market

Apr. 28–Nov. 18
Saturdays, 6 a.m.–1 p.m.
Sundays, 8 a.m.–1 p.m.
290 East Fifth St.
651.227.8101
www.stpaulfarmersmarket.com
Local growers sell their fresh produce directly to you.

Saint Paul (Seventh Place) Farmers' Market

June–Sept.
Tuesdays and Thursdays
Seventh Place, 10–2 p.m.
651.227.8101
www.stpaulfarmersmarket.com
Local growers sell their fresh produce directly to you.

Summer Flower Show

Through Sept. 30
Conservatory, Como Park
651.487.8200
www.comozooconservatory.org
Roses, statice, geraniums, Asiatic lilies, heliotrope, New Guinea impatiens, petunias, and caladiums bloom throughout the season.

Hmong International Sports Tournament and Freedom Festival

July 2–4
Como Park
651.266.6400
Largest Hmong community sporting event in the nation. Volleyball, soccer, kato, and tops tournaments; food, retail, and music.

Nine Nights of Music Series

July 3, 10, 17, 24, and 31, 6:30–8 p.m.
Minnesota History Center
651.259.3000
www.mnhs.org
Every Tuesday in July and August. Bring a lawn chair and pack a picnic, or purchase food from the Café Minnesota terrace grill. In case of rain, concerts will be held inside the History Center.

St. Anthony Park Fourth of July Parade

July 4
Como Ave. and Luther Place
sapcc.org
Race at 9 a.m., parade starts at 11 a.m., followed by food and celebrations at Langford Park.

Music and Movies, *District del Sol*

Thursdays, July 5, 12, 19, and 26, 6:30 p.m.
Parque Castillo, 149 Cesar Chavez Rd.
651.222.6347
www.districtdelsol.com
Youth activities at 6:30 p.m., music at 7 p.m., and movies at dusk. Beer,

May Lee Yang at a Saint Paul Almanac Lowertown Reading Jam

food, and gift vendors. Come and go as you please. No coolers, but bring your lawn chair.

Dragon Festival and Dragon Boat Races

July 9–10
Lake Phalen
651.646.7717
www.dragonfestival.org
Asian cultural festival with performances, food vendors, and dragon boat races with paddlers following the drumbeats.

Saint Paul Almanac Lowertown Reading Jam

July 9, 7–8:30 p.m.
Black Dog Café
651.785.6268
www.saintpaulalmanac.com
Selected writers curate readings around a theme they have chosen and invite other writers and artists to perform with them.

Music in Mears Park

Thursdays, July 12, 19, and 26, 6–9 p.m.
Mears Park
651.291.9128
www.musicinmears.com
Enjoy the sounds of summer in the beautiful outdoors.

Sunset Affair

July 19, dusk
Conservatory, Como Park
651.487.8200
www.comozooconservatory.org
A benefit for Como Zoo and the conservatory.

Highland Fest

July 20–22
Highland Village
651.699.9042
www.highlandfest.com
Three-day outdoor festival. Food, art vendors, and live entertainment on two stages. Fireworks Friday and Saturday.

Rondo Days

July 21
www.rondodays.com
Rondo Days are a central gathering time for celebrating the unique heritage of Saint Paul's historic Black community. The festival remembers Rondo with a senior citizens' dinner, one-day festival, famous drill team competition, parade, music, food, and art.

Rice Street Festival

July 26–28
651.285.4101
www.ricestreetfestival.org
Celebrate Rice Street. Parade on Thursday, July 26, begins at 6:30 p.m.

Car Craft Summer Nationals
July 27–29
Minnesota State Fairgrounds
877.413.6515
www.carcraft.com
Showcases over 4,000 street machines and muscle cars.

Fourth Friday at the Movies
Hosted by Mahmoud El-Kati
July 27
Golden Thyme Coffee Café
651.645.1340
Social hour at 6:30 p.m. and film at 7 p.m.

AUGUST

Downtown Saint Paul Farmers' Market
Apr. 28–Nov. 18
Saturdays, 6 a.m.–1 p.m.
Sundays, 8 a.m.–1 p.m.
290 East Fifth St.
651.227.8101
www.stpaulfarmersmarket.com
Local growers sell their fresh produce directly to you.

Saint Paul (Seventh Place) Farmers' Market
June–Sept.
Tuesdays and Thursdays
10–2 p.m., Seventh Place
651.227.8101
www.stpaulfarmersmarket.com
Local growers sell their fresh produce directly to you.

Summer Flower Show
Through Sept. 30
Conservatory, Como Park
651.487.8200
www.comozooconservatory.org

Roses, statice, geraniums, Asiatic lilies, heliotrope, New Guinea impatiens, petunias, and caladiums bloom throughout the season.

Circus Juventas
Aug. 2–14
651.699.8229
www.circusjuventas.org
Youth performers create a spectacular Cirque du Soleil–style show. Afternoon and evening shows.

Music in Mears Park
Thursdays, Aug. 2, 9, 16, 23, and 25, 6–9 p.m.
Mears Park
651.291.9128
www.musicinmears.com
Enjoy the sounds of summer in the beautiful outdoors.

Nine Nights of Music Series
Aug. 7, 14, 21, and 28
6:30–8 p.m.
Minnesota History Center
651.259.3000
www.mnhs.org
Every Tuesday in July and August. Bring a lawn chair and pack a picnic, or purchase food from the Café Minnesota terrace grill. In case of rain, concerts will be held inside the History Center.

Irish Fair
Aug. 10–12
Harriet Island
952.474.7411
www.irishfair.com
Upper Midwest's largest Irish festival. Lots of music, dance, history, food, and theater.

Tish Jones at a Saint Paul Almanac
Lowertown Reading Jam

Illustration © Lara Hanson

Minnesota State Fair
Aug. 23–Sept. 3
Minnesota State Fairgrounds
651.288.4400
www.mnstatefair.org
*The biggest state fair in the Midwest.
Lots of food on sticks.*

Fourth Friday at the Movies
Hosted by Mahmoud El-Kati
Aug. 24
Golden Thyme Coffee Café
651.645.1340
*Social hour at 6:30 p.m. and film at
7 p.m.*

SEPTEMBER

Downtown Saint Paul Farmers' Market
Apr. 28–Nov. 18
Saturdays, 6 a.m.–1 p.m.
Sundays, 8 a.m.–1 p.m.
290 East Fifth St.
651.227.8101
www.stpaulfarmersmarket.com
*Local growers sell their fresh produce
directly to you.*

Saint Paul (Seventh Place) Farmers' Market
June–Sept.
Tuesdays and Thursdays
10–2 p.m.
Seventh Place
651.227.8101
www.stpaulfarmersmarket.com
*Local growers sell their fresh produce
directly to you.*

Summer Flower Show
Continues through Sept. 30
Conservatory, Como Park

Japanese Lantern Lighting Festival
Aug. 19, 4 p.m.–dusk
Conservatory, Como Park
651.487.8200
www.comozooconservatory.org
*Lanterns float in the Japanese garden
ponds to celebrate Obon, the Japanese
festival honoring ancestors. Japanese
food and entertainment.*

University Avenue Community Parade
Aug. 18, 10 a.m.
University Ave.
*Parade starts north of University
Ave. in the Frogtown neighborhood
and ends at the Western Sculpture
Garden to help kick off the Hmong
Arts and Music Festival.*

Hmong Arts and Music Festival
Aug. 18
Western Sculpture Garden
651.603.6971
www.aboutchat.org
Theater, music, and art all day.

651.487.8200
www.comozooconservatory.org
*Roses, statice, geraniums, Asiatic lilies,
heliotrope, New Guinea impatiens,
petunias, and caladiums bloom
throughout the season.*

Minnesota State Fair

Aug. 23–Sept. 3
Minnesota State Fairgrounds
651.288.4400
www.mnstatefair.org

Concrete and Grass

Sept. 7–8
Mears Park
www.concreteandgrass.com
*Lowertown Music Festival features a
range of genres, including jazz, opera,
chamber music, rock, dance, roots, and
world music.*

Selby Avenue JazzFest

Sept. 8, 11 a.m.–7 p.m.
Corner of Selby and Milton
www.selbyareacdc.org
*Outdoor festival celebrating jazz music.
Bring the whole family. Delicious food,
including lots of Southern cuisine. Local
artisans and businesses too.*

Saint Paul Almanac Book Release Party

Sept. 13, 6–8:30 p.m.
Black Dog Café
651.785.6268
www.saintpaulalmanac.com
*Book release party for the 2013 Saint
Paul Almanac. Get your book signed by
authors and hear writers read their work.*

Fourth Friday at the Movies

Hosted by Mahmoud El-Kati
Sept. 28

Golden Thyme Coffee Café
651.645.1340
*Social hour at 6:30 p.m. and film
at 7 p.m.*

OCTOBER

Downtown Saint Paul Farmers' Market

Apr. 28–Nov. 18
Saturdays, 6 a.m.–1 p.m.
Sundays, 8 a.m.–1 p.m.
290 East Fifth St.
651.227.8101
www.stpaulfarmersmarket.com
*Local growers sell their fresh produce
directly to you.*

Saint Paul Art Crawl

Dates to be announced
Downtown Saint Paul
651.292.4373
www.artcrawl.org
*More than 200 artists open their
studios to the public.*

Saint Paul Oktoberfest

Dates to be announced
www.saintpauloktoberfest.org
*A fun family festival on Rice Street at the
corner of Rose and Geranium, featuring
live music for dancing and listening as
well as a wide array of German foods
and refreshments.*

Annual Twin Cities Black Film Festival

Dates to be announced
Various locations in Saint Paul
www.tcbff.com
*Opening and closing night premieres,
panel discussions, festival parties, 25
independent film projects, plus much
more.*

Illustration © Lara Hanson

*Ibé Kaba at a Saint Paul
Almanac Lowertown Reading Jam*

Fall Flower Show
Oct. 6–Nov. 25
Conservatory, Como Park
651.487.8200
www.comozooconservatory.org
*Hundreds of chrysanthemums,
ornamental grasses, and other
autumn garden favorites.*

Minnesota RollerGirls (Bout)
Oct. 16
Roy Wilkins Auditorium
651.265.4800
www.mnrollergirls.com

ZooBoo
Oct. 20–21 and Oct. 26–28,
4–7:30 p.m.
Como Park Zoo
651.487.8200
www.comozooconservatory.org
*Annual Halloween dress-up family
festival. A real treat for little ones.*

Fourth Friday at the Movies
Hosted by Mahmoud El-Kati
Oct. 26

Golden Thyme Coffee Café
651.645.1340
*Social hour at 6:30 p.m. and film at
7 p.m.*

**Dia de los Muertos Family
Fiesta**
Oct. 27
Minnesota History Center
651.259.3000
www.mnhs.org
Lots of calaveras, jollity, and costumes.

Great Pumpkin Festival
Date to be announced
Landmark Center
651.292.3225
www.landmarkcenter.org
*An autumn celebration for the whole
family, including costume contests,
music, and art projects. Usually held
the last Sunday in October.*

NOVEMBER

**Downtown Saint Paul Farmers'
Market**
Apr. 28–Nov. 18
Saturdays, 6 a.m.–1 p.m.
Sundays, 8 a.m–1 p.m.
290 East Fifth St.
651.227.8101
www.stpaulfarmersmarket.com
*Local growers sell their fresh produce
directly to you.*

Fall Flower Show
Oct. 8–Nov. 27
Conservatory, Como Park
651.487.8200
www.comozooconservatory.org
*Sunken Garden closed for mid-show
change, Nov.1–5.*

Illustration © Lara Hanson

Deborah Torraine at a Saint Paul Almanac Lowertown Reading Jam

Minnesota State High School League Girls' Volleyball Tournament

Nov. 8–10
Xcel Energy Center
763.560.2262
www.mshsl.org

Capital City Lights

Mid-Nov. to Mar.
Downtown Saint Paul
651.291.5600
www.capitalcitypartnership.com
Come downtown and enjoy the holiday lights in winter.

Minnesota RollerGirls (Bout)

Nov. 20
Roy Wilkins Auditorium
651.265.4800
www.mnrollergirls.com

Minnesota Hmong New Year

Nov. 23–25
Saint Paul RiverCentre
651.265.4800
www.rivercentre.org
Celebrate the Hmong New Year with dance, food, music, entertainment, and more.

Fourth Friday at the Movies

Hosted by Mahmoud El-Kati
Nov. 23
Golden Thyme Coffee Café
651.645.1340
Social hour at 6:30 p.m., film at 7 p.m.

DECEMBER

Downtown Saint Paul Winter Farmers' Market

Saturdays, 9 a.m.–1 p.m.
290 East Fifth St.
651.227.8101
www.stpaulfarmersmarket.com
Local growers sell their fresh foods directly to you.

Holiday Bazaar

Nov. 29–30, Dec. 1
Landmark Center
651.292.3225
www.landmarkcenter.org
More than 80 exhibits featuring local artists' work and gift items.

Holiday Flower Show

Dec. 1–Jan. 21
Conservatory, Como Park
651.487.8200
www.comozooconservatory.org
See the sunken garden decked out

with poinsettias and other seasonal favorites.

Grand Meander

Dec. 2, 8 a.m.–4 p.m.
Grand Ave., Dale to Fairview
651.699.0029
www.grandave.com

Minnesota RollerGirls (Bout)

Dec. 11
Roy Wilkins Auditorium
651.265.4800
www.mnrollergirls.com

Kwanzaa Family Celebration

Dec. 29
Minnesota History Center
651.259.3000
www.mnhs.org
Annual Kwanzaa celebration with crafts, stories, and music for all ages.

Health and Fitness Events

Teri J. Dwyer

Opportunities abound for outdoor recreation enthusiasts in Saint Paul, offering all of the conveniences of an urban setting plus many hidden (and not-so-hidden) treasures. Paved paths run along the river; bike lanes line major roads, parks, and lakes. Sidewalks, paths, and trails throughout the city provide wonderful places to enjoy many different outdoor recreational activities. Through snow, ice, rain, heat, and humidity, Saint Paul's most active citizens participate in a number of events throughout the year.

Here's a month-by-month look at some of the health and fitness events that make this city a great place to live, work, and work out.

JANUARY

New Year's Day Hopeful 5K
Jan. 1
Como Lake
charitieschallenge.org
One in a series of holiday-themed races around Como Lake.

Saint Paul Winter Carnival's Half Marathon and 5K
Jan. 28
Downtown Saint Paul
www.winter-carnival.com
Saint Paul heartily embraces winter by throwing a Winter Carnival each year. One of its many events is The Coolest Race on Earth, which begins and ends downtown, with a portion of each course following the Mississippi River.

Twin Cities Bicycling Club (TCBC)
Frequent group rides year round.
Various Saint Paul locations.
www.biketcbc.org
Join them for their Winter Warm-up, Think Spring, We Don't Need No Stinkin' Winter, Fridays on the Bike, and other events. They meet in various locations throughout the year.

FEBRUARY

The Frigid 5
Feb. 5
Minnesota State Fairgrounds
www.tslevents.com
The Frigid 5 is a 5K and 10K race circling the fairgrounds, with shorter races for the kids.

Valentine's Day Hearts 'r' Running 5K and 1.5–Mile Family and Friends Fun Walk
Feb. 12
Como Lake
www.charitieschallenge.org
One in a series of holiday-themed races around Como Lake.

Twin Cities Bicycling Club (TCBC)
www.biketcbc.org
See January for description.

MARCH

St. Pat's Irish Traditions 5K

Mar. 11
Como Lake
www.charitieschallenge.org
One in a series of holiday-themed races around Como Lake.

St. Patrick's Day Human Race

Mar. 18
Summit Avenue/University of Saint Thomas
www.tslevents.com
For more than three decades, runners and walkers in the region have equated the St. Patrick's Day Human Race running and walking events with the start of the spring racing season in Saint Paul. The event offers an 8K run, a 5K run/walk, and youth runs.

APRIL

Easter Sunday Rise 'n' Shine 5K

Apr. 8
Como Lake
www.charitieschallenge.org
Part of a series of holiday-themed races around Como Lake.

Challenge Obesity 5K

Apr. 14
Como Lake
www.charitieschallenge.org
One in a series of events together called Taking on All Challenges, which also include 1.5-mile and half-mile courses for families and children.

Joe Plant Memorial Living the Dream 5K Run and Walk

Apr. 14
Lake Phalen
www.charitieschallenge.org
A race in memory of Joe Plant, an avid runner, who died unexpectedly at age 24 of an undiagnosed likely congenital heart condition.

Annual Spring Parks Clean-Up

A Saturday in April
www.stpaul.gov/parks
Each year, Saint Paul Parks and Recreation hosts this event for families, groups, and individuals to help clean up the trash in Saint Paul's parks and recreation centers.

MAY

Menudo 5K

May 5
Saint Paul's West Side
www.andersonraces.com/events
The West Side, with its large Hispanic/Latino population, hosts a Cinco de Mayo celebration each spring on the weekend closest to May 5. The Menudo 5K takes place on the Saturday of this celebratory weekend.

Walk for Animals

May 5
Como Park
www.animalhumanesociety.org
Hosted by the Humane Society, this event kicks off the national Be Kind to Animals Week at Como Park.

Runners approach the halfway point of the Saint Patrick's Day Human Race 5K along historic Summit Avenue.

Mother's Day 5K

May 13
Como Lake
www.charitieschallenge.org
One in a series of holiday-themed races around Como Lake.

Challenge Hearts and Minds 5K

May 28
Como Lake
www.charitieschallenge.org
One in a series of events together called Taking on All Challenges, which also include 1.5-mile and half-mile courses for families and children.

Mississippi 10 Miler

May 28
Summit Ave. at East Mississippi River Blvd.
www.runmdra.org
This long-standing event is sponsored by MDRA (Minnesota Distance Running Association). The course is out and back along the Saint Paul side of the Mississippi River.

JUNE

Grand Old Day On the Go

June 3
Grand Ave. and Dale St.
www.tslevents.com
Grand Old Day (the largest one-day music, food, and entertainment festival in the U.S.) kicks off the summer festival season in Saint Paul. Grand Old Day On the Go events—an 8K in-line skate, 8K run, 5K run/walk, and youth run events begin Grand Old Day.

Weight Watchers Walk-It 5K

June 3
Como Lake
www.charitieschallenge.org
Charities Challenge, the Road Runners Club of America, and Weight Watchers have teamed up to highlight walking as America's most popular fitness activity.

Walk on the Wild Side

June 2
Como Lake

www.dakotacommunities.org
A 5K run/walk benefiting Dakota
Communities, an organization
providing a variety of services to
people with disabilities.

Running of the Pigs

June 9
Midway Stadium
www.tslevents.com
*This fun, festive 5K is on a loop
course in front of Midway Stadium,
home of the Saint Paul Saints, the
event's sponsor (hint: their mascot is
a large pink pig). The day's activities
also include youth runs. Be sure to
stay for the catered lunch afterward.*

Lederhosenlauf 5K Run and
1-Mile Fitness Walk

June 9
Summit Avenue
www.gai-mn.org
*Part of the Deutsche Tage Weekend
Festival at the Germanic-American
Institute on Summit Avenue. This
race course takes runners on a loop
around the Saint Paul Cathedral.*

American Lung Association Lung
Walk and 5K Run

June 10
Como Park
www.lungusa.org/associations/
states/minnesota
*Proceeds benefit the American Lung
Association.*

Nature Valley Bicycle Festival

June 13
Downtown Saint Paul
www.naturevalleybicyclefestival.
com

*This multi-day Minnesota festival
comes to downtown Saint Paul
for one day with the Saint Paul
Downtown Criterium. Proceeds
benefit Children's Hospitals and
Clinics of Minnesota.*

Father's Day 5K

June 17
Como Lake
www.charitieschallenge.org
*One in a series of holiday-themed
races around Como Lake.*

Time to Fly 10K and 5K

June 23
Harriet Island
www.childrenscancer.org
*Children's Cancer Research Fund
hosts the 10K and 5K races, plus a
2K and 1K kids' run.*

JULY

Langford Park Races

July 4
St. Anthony Park
*These very-low-key races (runners
choose a 2- or 4-mile option) have
had an entry fee of 50 cents since
they began, in 1974. The course is
a 2-mile loop on the streets of Saint
Paul's picturesque St. Anthony Park.
Races begin and end at Langford
Park.*

Free to Run 4 Miles

July 4
Harriet Island
www.charitieschallenge.org
*One in a series of holiday-themed
races (this one at Harriet Island).*

Finishers in the Grand Old Day On the Go youth run

Challenge Diabetes 5K

July 7

Como Lake

www.charitieschallenge.org

One in a series of events together called Taking on All Challenges, which also include 1.5-mile and half-mile courses for families and children.

Highland Fest 5K

July 21

Highland Park

www.highlandfest.com

This low-key, family-friendly fun run is part of the annual Highland Fest celebration, showcasing one of Saint Paul's many fine neighborhoods. The course follows the Mississippi River.

Rice Street Mile

July 28

Rice St. and Front Ave.

www.ricestreetfestival.org

The course is flat and point-to-point. Don't miss this opportunity to run one of the shortest road races offered

in Saint Paul. The race kicks off the parade for the annual Rice Street Festival.

Challenge Cancer 5K

July 29

Como Lake

www.charitieschallenge.org

One in a series of events together called Taking on All Challenges, which also include 1.5-mile and half-mile courses for families and children.

AUGUST

MDRA Cross-Country Runs

Aug. 1, 8, 15, 22, 29

Como Park

www.runmdra.org

Since 1974, MDRA has sponsored this series of cross-country races every Wednesday evening in August at Como Park in Saint Paul. The races are open to all ages and abilities.

Minnesota Half Marathon and 5K

Aug. 4
Downtown Saint Paul
www.minnesotahalfmarathon.com
In-line skaters and runners can all enjoy a course along the beautiful Mississippi River in Saint Paul. The half marathon is for skaters and runners, the 5K is for runners and walkers. The race ends in downtown Saint Paul at Mears Park.

Minnesota State Fair Milk Run 5K

Aug. 26
Minnesota State Fairgrounds
www.mnstatefair.org
Participants receive an admission ticket to the fair and a coupon for a free malt.

Saint Paul Triathlon

Aug. 19
Lake Phalen
www.frontrunnerusa.com/event/st-paul-triathlon
Participants choose the Sprint (1/2-mile swim, 20K bike, 5K run) or International (1 mile swim, 40K bike, 10K run).

Challenge Arthritis 5K

Aug. 25
Como Lake
www.charitieschallenge.org
One in a series of events together called Taking on All Challenges, which also include 1.5-mile and half-mile courses for families and children.

Minnesota Military Appreciation 5K Run and 2-Mile Walk

Aug. 25
Harriet Island
www.andersonraces.com

SEPTEMBER

Saint Paul Classic Bike Tour

Sept. 9
Throughout Saint Paul
www.bikeclassic.org
This event offers a rare opportunity to bicycle around and through the city of Saint Paul on streets free of car traffic. This family-friendly event offers a 15-mile tour of Saint Paul or a 30-mile ride.

Sharing Life Walk/Run

Sept. 15
Lake Phalen
www.sharinglife.org
This 3-mile, all-ages event includes special races and games for the kids. Support organ donation education and raise money for families going through the transplant process.

Race for Research

Sept. 23
Lake Phalen
www.mmrface.org
5K walk/run benefits the Multiple Myeloma Research Foundation.

OCTOBER

Twin Cities in Motion 10K, 5K, and Family events

Oct. 6
Summit Avenue
www.twincitiesmarathon.org

Grand Old Day On the Go 8K inline skate

The Twin Cities Marathon, a Twin Cities tradition for over 30 years, traverses the Mississippi River. On the Saturday before Sunday's big marathon, TCM hosts running events exclusively in Saint Paul. The races, starting and finishing near the Capitol, offer something for all ages and abilities.

Twin Cities Marathon and TC 10-Mile

Oct. 7
Summit Avenue
www.twincitiesmarathon.org
Traditionally called "The most beautiful urban marathon In America," TCM and the companion TC 10 Mile, begins in downtown Minneapolis, winding through a chain of Minneapolis parks, but the final six miles are run in Saint Paul, with a finish right in front of the State Capitol on the edge of downtown.

Challenge Aging 5K

Oct. 6
Como Lake

www.charitieschallenge.org
One in a series of events together called Taking on All Challenges, which also include 1.5-mile and half-mile courses for families and children.

MELSA 5K

Oct. 13
Harriet Island
www.andersonraces.com

CNHS A Boo Run Run Run

Oct. 20
Harriet Island
www.andersonraces.com

Halloween Fearless 5K and 1.5-Mile Fun Run

Oct. 27
Como Lake
www.charitieschallenge.org
One in a series of holiday-themed races around Como Lake.

NOVEMBER

Rocky's Run

Nov. 4

Les Bolstad University Golf Course
www.tslevents.com
This cross-country race offers the public a rare opportunity to run on the same course as the University of Minnesota men's and women's cross-country teams at the Les Bolstad University Golf Course. The 8K and 5K races benefit a scholarship in Rocky Racette's name for the women's track-and-field and cross-country teams at the U of M.

Turkey Run
Nov. 18
Como Lake
www.tslevents.com
A tradition for the Sunday before Thanksgiving each year, this family-friendly fun run encircles Como Lake, beginning and ending at warm indoor headquarters at Como Elementary School.

Giving Thanks 5K
Nov. 22
Como Lake
www.charitieschallenge.org
One in a series of holiday-themed races around Como Lake.

TCBC events
www.biketcbc.org
See January for description.

DECEMBER

JCC Dreidel Dash
Dec. 16
Jewish Community Center
www.stpauljcc.org/adults/dreidel_dash.lasso

Fifth Annual Joyful 5K Christmas Day
Dec. 25
Como Lake
www.charitieschallenge.org
One in a series of holiday-themed races around Como Lake.

TCBC events
www.biketcbc.org
See January for description.

Year-round Saint Paul Activities
The Saint Paul Hiking Club
www.stpaulhike.org
This group meets regularly at various locations throughout Saint Paul. Anyone is welcome. Check your local newspaper's recreation/events calendar for current hike locations and contact information.

Seasonal Activities
Rowing
www.boatclub.org
The Minnesota Boat Club—rowing in Saint Paul since 1870. Promoting health and fitness through the sport of rowing. Located on the shores of Raspberry Island, directly across from downtown Saint Paul. From novice to competitor, rowers of all ages and abilities can take part in classes, camps, and events of this well-established Mississippi tradition.

Star Swim Team

www.starswimteam.net
Programs for swimmers of all
ages and abilities. Outdoors in
summer at Highland Park pool.

Winter Activities
Cross-Country Skiing

www.stpaul.gov/parks
Saint Paul grooms trails at three
sites each winter: Como Golf
Course, Phalen Golf Course,
and the Highland 9-Hole Golf
Course. Lessons in classic
and skate skiing are available
through Saint Paul Parks and
Recreation.

Ice Skating Rinks

There are a variety of outdoor
ice skating rinks located
throughout the city. Amenities,
including availability of rental
skates, vary by location.
www.stpaul.gov/parks
www.capitalcitypartnership.com

Key:

4K (2.5 miles)
5K (3.1 miles)
6K (3.75 miles)
8K (4.97 miles)
10K (6.2 miles)
Half Marathon (13.1 miles)
Marathon (26.2 miles)

Coffeehouses and Tea Shops

Ai Hues Bakery and Deli
432B University Ave.
651.602.0231
A restaurant serving coffee and meals on the avenue during light rail construction.

Amore Coffee
879 Smith Ave. S.
651.330.0570
www.amorecoffee.com
Featuring award-winning coffee and authentic Italian gelato.

Bars Bakery
612 Selby Ave.
651.224.8300
www.barsbakery.com
Espresso, pour over, and brewed coffees, along with made-from-scratch baked goods featuring local organic ingredients.

Black Dog Café
308 Prince St.

651.228.9274
www.blackdogstpaul.com
Espresso and brewed coffees, wines, and local beers, with a breakfast, lunch, and dinner menu.

Bread & Chocolate
867 Grand Ave.
651.228.1017
www.cafelatte.com/bread
_chocolate.html
Coffee, sandwiches, and baked goods, including their famous brownies.

Cahoots Coffee Bar
1562 Selby Ave.
651.644.6778
Organic and fair trade coffee, Middle Eastern-inspired foods.

Coffee Bené
53 Cleveland Ave. S.
651.698.2266

Amore Coffee at 879 Smith Avenue South

Organic fair trade coffee from master roasters and yummy goods from the bakery.

The Coffee Grounds

1579 Hamline Ave. N.
651.644.9959
www.thecoffeegrounds.net
A friendly gathering place with a bridge club and creative beading group; ongoing open mic the first and third Sundays.

Coffee News Café

1662 Grand Ave.
651.698.3324
Small, busy shop for the neighborhood college crowd offering coffee, chai, wine and beer, and a full menu.

Dunn Bros

1569 Grand Ave.
651.698.0618
www.dunnbrosgrand.com
The original Dunn Bros Coffee features live music daily.

The Edge Coffee House

2399 University Ave. W.
651.641.1656
Soups, salads, and sandwiches under an arty, vintage tin ceiling; live music Saturday and Sunday mornings.

Espresso Royale

475 Fairview Ave. S.
651.699.1117
www.espressoroyale.com
A coffee shop plus extras: soups, sandwiches, frappes, and ice cream.

Fresh Grounds

1362 W. Seventh St.
651.224.2348
www.freshgroundscoffee.com
A nonprofit offering coffee and light meals, music and art, and job training for youth.

Ginkgo Coffeehouse

721 Snelling Ave. N.
651.645.2647
www.ginkgocoffee.com
Fair trade and organic coffees, tea and fruit smoothies, local food in season.

Golden Thyme Coffee Café

921 Selby Ave.
651.645.1340
www.twincitiesdiningguide
.com/pages/
goldenthymescoffeecafe.asp
A community hub offering drinks named after jazz legends (and a really great gumbo); meeting room available.

Groundswell Coffee

1342 Thomas Ave.
651.645.6466
groundswellcoffee.wordpress
.com
This neighborhood spot serving pizza and salads as well as coffee is operated by a community nonprofit.

Grumpy Steve's Coffee

215 Wabasha St. S.
651.224.1191
www.wabashastreetcaves.com
"Come start your morning with a snarl. Or put a little grouchy in your lunch" at the Wabasha Caves.

J & S Bean Factory

1518 Randolph Ave.
651.699.7788

Mad Hatter Coffee Café and Teahouse at 943 West Seventh Street

www.jsbeanfactory.com
Full-service roaster features the Obama blend, as well as many fair-trade and organic coffees; occasional live music.

Java Train Café
1341 Pascal St. N.
651.646.9179
www.javatraincafe.com
Family-friendly table service with Izzy's ice cream and a play area for children.

Jerabek's New Bohemian Coffeehouse and Bakery
63 Winifred St. W.
651.228.1245
www.jerabeks.com
A relaxed and casual coffeehouse serving flaky pastry specialties.

Kopplin's Coffee
490 Hamline Ave. S.
651.698.0457
www.kopplinscoffee.com

The local micro-culture for brewing connoisseurs offering seasonal beverage creations.

Lady Elegant's Tea Room
2230 Carter Ave.
651.645.6676
www.ladyelegantstea.com
Tea in the British tradition with three-, four-, and six-course events.

Lowertown Daily Perk
180 Fifth St. E., Ste. 266
651.228.9820
www.lowertowndailyperk.com
Formerly Executive Coffee and Tea; a skyway workday staple.

Mad Hatter Coffee Café and Teahouse
943 W. Seventh St.
651.227.2511
Social justice salons and acoustic music; St. Paul Gallery of Art adjoined.

Nina's Coffee Café
165 Western Ave. N.
651.292.9816

This art-friendly corner of Cathedral Hill hosts frequent art and literary events.

Polly's Coffee Cove
1382 Payne Ave.
651.771.5531
Comfortable kitsch and convenient boxed lunches; Polly is the bird.

Q Kindness Café
The Lowry
350 St. Peter St.
651.224.6440
www.QKindness.com
Feed your soul with kindness for breakfast and lunch; great for meetings.

Quixotic Coffee
769 Cleveland Ave. S.
651.699.5448
www.quixoticcoffee.com
Emphasizing both quality coffee and a supportive relationship with coffee farmers.

St. Paul Corner Drug
240 Snelling Ave. S.
651.698.8859
www.stpaulcornerdrug.com
A neighborhood pharmacy with five-cent coffee at the old-fashioned soda fountain.

Steep and Brew Coffee Shop
101 Fifth St. E. Ste. 296 (Skyway level)
651.221.9859
The sunniest corner in the skyway.

Sugar Rush
712 University Ave. W.
651.797.3354
Donuts too. Near the Sibley Bike Depot.

The Tea Garden
1692 Grand Ave.
651.690.3495
www.teagardeninc.com
Bubble tea delights with chewy tapioca.

TeaSource
752 Cleveland Ave. S.
651.690.9822
www.teasource.com
Extraordinary teas and Tuesday free samples; check the website for classes.

Restaurants

128 Café
128 Cleveland Ave. N.
651.645.4128
www.128cafe.net
Upscale dining with a changing menu
of fresh and seasonal ingredients. $$

Abu Nader Deli and Grocery
St. Anthony Park
2095 Como Ave.
651.647.5391
Small deli serving falafel and other
delights. $

American Burger Bar
354 N. Wabasha St.
651.222.2123
americanburgerbar.com
The ultimate handcrafted burger
den. $$

Aroma's Pizza
350 St. Peter St.
651.293.9040
aromascafe.com
Build your own pizza for dine-in or
take-out. $

Babani's Kurdish Restaurant
544 Saint Peter St.
651.602.9964
www.babanis.com
Authentic menu offers a Kurdish
take on cuisine. $

Bangkok Thai Deli
315 University Ave. W.
651.224.4300
When you see the mosaic-tiled
chimney, you've come to the right place
(one of the publisher's favorites). $

Barbary Fig
720 Grand Ave.
651.290.2085
www.thebarbaryfig.com
Grand Avenue location with inspired
Mediterranean cuisine. $$

Barrio Tequila Bar
235 E. Sixth St., No. 100
651.222.3250
www.barriotequila.com
Meet across from Mears Park for
happy hour: tacos, enchiladas,
seafood, chicken, ribs, or steak. $$

Bennett's Chop and Rail House
1305 W. Seventh St.
651.228.1408
wwwbennettschopandrailhouse
.com
A casual steakhouse atmosphere with
nightly specials for top-of-the-line cuts.
$$

Big Daddy's BBQ
625 University Ave.
651.222.2516
www.bigdaddysbbq-stpaul.com
Old-fashioned BBQ across from the
Rondo Library, in the heart of Frog-
town. $

Bin
400 Sibley St., Ste. 150
651.224.9463
www.binwinebar.com
Wine and light fare, exposed brick
and timbers, and an antique bar. $$

Black Bear Crossings on the Lake

1360 N. Lexington Pkwy.
651.488.4920
www.blackbearcrossings.com
Beautiful location in the historic Lake Como Pavilion serving breakfast, lunch, and dinner year round. $

Black Sea

737 Snelling Ave. N.
651.917.8832
www.blacksearestaurant.com
Offering fine Turkish cuisine from Ali's hometown of Akçaabat, Trabzon Province. $

Black Sheep Pizza

512 N. Robert St.
651.227.4337
www.blacksheeppizza.com
Coal-fired ovens and the best ingredients create the great American "pizza pioneer" experience. $

The Blue Door Pub

1811 Selby Ave.
651.493.1865
www.thebdp.com
Fun Americana décor and a menu featuring the Juicy Blucy (bleu cheese-stuffed burgers). $

Boca Chica Restaurante Mexicano & Cantina

11 Cesar Chavez St.
651.222.8499
www.bocachicarestaurant.com
Minutes from downtown in the District Del Sol of Saint Paul's West Side; patio dining and mariachi music. $ (lunch) $$ (dinner)

Bon Vie Café

518 Selby Ave.
651.287.0112
www.bonviecafe.net
Breakfast and lunch café that serves up "the good life" with a changing monthly menu. $

Brasa Premium Rotisserie

777 Grand Ave.
651.224.1302
www.brasa.us
Organic, local ingredients featuring slow-cooked rotisserie meats for dine-in or take-out. $

The Bulldog, Lowertown

237 E. Sixth St.
651.221.0750
www.thebulldoglowertown.com
Stop for lunch, after work, or on weekends for pub grub like Tater Tot Hotdish. $

Burger Moe's

242 W. Seventh St.
651.222.3100
www.burgermoes.com
A relaxed outdoor patio and more than 60 beers from around the world. $

Café Latté

850 Grand Ave.
651.224.5687
www.cafelatte.com
Cafeteria, bakery, and pizza wine bar; this Victoria Crossing landmark is three restaurants in one. $

Café Minnesota

Minnesota History Center
345 Kellogg Blvd. W.
651.651.259.3000

Cecils at 651 South Cleveland Avenue

www.mnhs.org/historycenter /cafemn
Cafeteria-style service, weekly Minnesota menus, free Wi-Fi. $

Caffè Biaggio

2356 University Ave. W.
651.917.7997
www.caffebiaggio.com
Country favorites and family recipes from all over Italy. $ (lunch) $$ (dinner)

Caribe Caribbean Bistro

791 Raymond Ave.
651.641.1446
www.caribemn.com
Colorful hot spot offering chef-driven fare from the islands. $

Caspers' Cherokee Sirloin Room

886 Smith Ave. S.
651.457.2729
www.cherokeesirloinroom.com
Traditional steaks, seafood, and spirits; open every day. $$

Cat Man Do

1659 Grand Ave.
651.528.7575
www.catmandorestaurant.com
The owners of Everest on Grand present the next level of Nepali cuisine: curries, choyla, and momo. $$

Cecils Delicatessen, Bakery, and Restaurant

651 Cleveland Ave. S.
651.698.6276 (Deli)
651.698.0334 (Restaurant)
www.cecilsdeli.com
Committed to quality delicatessen fare for three generations; delivery available. $

Chatterbox Pub

800 Cleveland Ave. S.
651.699.1154
www.chatterboxpub.net
A full-service neighborhood menu with old-school video games to "bring out the '80s kid in everyone." $

Cheeky Monkey Deli
525 Selby Ave.
651.224.6066
www.cheekymonkeydeli.com
A "deli by day and bistro by night"
with full table service after 5 p.m. $

Cheng Heng
448 University Ave. W.
651.222.5577
A photo album menu of authentic
Cambodian cuisine for those who are
weary of Americanized Asian. $

Christos
214 E. Fourth St.
651.224.6000
www.christos.com
Formal Greek dining or a weekday
lunch buffet in the breathtaking
Union Depot setting. $

Cossetta Italian Market & Pizza
211 W. Seventh St.
651.222.3476
Cafeteria-style classic Italian food
and a gourmet grocery shop. $

Costello's Bar & Grill
393 Selby Ave.
651.291.1015
www.costellosbar.com
A traditional Cathedral Hill
restaurant with a friendly
environment. $

Dari-ette Drive In
1440 Minnehaha Ave. E.
651.776.3470
Italian, American, and ice cream!
Family-owned and operated from
March to October for over 50 years.
$

Dar's Double Scoop
1046 Rice St.
651.489.2422
Over 40 tasty flavors of deluxe ice
cream from dairies in Minnesota and
Wisconsin, as well as sandwiches and
pizza. $

Day by Day Café
477 W. Seventh St.
651.227.0654
www.daybyday.com
Breakfast is their specialty all
day long; linger over coffee and
conversation. $

DeGidio's
425 W. Seventh St.
651.291.7105
www.degidios.com
Famous for pasta and a red sauce
made daily with ingredients imported
from Italy. $

Destiny Café
995 University Ave. W.
651.649.0394
Hmong deli and sit-down restaurant
located inside the Sunrise Market.
$$

Dixie's on Grand
695 Grand Ave.
651.222.7345
www.dixiesongrand.com
Casual dining and Southern comfort;
live jazz and soul throughout the
week. $$

Downtowner Woodfire Grill
253 W. Seventh St.
651.228.9500
www.downtownerwoodfire.com

Eden Pizza in the Midway

A comfortable retreat with classic cuts grilled over an oak fire. $$

Eagle Street Grille
174 W. Seventh St.
651.225.1382
www.eaglestreetgrille.net
Pre-event sports bar with a full menu and great views of downtown Saint Paul. $$

Eastside Thai
879 Payne Ave.
651.776.6599
Delicious Thai food in satisfying portions. $

Eden Pizza
629 Aldine St.
651.646.7616
www.edenpizza.com
Create your specialty pizza with a gluten-free crust: dine-in, take-out, or delivery. $

Egg & I
2550 University Ave. W.
651.647.1292
www.eggandimn.com

Open daily 'til 2 p.m. serving quality breakfast for over 20 years. $

El Burrito Mercado
175 Cesar Chavez St.
651.227.2192
www.elburritomercado.com
Shop and eat at this authentic Mexican taquer'a in the West Side Supermercado. $

Everest on Grand
1278 Grand Ave.
651.696.1666
www.everestongrand.com
A mix of tastes, from spicy North Indian curries to Tibetan dumplings and noodles. $$

Fabulous Fern's
400 Selby Ave.
651.225.9414
www.fabulousferns.com
Classic dishes as well as entrée salads, pastas, and sandwiches; kids' menu and weekly features. $$

FACES Mears Park
380 Jackson St.
651.209.7776
www.facesmearspark.com

American cuisine mixing modern and old-world artistry; bistro, wine bar, bottle shop, and bakery. $$

Fasika
510 Snelling Ave. N.
651.646.4747
www.fasika.com
Ethiopian fare with a variety of stewed, curried, and charbroiled meats (vegetarian entrées available). $

Flamingo
490 Syndicate St. N.
651.917.9332
Savory East African—Eritrean menu with specialty lamb and goat dishes. $

Forepaugh's
276 Exchange St. S.
651.224.5606
www.forepaughs.com
New American Cuisine and nine-teenth-century manners in a historic architectural setting. $$

Fuji Ya
465 Wabasha St. N.
651.310.0111
www.fujiyasushi.com
The Japanese food experience for lunch or dinner with an extensive happy-hour menu. $$

Glockenspiel
605 W. Seventh St.
651.292.9421
www.Glockenspielrestaurant
.com

Great chef specials and an exhaustive beer list at Saint Paul's German restaurant. $

Golden's Deli
275 Fourth St. E. Ste. 102
651.224.8888
www.goldensdeli.us
Homemade soups, sandwiches, and baked goods served with a healthy dose of green practices. $

Grand Ole Creamery
750 Grand Ave.
651.293.1655
www.grandolecreamery.com
A classic ice cream parlor and pizzeria. $

Grandview Grill
1818 Grand Ave.
651.698.2346
www.newgrandviewgrill.com
In pursuit of the perfect breakfast and lunch for more than 20 years. $

Great Waters Brewing Company
426 Saint Peter St.
651.224.2739
www.greatwatersbc.com
Award-winning brew pub and restaurant with a year-round patio. $ (lunch) $$ (dinner)

Happy Gnome
498 Selby Ave.
651.287.2018
www.thehappygnome.com
Craft beers and culinary adventure. $$

Heartland Restaurant and Farm Direct Market
289 E. Fifth St.

The Happy Gnome

651.699.3536
www.heartlandrestaurant.com
Lunch, dinner, and weekend brunch with an attached gourmet market of meats, produce, and dairy. $$

Highland Grill
771 Cleveland Ave. S.
651.690.1173
www.highlandgrill.com
Trendy comfort food prepared with flair. $

Ho Ho Gourmet Restaurant
1985 Old Hudson Rd.
651.731.0316
www.hohomn.com
Chinese buffet and à la carte items; memorable chicken wings and roast duck. $

India House
758 Grand Ave.
651.293.9124
www.indiahousesaintpaul.com
Try the lunch buffet from 11 to 2:30, or enjoy dinner with quality table service. $

Italian Pie Shoppe & Winery
1670 Grand Ave.
651.221.0093
www.italianpieshoppe.com
Award-winning pizzas and pasta since 1976 with online and dine-in specials. $

Izzy's Ice Cream Café
2034 Marshall Ave.
651.603.1458
www.izzysicecream.com
Artisan ice cream with inspired, quirky flavors. $

Keys Café & Bakery
767 Raymond Ave.
651.646.5756
500 N. Robert St.
651.222.4083
www.keyscafe.com
The made-from-scratch recipes "you grew up with" from a family restaurant favorite since 1973. $

Khyber Pass Café
1571 Grand Ave.
651.690.0505
www.khyberpasscafe.com
Authentic Afghan menu, which combines the best of several Asian cuisines, with special attention to chutneys. $$

Kincaid's Fish, Chop & Steakhouse
380 St. Peter St.
651.602.9000
www.kincaids.com
Classic American dining; every restaurant is uniquely local. $$$

Kolap Restaurant

601 Dale St. N.
651.222.2488
True Thai food in a warm and friendly space that is perfect for large groups. $

Krua Thailand

432 University Ave. W.
651.224.4053
Curries are a specialty at this BYOB restaurant. $

La Cucaracha

36 Dale St. S.
651.221.9682
www.lacucaracharestaurante
.com
Established Mexican restaurant with an ambitious list of tequilas. $$

La Grolla

452 Selby Ave.
651.221.1061
www.lagrollastpaul.com
Romance and garlic on Cathedral Hill; dine inside or on the patio. $ (lunch) $$ (dinner)

Lao-Thai Family Restaurant

501 University Ave.
651.224.5026
Traditional Lao-Thai cuisine like raw beef laab, yummy pad thai, and chicken wings. $

Lee's & Dee's Barbeque Express

161 North Victoria St.
651.225.9454
Ribs and catfish served up right by this welcoming husband-wife team. $

The Lexington

1096 Grand Ave.
651.222.5878
www.thelexongrand.com
A timeless Saint Paul landmark featuring steaks, seafood, and nostalgia. $$

The Liffey

175 W. Seventh St.
651.556.1420
www.theliffey.com
*Irish hospitality and an urban patio view of beautiful downtown.
$ (lunch) $$ (dinner)*

The Little Oven

1786 Minnehaha Ave. E.
651.735.4944
www.thelittleoven.com
Reasonably priced Italian fare with monthly coupons and specials that are easy on the wallet. $

Little Szechuan

422 University Ave. W.
651.222.1333
www.littleszechuan.com
Adventurous, eclectic Chinese dishes alongside traditional favorites. $

Luci Ancora

2060 Randolph Ave.
651.698.6889
www.ristoranteluci.com
Fresh and local gourmet Italian food prepared by traditional chefs. $$

The M St. Café

Saint Paul Hotel
350 Market St.
651.228.3855
www.mstcafe.com

Ngon Vietnamese Bistro at 799 University Avenue

Sophisticated yet casual with à la carte items or Euro-style sideboard servings; Sunday brunch. $$

Magnolias Restaurant
1081 Payne Ave.
651.774.3333
www.magnolias-stpaul.com
Quality family dining with home-cooked comfort food. $

Mai Village
394 University Ave. W.
651.290.2585
www.maivillage.net
Enjoy steaming meals and a full-service bar beside the koi pond and outdoor rose patio. $$

Malina's Sports Bar
691 Dale St. N.
651.488.7622
Late-night offerings of tasty papaya salad, beef laab, and chicken wings. $

Mama's Pizza
961 Rice St.
651.489.2005
www.mamaspizzaparlor.com

Italian and American eatery for lunch, dinner, and take-out. $

Mancini's Char House
531 W. Seventh St.
651.224.7345
www.mancinis.com
Featuring charbroiled steak and lobster with a lounge as classic as the day it was built. $$$

Mango Thai Restaurant
610 Selby Ave.
651.291.1414
www.mangothaimn.com
Mango spring rolls and pan-grilled tuna salad in a hip, visually appealing setting. BYOB. $$

Meritage
410 St. Peter St.
651.222.5670
www.meritage-stpaul.com
Sustainable and seasonal New American cuisine that tends toward the French. $$$

Mickey's Dining Car

36 W. Seventh St.
651.222.5633
www.mickeysdiningcar.com
An amusing Art Deco dining car on the National Register of Historic Places; open every day, 24 hours. $

Mirror of Korea

761 Snelling Ave. N.
651.647.9004
www.mirrorofkorea.com
Second-generation family-owned restaurant with summer and winter menus. $

Moscow on the Hill

371 Selby Ave.
651.291.1236
www.moscowonthehill.com
Post-perestroika Russian dining and the essential vodka bar. $$

Muddy Pig

162 Dale St. N.
651.254.1030
www.muddypig.com
Neighborhood bistro with an extensive beer list and "better than pub fare." $

Muffuletta

Milton Square
2260 Como Ave.
651.644.9116
www.muffuletta.com
An imaginative daily menu of seasonal ingredients, and a wine list tended by a sommelier. $ (lunch) $$ (dinner)

Ngon Vietnamese Bistro

799 University Ave. W.
651.222.3301
www.ngonbistro.com
Contemporary Vietnamese cuisine that holds true to the flavors of traditional dishes. patio. $, $$

The Nook

492 Hamline Ave. S.
651.698.4347
www.ngonbistro.com
After a fire gutted the place, the Nook is up and running again, cooking your favorite hamburger and scrumptious fries. $

Obb's Sports Bar & Grill

1347 Burns Ave.
651.776.7010
www.obbsbar.com
Watch your favorite sports, choose from a wide selection of draft or bottled beer and wine. $

Padelford Packet Boat Co.

Harriet Island
651.227.1100
www.riverrides.com
A variety of meal cruises, including a sunset dinner cruise, "Lunch and Lock," Sunday lunch, and special occasions. $$

Pad Thai Grand Café

1681 Grand Ave.
651.690.1393
Homemade Thai food, exposed brick and timbers, and service with a smile. $$

Palace's Pizza

1373 Maryland Ave.
651.771.3535
Pizza and Southeast Asian fare: egg rolls, laab, and sesame chicken. $

Try the "Lunch and Lock," Sunday lunch on the Padelford Packet Boat

Pappy's Chicago Style Eatery

1783 Maryland Ave. E.
651.771.4500
Philly cheese steaks, Italian beef, and the ubiquitous Chicago dog; stand in line to order and get your drink (it's worth the wait). $

Patrick McGovern's Pub

225 W. Seventh St.
651.224.5821
www.patmcgoverns.com
Pub food and drinks in a historic brick building, with a three-tiered outdoor dining patio. $

Pazzaluna

360 Saint Peter St.
651.223.7000
www.pazzaluna.com
Acclaimed Italian cuisine in a stylish downtown location; offers complimentary valet parking. $$

Pizza Luce

1183 Selby Ave.
651.288.0186
www.pizzaluce.com
Creative, artistic pizzas with vegan and gluten-free options for dine-in, take-out, or delivery. $

Punch Neapolitan Pizza

704 Cleveland Ave.
651.696.1066
769 Grand Ave.
651.602.6068
www.punchpizza.com
Gourmet pizzas cooked fresh in a wood-burning oven for a smoky crust flavor. $

Q Kindness Café

The Lowry
350 St. Peter St.
651.224.6440
www.QKindness.com
Feed your soul with kindness for breakfast and lunch; great for meetings. $

Que Nha Vietnamese Restaurant

849 University Ave. W.
651.290.8552
Unassuming décor belies noteworthy

dishes like goat curry and rice porridge. $

Ray's Mediterranean Restaurant

1199 W. Seventh St.
651.224.3883
Features a neighborhood Greek and Italian menu. $

Red's Savoy Inn and Pizza

421 E. Seventh St.
651.227.1437
520 White Bear Ave. N.
651.731.1068
Countless topping combinations on that famous red sauce. $

Ristorante Luci

470 Cleveland Ave. S.
651.699.8258
www.ristoranteluci.com
Romantic, classical Italian cuisine with a multi-course tasting menu. $$

River Boat Grill

Harriet Island Riverfront
105 Harriet Island Rd.
651.290.2363
www.riverboatgrill.com
Eat on the Mississippi; gaze at the Saint Paul skyline. Open spring through fall. $

Ruam Mit Thai Café

475 Saint Peter St.
651.222.7871
www.ruam-mit-thai.net
Convenient downtown location; family-friendly lunch buffet. $

Russian Tea House

1758 University Ave. W.
651.646.4144

Serving borscht, piroshki, cabbage rolls, and real Russian tea. $

Rusty Taco

508 Lexington Pkwy.
651.699.1833
www.rustytacomn.com
Breakfast tacos, Mex tacos, beer, and coffee at the corner of Lexington and Randolph. $

Saigon Restaurant

704 University Ave. W.
651.225.8751
Familiar Vietnamese favorites with pho, broken rice dishes, banh mi sandwiches, and more. $

St. Clair Broiler

1580 St. Clair Ave.
651.698.7055
www.stclairbroiler.com
Burgers, sandwiches, and buttermilk fried chicken in a classic American diner. $

St. Paul Cheese Shop

1573 Grand Ave.
651.698.3391
www.france44cheeseshop.com
An rBGH-free cheese list, cured-meat sandwiches, and delicious accompaniments. $

St. Paul Grill

The Saint Paul Hotel
350 Market St.
651.224.7455
www.stpaulgrill.com
Impeccable service and classic American entrées; Scotch, whiskey, and cognac for connoisseurs. $$$

Linda and Nikolai, co-owners of the Russian Tea House

Saji-Ya
695 Grand Ave.
651.292.0444
www.sajiya.com
Japanese sauté cooking with a bar and teppanyaki grill. $$

Sakura
350 St. Peter St.
651.224.0185
www.sakurastpaul.com
Timeless Japanese food and drink; begin an evening downtown at the full-length bar. $$

Salut Bar Américain
917 Grand Ave.
651.917.2345
www.salutbaramericain.com
French-inspired cuisine in an ooh-la-la dining venue. $$

Scusi
1806 St. Clair Ave.
651.789.7007
scusistpaul.com
A shared-plate approach to Italian cuisine. $

Señor Wong
111 Kellogg Blvd. E.
651.224.2019
www.senorwong.com
A convincing combination of Asian and Latin foods gives a unique twist to the menu. $ (lunch) $$ (dinner)

Serlin's Café
1124 Payne Ave.
651.776.9003
Homey goodness and old-fashioned comfort food at a step-back-in-time all-American café. $

Shamrock Grill
995 W. Seventh St.
651.228.9925
www.crshamrocks.com
A real Irish pub with live entertainment, serving famous Nook food. $

Skinners Pub & Eatery
919 Randolph Ave.
651.291-0146
www.skinnersmn.com
Fun for the whole family with Thursday bingo, Saturday night

tacos, and specials every day. $

The Strip Club

378 Maria Ave.

651.793.6247

www.domeats.com

Playful, sophisticated atmosphere for meat and fish dinners on Dayton's Bluff. $$

Supatra's Thai Cuisine

967 W. Seventh St.

651.222.5859

www.supatra.com

Chef and owner Supatra Johnson is the author of Crying Tiger: Thai Recipes from the Heart. *$*

Tanpopo Noodle Shop

308 Prince St.

651.209.6527

www.tanpoporestaurant.com

Simple, elegant, and affordable Japanese food. $

Taste of Thailand

1671 Selby Ave.

651.644.3997

www.tasteofthailandmn.com

Order with as much or as little spice as you want, but remember that hot means HOT. $

Tavern on Grand

656 Grand Ave.

651.228.9030

www.tavernongrand.com

Go for the fried walleye and log cabin décor. $$

Tavern on the Avenue

825 Jefferson Ave.

651.227.6315

www.tavontheavenue.com

No-frills neighborhood bar that offers food made from scratch. $

Tay Ho Restaurant

302 University Ave. W.

651.228.7216

Small dining space with big flavors in traditional and old-world Asian fare. $

The Tea House

1676 Suburban Ave.

651.771.1790

www.ourteahouse.com

A Szechuan gem on the East Side. $

Tom Reid's Hockey City Pub

258 W. Seventh St.

651.292.9916

tomreidshockeycitypub.com

Generous portions for lunch, dinner, and after the game; serves late at night. $

Trattoria da Vinci

400 Sibley St.

651.222.4050

www.trattoriadavinci.com

Fine Italian cuisine amid antique stone fountains and architectural elegance. $$

Trieu Chau Restaurant

500 University Ave. W.

651.222.6148

Busy shop with outstanding soups and tasty banh mi sandwiches. $

Trotter's Café & Bakery

232 Cleveland Ave. N.

651.645.8950

www.trotterscafe.com

Find local and organic food at this charming café in Merriam Park. $

Twisted Fork Grille

1342 Grand Ave.
651.690.5901
www.twistedforkgrille.com
*American-inspired recipes with
seasonal foods for breakfast, lunch,
and dinner. $*

W. A. Frost & Company

Dacotah Building
374 Selby Ave.
651.224.5715
www.wafrost.com

*Incomparable ambience and an old-
world wine cellar to complement the
artisanal cuisine. $$$*

Yarusso Bros.

635 Payne Ave.
651.776.4848
www.yarussos.com
*Family-owned Italian classic since
1933; famous for* Francesco's
sauce and Bocce Ball. $

Theaters

Actors Theater of Minnesota
350 Saint Peter St., Ste. 254
651.290.2290
www.actorsmn.org
Resident theater company offering annual (and extended!) seasons at the Lowry Lab and other venues.

Anodyne Theatre
825 Carleton St.
651.642.1684
www.anodyneart.org
A visual and performing arts center especially for artists with disabilities.

Ballet Minnesota
249 E. Fourth St.
651.222.7919
www.balletminnesota.org
Creating and sharing dance artistry "that enriches the human spirit."

Camp Cabaret
490 Robert St. N.
651.292.1844
camp-bar.net
5,000 square feet with a back mezzanine lounge, distinctive performance stage, and dance floor.

Canvass
1610 Hubbard Ave.
651.298.4393
www.canvas651.com
Workshops and events, materials and support for young writers, dancers, visual artists, and performers.

Center for Hmong Arts and Talent (CHAT)
995 University Ave W., Ste. 220
651.603.6971
www.aboutchat.org
CHAT empowers the local Hmong community through the arts.

Commedia Beauregard
1043 Grand Ave., No. 358
651.214.2905
www.cbtheatre.org
Making classic and modern works from around the world accessible to modern audiences.

Dreamland Arts
677 Hamline Ave. N.
651.645.5506
www.dreamlandarts.com
A gathering place for creative expression through art that builds healthy community.

Fitzgerald Theater
10 Exchange St. E.
651.290.1200
fitzgeraldtheater.publicradio.org
The city's oldest theater and home to A Prairie Home Companion.

Gremlin Theatre
2400 University Ave. W.
651.228.7008
www.gremlin-theatre.org
Intimate space for a "relevant, entertaining, and enjoyable theatrical experience."

Hamm Brewery
707 Minnehaha Ave. E.
651.776.0550
www.swedehollow.org

An East Side performance space for artists and art lovers alike.

The Historic Mounds Theatre
1029 Hudson Rd.
651.772.2253
www.moundstheatre.org
An Art Deco landmark on Dayton's Bluff that benefits Portage for Youth.

History Theatre
30 E. Tenth St.
651.292.4323
www.historytheatre.com
Producing new works based on Minnesota's past and the American experience; Sample Night Live the first Wednesday of the month.

Lex-Ham Community Theater
1184 Portland Ave.
651.644.3366
www.LexHamArts.org
Quality theater activities by and for the residents of the Lexington-Hamline and surrounding neighborhoods.

Lowry Lab/Theater Space Project
350 Saint Peter St.
651.222.0149
www.theaterspaceproject.org
Offering affordable, convenient performance space in downtown Saint Paul.

Minnesota Jewish Theatre Company
1978 Ford Pkwy.
651.647.4315
www.mnjewishtheatre.org
Performances at Hillcrest Center. "Igniting your mind by touching your heart (even if you're not Jewish!)."

Nautilus Music-Theater
308 Prince St., Ste. 250
651.298.9913
www.nautilusmusictheater.org
Dedicated to new operas and innovative productions of existing works.

Ordway Center for Performing Arts
345 Washington St.
651.224.4222
www.ordway.org
Broadway-style shows, music, and dance.

Padelford Packet Boat Company
Harriet Island
651.227.110
www.riverrides.com
Come aboard the Showboat for stand-up comedy and live theater.

Park Square Theatre
20 West Seventh Place
651.291.7005
www.parksquaretheatre.org
Exceptional downtown theater staging a balance of familiar favorites and fresh new stories.

Penumbra Theatre Company
270 Kent St. N.
651.224.3180
www.penumbratheatre.org
Productions illuminating "the human condition through the prism of the African American experience."

Saint Paul City Ballet
1680 Grand Ave.
651.690.1588
www.spcballet.org

Sendero Flamenco dancing at the Mississippi River

Classical training and extraordinary performances.

Sendero Flamenco
153 E. 10th St.
612.203.6188
www.sendero-flamenco.com
Traditional flamenco dance and acoustic guitar.

Skylark Opera
Landmark Center, Ste. 414
75 W. Fifth St.
651.292.4309
www.skylarkopera.org
Familiar favorites and "off-the-beaten-path adventures" at the E. M. Pearson Theatre of Concordia University.

SteppingStone Theatre
55 Victoria St. N.
651.225.9265
www.steppingstonetheatre.org
Youth-centered theater art; family entertainment that feeds the mind.

Teatro del Pueblo
209 Page St. W., Ste. 208
651.224.8806
www.teatrodelpueblo.org
Serving communities across the state with educational residencies and touring shows.

Music Venues

Arnellia's
1183 University Ave. W.
651.642.5975
The "Legendary Club Apollo" of Minnesota.

Baroque Room
275 E. Fourth St., Ste. 280
651.705.6772
www.thebaroqueroom.com
The new downtown performance venue for chamber music.

Artists' Quarter
408 St. Peter St.
651.292.1359
www.artistsquarter.com
Located in the basement of the historic Hamm Building with a subterranean classic jazz vibe.

Black Dog Coffee & Wine Bar
308 Prince St.
651.228.9274
www.blackdogstpaul.com
A Lowertown meeting place for music, ideas, and good food.

Dubliner Pub
2162 University Ave. W.
651.646.5551
www.myspace.com
/DublinerMN
No-frills Irish bar: whiskey, scotch, beer, and an up-to-the-minute music calendar.

Eagles Club 33
287 Maria Ave.
651.774.7643
stpaulaeriearts.blogspot.com

St Paul Aerie for the Arts with music most Friday nights.

Ginkgo Coffeehouse
721 Snelling Ave. N.
651.645.2647
www.ginkgocoffee.com
Corner café offering fair trade and organic products with a diverse mix of music and clientele.

Half Time Rec
1013 Front St.
651.488.8245
www.halftimerec.com
A neighborhood nightclub with a variety of music and the only indoor bocce ball courts in Saint Paul.

Hat Trick Lounge
134 E. Fifth St.
651.228.1347
www.robincommunications
.com/hat_trick_lounge.htm
Classic saloon offering rock and roll, blues, country, folk, jazz, and pop.

Minnesota Music Café
499 Payne Ave.
651.776.4699
www.minnesotamusiccafe.com
"Where the food's great and the music's cooking!"

Music in Mears
221 E. Fifth St.
651.248.0857
www.musicinmears.com
Thursday evening outdoor concerts, June through August, from 6 to 9 p.m.

Zeitgeist's Studio Z in the Northwestern Building

O'Gara's Bar & Grill
164 Snelling Ave. N.
651.644.3333
www.ogaras.com
Neighborhood pub with music, grill food, and the free Shamrock Shuttle to sports events, including the Wild and Minnesota RollerGirls.

Shamrock's
995 W. Seventh St.
651.228.9925
www.crnook.com
A loyal customer following for bands Soul Tree, Mouldy Figs, Loose Cannon, and more.

SPCO Music Room / Saint Paul Chamber Orchestra
Historic Hamm Building
408 St. Peter St., third floor
651.291.1144
www.thespco.org
An intimate performance space for the nation's only full-time professional chamber orchestra.

Station 4
201 E. Fourth St.
651.224.6372
www.station-4.com

This vintage downtown club puts a variety of cult artists onstage.

Studio Z / Zeitgeist
275 E. Fourth St.
651.755.1600
www.zeitgeistnewmusic.org
A small ensemble of percussion, piano, and woodwinds performing a diverse range of new music.

Tavern on the Avenue
825 Jefferson Ave.
651.227.6315
www.tavontheavenue.com
Cozy venue; classic rock and roll, rhythm, blues, and soul.

Turf Club
1601 University Ave. W.
651.647.0486
www.turfclub.net
The newest music performed in a gritty relic of old-school Saint Paul: "The best remnant of the '40s."

Wilebski's Blues Saloon
1638 Rice St.
651.331.0929
www.wilebskiblues.com
Hardwood floors and out-of-this-world blues.

Dance Venues

Abetto's

560 Como Ave.
651.488.8588
www.abettos.com
Third Saturday Tango Milonga and lesson.

Celtic Junction

836 Prior Ave.
612.722.7000
www.thecelticjunction.com
Third Saturday night céili with the Twin Cities Céili Band.

Dubliner Pub

2162 University Ave. W.
651.646.5551
www.thedublinerpub.com
First Saturday afternoon céili (under 12 free).

Half Time Rec

1013 Front St.
651.488.8245
www.halftimecajun.com
Cajun and Zydeco every Sunday.

Oddfellows' Hall

2380 Hampden Ave.
651.222.5475
www.wildgoosechasecloggers
.com/local.html
First Saturday night New England Contra Dance.

Señor Wong

111 Kellogg Blvd. E.
651.224.2019
www.senorwong.com
Hold Tight DJ Saturdays with R&B, funk, hip-hop, remixes, classic and new jams.

Wabasha Street Caves

215 Wabasha St. S.
651.224.1191
www.wabashastreetcaves.com
Thursday night Swing dance.

Photo courtesy of Wabasha Caves

Swing dancing on Thursday nights at the Wabasha Caves

Art Galleries

*private (sell)

AAW Gallery of Wood Art
222 Landmark Center
75 Fifth St. W.
651.484.9094
www.galleryofwoodart.org
Sponsored by the American Association of Woodturners.

Artist Mercantile*
24 West Seventh Place
651.222.0053
www.artistmerc.com
An eclectic mix of art and gifts with a focus on regional artists.

AZ Gallery*
308 Prince St., No. 130
651.224.3757
www.theazgallery.org
A fine arts co-op in Lowertown.

Catherine G. Murphy Gallery
St. Catherine University
2004 Randolph Ave.
651.690.6644
www.stkate.edu/gallery
Visual arts that support the mission of the university.

Concordia Arts Center
Concordia University
275 Syndicate St. N.
651.641.8230
www.csp.edu/art
Showing local and national artists as well as juried student and senior exhibitions.

CVA Gallery
College of Visual Arts
173 Western Ave. N.
651.757.4080
www.cva.edu/gallery
Balances academic and community priorities to showcase all disciplines at the College of Visual Arts.

Evoke Gallery*
275 Fourth St. E., Ste. 260
612.839.3079
www.evokegallery.com
A mix of fair trade and eco-friendly gifts, handmade jewelry, and fine art.

The FrameWorks Gallery*
2022A Ford Pkwy.
651.698.3372
www.frameworksmn.com
An ongoing exhibition of works by local artists, with a featured artist that changes every six weeks.

The Grand Hand Gallery*
619 Grand Ave.
651.312.1122
www.thegrandhand.com
Contemporary fine American craft, mostly from local and regional artists, in a variety of media.

Gordon Parks Gallery
Metro State University
645 Seventh St. E.
651.793.1631
www.metrostate.edu/cas/cwa/gallery
Supports the arts curriculum and cultural activities of the university, and preserves the legacy of twentieth-century artist Gordon Parks.

Hosko Gallery*
56 E. Sixth St., Ste. 305

651.222.4767
www.billhosko.com
Architectural art and photography that features Saint Paul.

Johnson Gallery
Bethel University, Clausen Center, second floor
3900 Bethel Dr.
651.638.6400
www.bethel.edu/galleries
Works by students as well as local and national artists.

Larson Art Gallery
University of Minnesota Student Center, lower level
2017 Buford Ave.
612.625.7281
sua.umn.edu/events/arts
Curated, designed, installed, and promoted by the Visual Arts Committee of the student union's Program Board.

Lift Kids at Global Village
Produce Exchange Building
153 E. 10th St.
651.298.9200
www.liftkids.org
An art gallery serving coffee, tea, and social responsibility to increase peace and justice for people of all ages.

Macalester College Art Gallery
Located in "The Duplex" until fall 2012, while the Janet Wallace Fine Arts Center is being renovated
1665 Princeton Ave.
651.696.6416
www.macalester.edu/gallery
Emphasis on contemporary art with exhibitions on a wide range of historical and sociological topics.

Olson Gallery*
Bethel University, Community Life Center, second floor
3900 Bethel Dr.
651.638.6400
www.bethel.edu/galleries
Encouraging public dialogue on issues of art, faith, and culture.

Raymond Avenue Gallery*
761 Raymond Ave.
651.644.9200
The works of recognized regional artists in a variety of media, from pottery to fiber.

Soeffker Gallery
Hamline University, Drew Fine Arts Center
1536 Hewitt Ave.
651.523.2800
www.hamline.edu/features/tour/drew_fine_arts.html
Houses the permanent collection and hosts touring exhibitions.

UST Department of Art History/Exhibitions
University of St. Thomas
2115 Summit Ave.
651.962.5560
www.stthomas.edu/arthistory/exhibitions
Hosts three exhibitions a year featuring emerging and established artists working in a variety of media.

Water and Oil Art Gallery*
506 Kenny Rd.
651.774.2260
www.waterandoil.com
Bringing the art of Europe to the heart of Minnesota.

Bookstores

Common Good Books
165 Western Ave. N.
651.225.8989
www.commongoodbooks.com
A nice local store to buy a book or two.

Hmong ABC
Two locations: 217 Como Ave.
and 1001 Johnson Pkwy.
651.293.0019
www.hmongabc.com
*Also sells handmade crafts, clothing,
and jewelry.*

Micawber's Books
2238 Carter Ave.
651.646.5506
www.micawbers.com
Everyone's neighborhood bookstore.

Midway Books
1579 University Ave. W.
651.644.7605
www.midwaybook.com

*Rare, used, and out-of-print books
and comics, with a wide array of
memorabilia.*

Red Balloon Bookshop
891 Grand Ave.
651.224.8320
www.redballoonbookshop.com
*A children's bookstore with frequent
author readings and a terrific
selection of hand puppets.*

Sixth Chamber Used Books
1332 Grand Ave.
651.690.9463
www.sixthchamber.com
*A searchable online inventory and
convenient on-street parking.*

Rab Balloon Bookshop

Photo © Dan Tilsen

Museums, Historical Sites, and Tours

Alexander Ramsey House
265 Exchange St. S.
651.296.8760
www.mnhs.org/ramseyhouse
Near Irvine Park, the 19th century
Victorian home of Alexander
Ramsey offers "a glimpse into family
and servant life" with guided tours;
closed January 2 to May 31.

Assumption Church
51 Seventh St. W.
651.224.7536
www.assumptionsp.org
A Roman Catholic church built
in 1871 with a self-guided tour
brochure available online.

Cathedral of Saint Paul
239 Selby Ave.
651.228.1766
www.cathedralsaintpaul.org
One of the city's most recognizable
buildings since it was completed in
1915; tours most weekdays at 1 p.m.

Gibbs Museum
2097 Larpenteur Ave. W.
651.646.8629
www.rchs.com
Summer Day Camps re-create the
pioneer and Dakota life; closed
mid–November to mid–April.

Goldstein Museum of Design
University of Minnesota,
McNeal Hall
1985 Buford Avenue
612.624.7801
goldstein.design.umn.edu
The only design museum in the Upper
Midwest.

Governor's Residence
1006 Summit Ave.
651.297.2161
www.admin.state.mn.us/govres
Summer tours in June, July, and Au-
gust; holiday tours in December.

Historic Fort Snelling
200 Tower Avenue (Hwys 5 & 55)
612.726.1171
www.mnhs.org/fortsnelling
1820s military post and prison with
costumed guides and demos; open
Memorial Day Weekend through
Labor Day.

Jackson Street Roundhouse
Minnesota Transportation
Museum
193 Pennsylvania Ave. E.
651.228.0263
www.mtmuseum.org
Kids of all ages enjoy the railroading
experience at this former steam
engine maintenance facility; open
Wednesday and Saturday year
round.

James J. Hill House
240 Summit Ave.
651.297.2555
www.mnhs.org/hillhouse
Hill's red sandstone mansion from
the gilded age was completed in
1891; 75-minute guided tours
Wednesday through Saturday.

Julian H. Sleeper House
66 St. Albans St. S.
651.225.1505
www.julianhsleeperhouse.com

Tour the dream home of this Saint Paul entrepreneur, real estate speculator, and theatrical promoter; nine decorative exhibition rooms (by appointment only).

Minnesota Children's Museum

10 Seventh St. W.
651.225.6000
www.mcm.org
A hands-on learning environment for children age six months to 10 years; closed Monday.

Minnesota History Center

345 Kellogg Blvd. W.
651.259.3000
www.mnhs.org
An interactive museum with changing exhibits that inform and inspire; free admission on Tuesday from 5 to 8 p.m.

Minnesota Korean War Veterans' Memorial

State Capitol Grounds
www.mdva.state.mn.us
/memorials/capitol/
koreanwarveterans.htm
Installed in 1998, the complex bronze statues and paving stones stand in memory of the war years from 1950 to 1955.

Minnesota Museum of American Art

Landmark Center
75 Fifth St. W., Ste. 224
651.783.5690
www.mmaa.org
The gallery is closed and working to secure a permanent site, but they do curate occasional off-site exhibitions.

Minnesota State Capitol

75 Rev. Dr. Martin Luther King Jr. Blvd.
651.296.2881
www.mnhs.org/statecapitol
Designed by architect Cass Gilbert and opened in 1905; plan ahead for a theme tour, or choose the 45-minute overview (free, on the hour).

Minnesota Vietnam Veterans' Memorial

State Capitol Grounds
www.mvvm.org
Dedicated in 1992, the solemn granite memorial honors the 68,000 Minnesotans who served.

Old Muskego Church

Luther Seminary
2481 Como Ave.
651.641.3456
www2.luthersem.edu/tour/
visitor/muskego.asp
Built in Racine, Wis., by Norwegian immigrants, the log church was moved to Luther in 1904; contact the information desk for tour information.

Ramsey County Courthouse and Saint Paul City Hall

15 Kellogg Blvd. W.
651.266.8002
www.co.ramsey.mn.us/cm
/manager/CourthouseTours.
htm
Built in 1932, this 21-story art deco high-rise includes Carl Milles' imposing statue, Vision of Peace; *self-guided tours and by appointment during weekday work hours.*

Roy Wilkins Memorial on the State Capitol grounds

Raptor Center
University of Minnesota
1920 Fitch Ave.
612.624.4745
www.raptor.cvm.umn.edu
*A learning center that's hospital
and home to birds of prey; closed
Mondays and University holidays.*

Roy Wilkins Memorial
State Capitol Grounds
*Designed by Curtis Patterson and
erected in 1995 to honor civil rights
leader Roy Wilkins.*

Saint Paul Central Library
90 Fourth St. W.
651.266.7000
www.stpaul.lib.mn.us
*Italian Renaissance revival building
completed in 1917; guided tours
available the first Sunday of the month
at 1:30 p.m.*

The Schubert Club Museum
Landmark Center
75 Fifth St. W.
651.292.3267
www.schubert.org
*An interpretive guide to keyboards,
the recital tradition, and an Ordway*
*manuscript collection; Sunday
through Friday, 12 to 4 p.m. (free).*

Science Museum of Minnesota
120 Kellogg Blvd. W.
651.221.9444
www.smm.org
*Dynamic traveling exhibits
and science movie thrills at the
Omnitheater.*

Twin City Model Railroad Museum
Bandana Square, Ste. 222
1021 East Bandana Blvd.
651.647.9628
www.tcmrm.org
*State-of-the-art miniature railroads,
plus a toy train division; American
Flyer, Lionel, K-Line, MTH, and other
formats; free parking.*

Wabasha Street Caves
215 Wabasha St. South
651.292.1220
www.wabashastreetcaves.com
*Cave tours Thursday at 5 p.m.,
Saturday and Sunday, 11 a.m.;
Gangster tours Saturday at noon.*

Food Co-ops

The UN has declared 2012 the International Year of Cooperatives; see www.ica.coop

Mississippi Market Food Co-ops

1500 Seventh St. W.
651.690.0507

622 Selby Ave.
651.310.9499
www.msmarket.coop
Delis and healthy, sustainable shopping, with an emphasis on organic and local foods.

Hampden Park Food Co-op

928 Raymond Ave.
651.646.6686
www.hampdenparkcoop.com
Organic, unprocessed, bulk, fresh foods and working member discounts.

Hampden Park Co-op at 928 Raymond Avenue

Sports and Competiton

Minnesota Boat Club

1 Wabasha S.
651.228.1602
www.boatclub.org
Learn to row on Raspberry Island.

Minnesota Men's Roller Derby

600 Cedar St.
www.tcterrors.com
Destruction Workers, Skate Pauli Boys, and TC Terrors, at the "Terrordome," a.k.a. the armory.

Minnesota RollerGirls

175 Kellogg Blvd. W., Ste. 501
651.265.4899
www.mnrollergirls.com
Fast-paced action at Roy Wilkins Auditorium with the hard-hitting women's roller derby league.

Minnesota Swarm

317 Washington St.
888.MN.SWARM
www.mnswarm.com
Lacrosse for the whole family.

Minnesota Wild

317 Washington St.
651.222.WILD (box office)
www.wild.com
The State of Hockey's NHL games at the Civic Center.

Saint Paul Bicycle Racing Club

www.spbrc.org
Bringing all levels of cyclists together for fun and competition.

St. Paul Blackhawks Soccer Club

875 Orchard Ave.
651.894.2437
www.blackhawksoccer.org
A year-round soccer development and training center.

Saint Paul Curling Club

470 Selby Ave.
651.224.7408
www.stpaulcurlingclub.org
Pull up a chair at the viewing windows.

Saint Paul Saints

1771 Energy Park Dr.
651.644.6659
www.saintsbaseball.com
Saint Paul's minor league baseball games at Midway Stadium.

St. Paul Pioneers

Humboldt High School Stadium
30 East Baker St.
www.pioneersfootball.org
Saint Paul's semi-pro football team with home games at Humboldt High School Stadium.

Saint Paul Public Libraries

The Saint Paul library system provides resources for everyone, from children studying a beloved subject to adults reading their favorite newspaper on a day off from work. Offering many literary, historical, and cultural events, Saint Paul libraries also provide further learning for eager minds of the city. Each library provides a calm, safe learning environment to read, study, surf the Web, or search for information. The following is a listing of all Saint Paul's libraries, locations, and hours. All locations are handicapped-accessible. For further information visit http://www.stpaul.lib.mn.us.

Arlington Hills
1105 Greenbrier St.
651.793.3930

M	12:00 p.m.–8:00 p.m.
T	10:00 a.m.–5:30 p.m.
W	12:00 p.m.–8:00 p.m.
TH	10:00 a.m.–5:30 p.m.
F	10:00 a.m.–5:30 p.m.
SA	11:00 a.m.–5:30 p.m.
SU	CLOSED

Central Library
90 West Fourth St.
651.266.7000

M	12:00 p.m.–8:00 p.m.
T	9:30 a.m.–5:30 p.m.
W	9:30 a.m.–5:30 p.m.
TH	9:30 a.m.–5:30 p.m.
F	9:30 a.m.–5:30 p.m.
SA	9:30 a.m.–5:30 p.m.
SU	1:00 p.m.–5:00 p.m.

Dayton's Bluff
645 East 7th St.
651.793.1699

M	12:00 p.m.–8:00 p.m.
T	10:00 a.m.–5:30 p.m.
W	12:00 p.m.–8:00 p.m.
TH	10:00 a.m.–5:30 p.m.
F	10:00 a.m.–5:30 p.m.
SA	11:00 a.m.–5:30 p.m.
SU	1:00 p.m.–5:00 p.m.

Hamline Midway
1558 West Minnehaha Ave.
651.642.0293

M	12:00 p.m.–8:00 p.m.
T	10:00 a.m.–5:30 p.m.
W	12:00 p.m.–8:00 p.m.
TH	10:00 a.m.–5:30 p.m.
F	10:00 a.m.–5:30 p.m.
SA	11:00 a.m.–5:30 p.m.
SU	CLOSED

Hayden Heights
1456 White Bear Ave.
651.793.3934

M 12:00 p.m.–8:00 p.m.
T 10:00 a.m.–8:00 p.m.
W 12:00 p.m.–8:00 p.m.
TH 10:00 a.m.–5:30 p.m.
F 10:00 a.m.–5:30 p.m.
SA 10:00 a.m.–5:30 p.m.
SU CLOSED

Highland Park
1974 Ford Pkwy.
651.695.3700

M 10:00 a.m.–9:00 p.m.
T 10:00 a.m.–9:00 p.m.
W 10:00 a.m.–9:00 p.m.
TH 10:00 a.m.–9:00 p.m.
F 10:00 a.m.–5:30 p.m.
SA 10:00 a.m.–5:30 p.m.
SU 1:00 p.m.–5:00 p.m.

Merriam Park
1831 Marshall Ave.
651.642.0385
TTY: 651.298.4184

M 12:00 p.m.–8:00 p.m.
T 10:00 a.m.–8:00 p.m.
W 12:00 p.m.–8:00 p.m.
TH 10:00 a.m.–5:30 p.m.
F 10:00 a.m.–5:30 p.m.
SA 10:00 a.m.–5:30 p.m.
SU CLOSED

Rice Street
1011 Rice St.
651.558.2223

M 12:00 p.m.–8:00 p.m.
T 10:00 a.m.–8:00 p.m.
W 12:00 p.m.–8:00 p.m.
TH 10:00 a.m.–5:30 p.m.
F 10:00 a.m.–5:30 p.m.
SA 10:00 a.m.–5:30 p.m.
SU 1:00 p.m.–5:00 p.m.

Riverview
1 East George St.
651.292.6626

M 12:00 p.m.–8:00 p.m.
T 10:00 a.m.–5:30 p.m.
W 12:00 p.m.–8:00 p.m.
TH 10:00 a.m.–5:30 p.m.
F 10:00 a.m.–5:30 p.m.
SA 11:00 a.m.–5:30 p.m.
SU CLOSED

Rondo Community Outreach
461 North Dale St.
651.266.7400
TTY: 651.266.7485

M 10:00 a.m.–9:00 p.m.
T 10:00 a.m.–9:00 p.m.
W 10:00 a.m.–9:00 p.m.
TH 10:00 a.m.–9:00 p.m.
F 10:00 a.m.–5:30 p.m.
SA 10:00 a.m.–5:30 p.m.
SU 1:00 p.m.–5:00 p.m.

Saint Anthony Park
2245 Como Ave.
651.642.0411

M	12:00 p.m.–8:00 p.m.
T	10:00 a.m.–8:00 p.m.
W	12:00 p.m.–8:00 p.m.
TH	10:00 a.m.–5:30 p.m.
F	10:00 a.m.–5:30 p.m.
SA	10:00 a.m.–5:30 p.m.
SU	CLOSED

West Seventh
265 Oneida St.
651.298.5516

M	12:30 p.m.–8:00 p.m.
T	11:30 a.m.–5:30 p.m.
W	10:00 a.m.–5:30 p.m.
TH	12:30 p.m.–8:00 p.m.
F	10:00 a.m.–5:30 p.m.
SA	CLOSED
SU	CLOSED

Sun Ray
2105 Wilson Ave.
651.501.6300

M	10:00 a.m.–9:00 p.m.
T	10:00 a.m.–9:00 p.m.
W	10:00 a.m.–9:00 p.m.
TH	10:00 a.m.–9:00 p.m.
F	10:00 a.m.–5:30 p.m.
SA	10:00 a.m.–5:30 p.m.
SU	1:00 p.m.–5:00 p.m.

Saint Paul Central Library banner

Saint Paul District Councils

The district council planning process was created over thirty years ago to help support each of Saint Paul's unique neighborhoods. There are seventeen councils in Saint Paul. Their responsibilities include developing the community geographically, socially, and economically, and planning and sponsoring community events. It is easy and satisfying to take part in your council. Find your district below and get involved today. A map with more information is available at www.stpaul.gov/index .aspx?NID=1212.

District 1
Eastview, Conway, Battle Creek, and Highwood Hills neighborhoods.
2105 ½ Old Hudson Rd.
55119
651.578.7600
www.district1council.org

District 2
Beaver Lake Heights, East Phalen, Frost Lake, Hayden Heights. Hazel Park, Hillcrest, Lincoln Park, Parkway/Greenbrier, Phalen Village, and Prosperity Heights neighborhoods.
1961 Sherwood Ave.
55119
651.774.2220
www.district2council.org

District 3
West Side Citizens Organization
127 Winifred St. W.
55107
651-293-1708
www.wsco.org

District 4
Dayton's Bluff Community Council
798 E. Seventh St.
55106

651.772.2075
www.daytonsbluff.org

District 5
Payne-Phalen Planning Council
506 Kenny Rd., Ste. 130
55130
651.774.5234
www.paynephalen.org

District 6
North End and South Como neighborhoods.
213 Front Ave.
55117
651.488.4485
www.district6stpaul.org

District 7
East Midway, Frogtown, Mt. Airy, and Capitol Heights neighborhoods.
685 Minnehaha Ave. W.
55104
651.789.7480
www.frogtownmn.org

District 8
Summit-University Planning Council
627 Selby Ave.
55104
Phone: 651.228.1855
www.summit-u.com

District 9

West Seventh/Fort Road Federation
974 W. Seventh St.
55102
651.298.5599
www.fortroadfederation.org

District 10

*Como Park, Energy Park, and Como
Campus (zoo, park, and lake)
neighborhoods*
1224 Lexington Pkwy. N.
55103
651.644.3889
www.district10comopark.org

District 11

Hamline Midway Coalition
1564 Lafond Ave.
55104
651.646.1986
www.hamlinemidway.org

District 12

St. Anthony Park Community Council
890 Cromwell Ave.
55114
651.649.5992
www.sapcc.org

District 13

Union Park District Council
1570 Concordia Ave., Ste. LL100
55104
651.645.6887
www.unionparkdc.org

District 14

*Macalester-Groveland Community
Council*
320 Griggs St. S.
55105
651.695.4000
www.macgrove.org

District 15

Highland District Council
1978 Ford Pkwy.
55116
651.695.4005
www.highlanddistrictcouncil
.org

District 16

Summit Hill Association
860 St. Clair Ave.
55105
651.222.1222
www.summithillassociation.org

District 17

CapitolRiver Council
101 E. Fifth St., Ste. 240
55101
651.221.0488
www.capitolrivercouncil.org

Voter Registration

Ramsey County Elections Office
90 West Plato Blvd., Suite 160
Saint Paul, MN 55107
651.266.2171

To learn about your precinct location and caucus location, view the election calendar or see a sample ballot, and for all other voting information, visit www.co.ramsey.mn.us/elections.

For online voter registration, also visit www.projectvote.org or www.rockthevote.com. Remember to vote!

Saint Paul Parks

The city of Saint Paul is home to one of the best park systems in the country, and features some of the most well-kept and beautiful hiking trails, sports facilities, woods, picnic areas, fishing, and scenic beauty in the world. Saint Paul offers so many parks that this publication was unable to include them all in its listings. The following is a compilation of community and regional parks that best represent Saint Paul: a list of natural retreats (often including facilities and amenities) that offer something unique for the joggers, sunbathers, anglers, sports fanatics, nature enthusiasts, children young and old, and the child within us all. For a full listing of parks and more visit http://www.stpaul.gov/index.aspx?nid=245

Arlington/Arkwright Park (Community)
400 Arlington Ave. East
651.632.5111
Known for the large Off-Leash Dog Area, this park includes wooded trails, open space, and a large rounded slope perfect for summer and winter play, tucked away in a quiet residential neighborhood. Also features a baseball and soccer field nearby and a recreational facility for those cold or rainy days.

Como Park (Regional)
1199 Midway Parkway
(Pavilion)
651.632.5111
A Saint Paul jewel for over 100 years, Como Park still plays a vital role in meeting the recreational needs of the city. Features Como Shelter and Como Pavilion, which provide electricity and seating for events, as well as Como Lake, Zoo, and historic streetcar station. Voted best tourist destination in Minnesota.

Crosby Farm Park (Regional)
2595 Crosby Farm Rd.
651.632.5111
Crosby Park, once a 160-acre farm staked out by English immigrant Thomas Crosby in 1858, now offers multiple trails for hiking, biking, and jogging, as well as fishing, and a shelter with seating, electricity, grills, and a fire pit.

Harriet Island Park (Regional)
200 Dr. Justus Ohage Blvd.
651.292.7010
Famed Harriet Island, home of various events throughout the year, is the perfect summer getaway located just across the Mississippi from downtown Saint Paul. Perfect for walks, boat rides from the shore, and live music at the bandstand.

Hidden Falls (Regional)
1415 Mississippi River Blvd. South
651.632.5111

Immensely beautiful, with spacious grounds, towering trees, and the river just down the slope, Hidden Falls is a park for both summer and winter activities. The waterfall, from which the park gets its name, is worth the visit alone for its scenic beauty. Includes a section for boat launching, as well as hiking and general picnic area.

Highland Park

1200 Montreal Ave.
651.632.5111
Highland Park, acquired as a completely undeveloped park in 1925, now features an 18-hole golf course, aquatic center, pavilion, picnic shelters, and a Frisbee golf course, most of which is still standing from the 1930s.

Indian Mounds Park (Regional)

10 Mounds Blvd.
651.632.5111
An integral part of Minnesota's history, Mounds Park features Native American burial grounds, some of which date back 2,000 years or more. Mounds Park offers beautiful grounds and trails, sitting high on a bluff overlooking the city. A perfect place to enjoy a stroll and be a part of Saint Paul's past.

Irvine Park (Neighborhood)

251 Walnut St.
651.632.5111
A beautifully ornate fountain is the central feature of this popular park for weddings and picnics. Offers shelter, seating, and electricity. This park is nestled in a residential area just west of downtown.

Kellogg Mall (Neighborhood)

62 Kellogg Blvd. East
651.632.5111
One of the greatest views of the Mississippi can be found at this park, which also has two fountains and an arbor for visitors to enjoy. Located in downtown Saint Paul, Kellogg Mall offers perfect views of both cityscape and America's natural gem, the Mississippi.

Lilydale Park (Regional)

950 Lilydale Rd.
651.632.5111
Fossil hunting is available. Bring the whole family and spend the day enjoying the beautiful paths and forest, and searching for ancient pieces of Saint Paul's past.

Marydale Park (Community)

542 Maryland Ave. West
651.632.5111
Beautiful greenery fills this community park surrounding Loeb Lake. Offers barbeque grills, restrooms, and fishing pier, where anglers can try for crappies and bluegills, and sometimes bullheads and bass as well. The lake is designated as a children's fishing pond by the Minnesota Department of Natural Resources.

Mears Park (Community)

221 5th St. East
651.632.5111
Lowertown's gem, this park has a covered bandstand for summer music and a picturesque stream running from one corner to the other. Surrounded by new hot spots Barrio, the Bulldog, and

Bin Wine Bar, this park is a retreat in downtown Saint Paul.

Newell Park (Community)

900 North Fairview Ave.
651.632.5111
Newell Park is one of the oldest in Saint Paul. Covered in hills and old oak trees, the 10-acre plot is a good place to have a summer picnic, play Frisbee with friends, or to sit under a tree and read a book. The pavilion, a perfect place for a family get-together, has been standing since 1929.

Phalen Park (Regional)

1615 Phalen Dr.
651.632.5111
A beautiful lagoon rests next to the family-friendly Phalen amphitheater. With Lake Phalen just a few yards

beyond, this east Saint Paul park and recreational area offers something for everyone.

Western Park (Community)

387 Marion St.
651.632.5111
Features a sculpture garden, including the "Democracy Speaks" sculpture, recently created by John Hock and Andrew MacGuffie. The sculpture is 17 feet tall and built out of fabricated and painted steel.

Photo © Henry Jackson

One of the oldest parks in Saint Paul, Newell was dedicated in 1908

Contributors' Biographies

Rashidah Ismaili AbuBakr is now retired but teaches in a low-residence creative writing MA and MFA program at Wilkes University in Pennsylvania. She is now writing full time in all genres. Her apartment is home to Salon d'Afrique, where she holds soirees with visiting artists and Harlemites.

Suzel Aburto attends English classes at the Minnesota Literacy Center on the East Side.

Mathal Al-Azawi is from Iraq. She is forty years old, married, and has a beautiful family, especially her daughter. She lives in Saint Paul, and has been learning English at the Minnesota Literacy Council. She likes the freedom and safety of the U.S.

Hannah Anderson attends sixth grade in Saint Paul Public Schools. Hannah started playing the Irish whistle in third grade, and the cello in fourth. Not that long ago she began Irish singing. In her free time, she likes to read, write, and draw.

Margaret Anzevino grew up on Railroad Island just blocks from both the first St. Ambrose on Payne Avenue and then the second on Burr and Minnehaha. She taught in the Roseville School District for thirty-seven of her thirty-nine years in education. Knitting, reading, writing, travel, and politics are some of her interests. She loves Saint Paul. If and when she wins the lottery, the first thing she will do is move to a condo in downtown Saint Paul.

Rudy Arnold is an artist who documented five small businesses on the corner of Hamline Avenue and Thomas Avenue in Saint Paul to show how the relationships between the owners and their customers nurture a community. See more of his work at www.rudyarnold.com.

Sasha Aslanian is a lifelong Saint Paul resident, although she will admit to being born in Minneapolis. She now lives on Saint Paul's West Side with her husband and two daughters. She enjoys walking over the Wabasha Street Bridge to her job as a documentary radio producer at Minnesota Public Radio.

Scott Bade is a Metropolitan State University English major graduate and, with his lovely wife, Erika, soon to welcome his first child into the world. They're waiting until the child is born to know the gender. As long as he or she is a pro-golfer, he'll be happy.

Mehari Baheru was born in Asmera, Eritrea. He likes to eat injera. Mehari has been living in Saint Paul for two years. He studies at the Hubbs Center for Lifelong Learning, which he likes, and thinks it is a good place for adult learning. He has learned English, writing, listening, vocabulary, and grammar there, and also took a Certified Nursing Assistant class in 2009. He passed the test to get his license, and now works as a CNA.

Aleli Balagtas lives near Como Park. She walks around the lake twice a week all year round, even when it's really cold.

Susele Barrios is from Mexico and has lived in Saint Paul for several years. When she isn't working, she attends Advanced English classes at the Minnesota Literacy Council's Arlington Hills Learning Center on the East Side of Saint Paul.

Arlo Beckman attends sixth grade in Saint Paul Public Schools. Arlo's favorite hobby is baseball. He used to live in San Francisco, California, but then his dad was offered a better job in Minnesota, so he moved. He has many friends in Saint Paul and likes it here.

Maya Beecham, a second-generation native Saint Paulite, was born in the historic Rondo neighborhood, graduated from Cretin-Derham Hall High School, and earned a bachelor of arts in communication studies at Hamline University. Currently, she works for a national nonprofit organization in Saint Paul and as a freelance writer.

Gloria Bengtson is an editor who has worked in publishing for over twenty years. Recently, she has taken up writing poetry, with running as her muse. She lives and gardens in Saint Paul.

Carol Pearce Bjorlie grew up in Richmond, Virginia, which she considers the source of her writer's voice. She has a bachelor of music degree in cello performance from East

Carolina University and an MFA in writing from Hamline University. She teaches music at the University of Wisconsin, River Falls, and writing at The Loft Literary Center. Carol continues to perform and have her work published, including, most recently, a poem in a 2010 anthology, *The Wind Blows, The Ice Breaks: Poems of Loss and Renewal by Minnesota Poets*, from Nodin Press.

Patricia Black continues to work with Aurora/St. Anthony Neighborhood Development Corporation because the organization works to preserve this historic community and, also, teaches Black people to have pride in themselves. That is very important.

Patricia Bour-Schilla is a wife, mother, and full-time student who loves to bike ride, hike, take photos of everything, and spend lots of time with family and friends.

Jill Breckenridge has published three books of poetry. *How To Be Lucky* won the Bluestem Award, judged by William Stafford, and *Civil Blood* was nominated for the American Library Association's Notable Books of the year. Her latest collection, *The Gravity of Flesh,* won a 2009 Northeastern Minnesota Book Award. Jill's memoir, *Miss Priss and the Con Man*, will be published in the fall of 2011.

Rich Broderick lives in Saint Paul and teaches journalism at Anoka-Ramsey Community College. Rich is a writer, poet, and social activist.

Wendy Brown-Baez is a writer, teacher, performance poet, and installation artist. She is the author of the poetry collections *Ceremonies of the Spirit* and *Transparencies of Light.* Wendy is the creator of Writing Circles for Healing and teaches an after-school writing workshop for at-risk youth in Saint Paul, where she is kept on her toes.

Destiny SaNaa' Carter was born on April 18, 2002, in Marshall, Texas. She is currently a third grader at J. J. Hill Montessori School. Her hobbies are singing, writing, reading, and socializing with her friends. She has had a passion for writing poems since she learned how to write in cursive in the first grade. When Destiny grows up, she would like to go to college and then become a singer/writer.

Kate Cavett has spent hundreds of hours listening to over 200 individuals share their reflections on Saint Paul, careers, racism, passions, sorrows, challenges, and successes. Her book Voices of Rondo: Oral Histories of Saint Paul's Historic Black Community won the 2006 Minnesota Book Award. She continues her dedication to document the stories of ordinary people with extra ordinary lives.

Sharon Chmielarz has had poems published in many literary magazines, she's had three children's picture books published, and her travel memoirs have been included in several anthologies. She has been awarded a Jerome Foundation Fellowship, and Minnesota State Arts Board and Region 2 grants; her work has been a finalist in the National Poetry Series, nominated for a Pushcart Prize five times, and has been translated into French and Polish. She's served as readings coordinator for SASE at the Banfill-Locke Center for the Arts. Her poem *The Other Mozart* has been made into a two-part opera. Her most recent books of poetry are *Calling,* from Loonfeather Press, and *The Sky is Great, The Sky is Blue,* from Whistling Shade Press.

Elena Cisneros is an MFA student at Hamline University in Saint Paul.

John Lee Clark was born deaf and became blind in adolescence. His poetry has appeared in many publications, including *The Hollins Critic, McSweeney's, Poetry,* and *The Seneca Review.* His chapbook of poems, *Suddenly Slow,* was published by Handtype Press in 2008; he edited the definitive anthology *Deaf American Poetry* for Gallaudet University Press in 2009. He and his wife, the cartoonist Adrean Clark, run an online publication, *Clerc Scar,* at www.clercscar.com, and they live in Saint Paul with their three sons.

Sarah Clark and her husband have lived in the St. Anthony Park neighborhood of Saint Paul for five years. She graduated from Luther College in 2005 and Luther Seminary in 2010. Sarah is an ELCA pastor who is seriously addicted to good food, the Minnesota

Public Radio station The Current, and the Boundary Waters Canoe Area in northern Minnesota.

Patrick Coleman is the Minnesota Historical Society acquisitions librarian. He was honored with the prestigious Kay Sexton Award at the twenty-first annual Minnesota Book Awards gala, serves on the board of Coffee House Press, and is a longtime member of the Ampersand Club and the Manuscript Society. He writes the 150 Best Minnesota Books Blog, highlighting books that are important to the intellectual life and identity of the state. Due to his work, the MHS library is one of the preeminent research libraries in the nation.

Carol Connolly was appointed by Mayor Chris Coleman as Saint Paul's first poet laureate. She is a longtime media columnist, and curates and hosts the monthly Readings by Writers series, now in its twelfth year, at the historic University Club of Saint Paul. Her book of poems, *Payments Due,* is in its fifth printing from Midwest Villages and Voices, a press founded by the late great poet Meridel Le Sueur. Connolly's recent book of poems is *All This and More* (Nodin Press).

Greg Cosimini has lived in Dayton's Bluff all his life, as did his parents. His four grandparents emigrated from Italy just to live there too. Greg wandered off to the U of M to study electrical things but always came back at night. He then worked in the exotic suburbs of Eagan and Eden Prairie before realizing there is no place like home.

Paul Creager is the curriculum and media arts coordinator for Gordon Parks High School.

Patricia Cummings grew up in Saint Paul. She graduated from the College of St. Catherine (now St. Catherine University) and did what women of her generation were supposed to do—got married and had three children. Eventually, Pat went back to work and made a career in philanthropy for twenty-five years. Now retired, Pat spends many happy hours at her computer, writing prose and poetry.

Lawrence Daniels saved money from his summer job to buy a 35mm camera his freshman year in high school. Since that time, he has sustained an interest in writing, photography, video production, and the arts. When in the seventh grade, he set a city record for polevault (thirteen feet) that stands to this day.

Barbara Davis is director of Great River T'ai Chi in Minneapolis, editor of *Taijiquan Journal* and author of *The Taijiquan Classics: An Annotated Translation.*

Sharon M. Day is Ojibwe, a Bois Forte enrollee. An artist and musician, she has spent forty-six years as a Saint Paulite.

Brittany "Rittan" Delaney is an activist and spoken word artist, born and raised in Minnesota. Having been on the scene for going on nine years. In the past, she has participated in spoken word groups such as The Minnesota Spoken Word Association, Quest for the Voice, Teens Rock the Mic, and university-based establishments. She's currently working as an arts literacy facilitator at Gordon Parks High School, and continues residencies and workshops. Her focus is on promoting literacy and safe-space learning environments. She is working on her first book as a teaching artist and plans to release it in the next year.

Martin Devaney is a songwriter born and raised in Saint Paul. Nicknamed "The Mayor," he has released five full-length albums, including most recently *The West End*, and studied creative writing at the U of M. His website is martindevaney.com.

Gayathri Dileepan attends sixth grade in Saint Paul Public Schools. Gayathri was born in Colombo, Sri Lanka. Gayathri enjoys reading, especially fiction; often, she feels as if she is in the story as the main character. She also enjoys writing, which is just the opposite of reading. She has a journal in which she records the important events in her life.

Virginia Dippel has decided to self-publish a book of poetry, inspired by the *Saint Paul Almanac*'s acceptance of some her poems and articles. She has been writing for many years and figured that, at the age of seventy-three, she may not have many more years to get her work out to the public—this has given her a fresh sense of urgency. She wants her book, *A Simple View,* to leave behind a memory of who she is. She intends to give copies to her children, grandchildren, various relatives, and anyone else who may be standing around and interested. She wants to thank the *Saint Paul Almanac* for its help and motivation.

Louis DiSanto is a retired keeper from Como Zoo who enjoys photography, writing children's stories, classical music (especially DeBussy), and long walks. He also worked as a newspaper reporter, playground assistant, and one summer at a cemetery. Passionate about nostalgia, Louis loves to reminisce with friends about the fun they had as kids, like taking the bus downtown to see movies, eating ice cream at Bridgeman's, and sneaking into Harkin's pool hall on West Seventh Street.

Norita Dittberner-Jax is a poet whose work has been widely published. She has an abiding love for Saint Paul, having been raised in Frogtown, taught English in its schools, and continues to live in this lovely city. Her books of poems include *The Watch* and *What They Always Were.*

Matt Ehling is a Saint Paul–based television producer and writer. He has produced work for PBS stations and has written for a variety of Twin Cities publications, including Minnpost.com.

Gayla Ellis is a Minneapolis resident who was a legal secretary in many different offices in downtown Saint Paul for many years, and prefers that city's scene to downtown Minneapolis.

Donald Empson is a local historian who lives in Stillwater.

Joanne A. Englund moved to Grandma's 1910 homestead in 1933. She was three. As an adult, she moved to Shoreview, then back to Saint Paul, and back to Midway. Her mom lived in the house till 2000. Writing, photography, genealogy, and Google compete with kids and grandkids for her time.

Sandra Erskine uses her old kitchen table as a desk.

Nimo Farah loves orators and storytellers. Her ideal vacation is visiting remote villages in Somalia and listening to the stories of elders and children under the dancing stars and full moon while drinking tea. She has an inner child that recently turned four years old and can doodle and dream for hours (she looks forward to a day dedicated to dreaming). She lives in many places in Minneapolis and Saint Paul, including her car (she's always driving and up for any adventure) and thinks of herself as a Twin Cities nomad. Being the ninth of eleven children allows her to live and eat at many homes and run around with lots of nieces and nephews to burn the calories from all that Somali food. She recently began writing and is an aspiring storyteller.

William (Bill) Fietzer has celebrated the beauties, pleasures, and friendships of Saint Paul for the past twelve years. An ardent patron of the arts and of the parks that make the city unique, he often can be spotted perfecting his chipping game at one of Saint Paul's municipal golf courses.

Mike Finley arrived in Saint Paul to live in 1969, and has loved it ever since.

Kari Fisher is a native Minnesotan who has lived in six other states. She currently teaches at Normandale Community College, but taught adult basic education in Saint Paul for more than five years. When not busy working on her MFA in creative writing from Pacific Lutheran University in Tacoma, Washington, she likes to torment her wonderful family by listening to roots music and referring to herself in the third person.

Beth Fryxell attends sixth grade in Saint Paul Public Schools. Beth takes violin lessons. Beth is also taking percussion and gymnastic classes. In her free time, she enjoys reading, writing, and playing with her pet rat.

Carrie Gagne is a native of Minnesota and a graduate of Hamline University, where she earned her degree in English and creative writing. Her favorite food to eat at the State Fair is Sweet Martha's Cookies.

Bertha Douglas Givins, the eighth of ten children, resided with her family in the 400 block of Rondo Avenue beginning in 1937. She recalls Rondo as being a close-knit community where everyone knew each other, walked to get where they needed to go, and contributed to the engagement and fraternization of the citizens as they went about their daily business. It was a self-contained community and the children were well-behaved. Mrs. Bertha Givins has a third career as a writer.

Caprice Kueffner Glaser attends sixth grade in Saint Paul Public Schools.

Kitty Gogins, the daughter of Olga Zoltai, has been fascinated from an early age with her parents' experiences as refugees and new Americans. Her story in this issue of the *Almanac* is from her book about her parents' journey, *My Flag Grew Stars: World War II Refugees' Journey to America.*

Beverly Schultz Golberg is a lifelong resident of Saint Paul. Her essays have appeared in the literary journals *Ars Medica* and *Willard & Maple*, the magazine *Cottage Life*, anthologies *Cup of Comfort* and *Chicken Soup for the Soul*, and the *St. Paul Pioneer Press*. She reads her work at the Wild Yam Cabaret in Saint Paul.

Lenore Gollop grew up in the Macalester-Groveland neighborhood of Saint Paul and attended Groveland grade school, which was, and still is, near and dear to her heart. She remembers planting carrots outside the kindergarten room, and that it was so much more exciting than the watercolors, clay, and naps.

Kenia Guadarrama is twenty years old and has two wonderful boys. Life has been such a roller coaster ride so far, but she's happy with the life she has.

Armando Gutierrez attends sixth grade in Saint Paul Public Schools.

Janet Lunder Hanafin grew up on a South Dakota farm and was transplanted to Minnesota for her college years. She and her husband have two grown children and three grandchildren (all above average), and enjoy the companionship of two very fine cats.

Eric Charles Hansen studied with Carol Bly while earning his Master of Fine Arts in writing at Hamline University. He lives with his wife, Alison, and two children, Fiona and Miles, in the Battle Creek neighborhood of Saint Paul.

Phebe Hanson has been keeping a diary since she was ten, writing poems since she was forty-seven, and emailing since she was sixty-nine. She is a Bush Literary Fellow who has published two books of poetry (*Sacred Hearts* and *Why Still Dance*), and co-authored a travel-friendship memoir, *Not So Fast,* with Joan Murphy Pride. She is working on a book of poems about her mother, who died at age thirty-one, when Phebe was eight. Phebe is the proud mother of three grown children, nine grandchildren, and the great-grandmother of two.

Barbara Haselbeck calls the East Side home, edits for a living, writes for discovery, and feels ambivalent about shoveling snow.

Margaret Hasse, who lives in Saint Paul, once said to elementary school students during a poets-in-the-schools residency in rural Minnesota, "I'm a poet. Do you know what a poet is?" to which a little boy responded with great certainty, "It's a young chicken." The teacher later explained, "His family farms. He thought you said you were a pullet."

Media Mike Hazard is a filmmaker, photographer, and poet who decided to make a picture story of a person every day for a year, posting them on Facebook in an album called 365 Friends. He's had so much fun, he can't stop.

Dave Healy is a lifelong resident of Saint Paul. He lives with his wife, Nancy, within walking distance of the Minnesota State Fairgrounds. Their two sons grew up in Saint Paul but now live in Brooklyn. Their parents have forgiven them.

Diane Helander has been writing her whole life—from feature articles, newsletters, and humorous columns, to computer manuals and, currently, short humorous fiction. Through it all, her greatest inspiration has been her family: Denny, Lori, Amy, David, and Steve, and her glorious grandchildren, Julia, Sam, Abby, Anna, and Paige. Life is good.

Kara Hendershot is an artist who uses a style that consists of realistic images with implications of abstraction. She explores the relationships between people and their connection to, or detachment from, their surroundings. The abstraction in the work creates an act of spontaneity that carries elements of uncertainty and mystery, lending faded detail to the narrative in each piece. See more of her work at karahendershot.com.

Margie Hendriksen is a retired attorney and history buff.

Kofi Bobby Hickman was born and raised in Saint Paul, and has remained a lifelong resident of the city. He directed the Inner City Youth League for twenty years

Maria I. is from Ecuador and also a student at the Hubbs Center for Lifelong Learning in Saint Paul. She likes playing soccer with her kids.

Henry Jackson is an artist who has been involved in the field of photography practically an entire lifetime. As a young man, he was the first African American to work for a daily newspaper in Saint Joseph, Missouri, where he became a staff photographer. Since that time his passion for camera work has only grown. His work includes weddings, portraits, and candid shots. Henry has made his home in Saint Paul for several years. He says Saint Paul is one of the greatest places in the country to live. Henry's email is pichen50@yahoo.com.

Karen Jeffords-Brown moved to Minnesota from the East Coast in 1976 to attend graduate school in Mankato, where the wind-chill factors hit 100 below her first winter here, much to her dismay. She decided to settle here and eventually embraced the climate, becoming involved in recreational dogsled racing for five years, with her son and their three Huskies. Ms. Jeffords-Brown lives in Saint Paul and is a psychologist in private practice. She has written a screenplay and personal essays but until now publication has eluded her.

Noah Johnston attends sixth grade in Saint Paul Public Schools. Noah has a sister named Anna, whom he loves very much. His main hobbies are video games and reading. His favorite book is *The Giver,* by Lois Lowry, whom he has met.

Daryl Jorgenson will hesitate to admit it but he was born in Minneapolis in 1983. Thankfully, before long he moved to the beautiful city of Saint Paul and has lived there for most of his life. One day, Daryl would like to be considered a writer.

Karen Karsten lived in the Irvine Park area for a good part of her pre-adult years. Karen feels it is a writer's job to bear witness to the world in which they live from both a personal and political point of view. She believes that it is never too late to be who you always wanted to be and that you should try things even if you have been told you are bad at them. Taking her own advice, she recently finished her first year of drawing badly and is happy to report that progress has been made. She is now starting a year of drawing not-so-badly and invites you to do the same.

Pat Kaufman-Knapp was born and raised in Saint Paul, and attended St. Joseph's Academy, as has her mother's family for over 100 years. She served seven years in the Navy WAVES, moved to Nashville, Tennessee, and quickly became involved in volunteering there as a Civil War guide, teaching a writing class, writing newsletters, and doing public speaking.

Garrison Keillor is the host and writer of *A Prairie Home Companion*; the author of many books, including the Lake Wobegon novels and *Daddy's Girl*; and the editor of *Good Poems* and *Good Poems for Hard Times*. He has most recently edited and published *Good Poems, American Places.* A member of the Academy of American Arts and Letters, he lives in Saint Paul.

Patricia Kirkpatrick has published *Century's Road* and the picture book *Plowie: A Story from the Prairie*, illustrated by Joey Kirkpatrick. Her awards include fellowships from the National

Endowment for the Arts, the Bush Foundation, and the McKnight Loft Award. She teaches at Hamline University and is poetry editor for *Water-Stone Review*.

Evelyn D. Klein is a freelance writer, editor, poetry judge, and artist. She taught writing at The Loft, teaches at Century College, and presents workshops, programs, and readings of her work. Her articles and poetry have appeared in numerous publications. A prize-winning poet, she edited and published the anthology *Stage Two: Poetic Lives* in 1994; her poetry memoir, *From Here Across the Bridge*, including art by her father, Wolfgang Klein, came out in 2006; and her second book of prose, poetry, and her own drawings, *Once upon a Neighborhood*, was published in 2009.

Kathryn Knudson's fiction, poetry, and travel writing have been published in a variety of print and Web publications. She lives across the river in Minneapolis.

Susan Koefod still remembers reading elephant joke books as a child. She writes and publishes in various genres, was born in Saint Paul, and has lived in and around Saint Paul her entire life. Her debut novel, *Washed Up*, was published by North Star Press in 2011.

Jennifer LaCasse's is an artist whose recent work explores the idea of home, belonging, and where we come from. She is very interested in the stories that are passed along by earlier generations, and how those stories become mythologies. Saint Paul has been her artistic home since she began studying at the College of Visual arts in 2003. Her years living and working in the beautiful Summit Hill neighborhood were very formative in the development of her artistic career. She has also been involved with the vibrant arts community in Lowertown, and looks forward to doing so again. She has fallen in love with Saint Paul and will always consider it her home, wherever life takes her. See more of Jennifer's work at www.mnartists.org/Jennifer_LaCasse.

Andrea Langworthy writes a weekly column for the *Rosemount Town Pages* newspaper and teaches at The Loft Literary Center. In a previous life, for nearly thirty years, she sold cars and trucks in the Twin Cities area and says that the cast of characters from that career would make Stephen King shudder.

Light the Underground is a Minnesota-born photographer who focuses on light painting and urban exploration photography. See more of his work at www.flickr.com/photos/light_the_underground.

Chia (Chilli) Lor was born in Chiang Kham refugee camp, Thailand, in 1992. She graduated with honors from St. Paul Central High School and is currently attending St. Catherine University. As an emerging Hmong community organizer, poet, hip-hop artist, and b-girl, Chia has a vision of changing the lives of youth and women through performing arts.

Charles Matson Lume's art has been exhibited at institutions such as the Irish Museum of Modern Art, Minnesota Museum of American Art, Urban Institute of Contemporary Art in Michigan, and others. Charles has been awarded fellowships from the Bush Foundation, Jerome Foundation, and the Minnesota State Arts Board. Currently, he is an associate professor of art at the University of Wisconsin-Stout. Charles lives with his wife, Sarah, and daughter, Helena, in Saint Paul.

Brenda Manthe is an active artist living in Saint Paul and concentrating on urban abstract photography. Her photo was taken at the Minnesota Street Rod Association Back to the Fifties classic car show. See more of her work at www.brendamanthe.com.

Megan Marsnik studied poetry and writing at Hamline University and at The Naropa Institute in Boulder, Colorado. She is currently working on a novel about the role of women in the 1916 strike in northern Minnesota. She lives in Saint Paul with her husband and two daughters.

David Mather attends sixth grade in the Saint Paul Public Schools.

David McKay is a media activist with a special interest in Saint Paul history. He rides a Harley Dyna low rider and is often inspired by his poet/writer wife Linda Back McKay.

Linda Back McKay is a poet, writer, and teacher whose work has appeared in many magazines and literary publications in the U.S. and Canada, with a wide range of awards. McKay is also an independent advertising creative director/writer and lives with David McKay, the neighbor's pushy cat, and their red-hot motorcycle in Minneapolis. Their four grown children include Becka, a writer and editor; Michele, an officer in the Foreign Service; Joel, an art student; and Katie, a social service worker. The McKays treasure every moment with Linda's birth son and his family, which includes grandchildren Allie Rose and Nicholas Leon.

James McKenzie has only been appreciating Saint Paul's murals for seven years now, since moving here from North Dakota. His own artistic abilities are limited to creative nonfiction; portions of his work-in-progress have appeared in *Notre Dame Review, Western Pennsylvania History,* and *Whistling Shade,* among other places. His unpublished memoir is *Speaking Over Graves*

Ethna McKiernan is a 2011 recipient of an Artist Initiative Grant from the Minnesota State Arts Board. Her newest book, *Sky Thick with Fireflies,* is due out October 2011. She works for a nonprofit serving the downtown Minneapolis homeless population.

Marianne McNamara, poet and third-generation Saint Paulite, has lived in Macalester-Groveland for over thirty-five years. She loves all things Saint Paul, from the State Capitol building to the State Fair.

Annie Mikel lives in North Saint Paul with her husband and their two boxers, Cassie and Mosely. All four of them welcomed a baby girl into the family at the end of March. She loves the color pink, her family, and all things Irish.

John Minczeski, a longtime poet in the schools, has also taught at The Loft, Macalester College, Hamline University, the College of St. Thomas, St. Cloud State University, and the University of Minnesota. His recent poems may be found online at *Cerise Press, Big City Lit, Poetry Magazine.com,* and in print journals such as *The Connecticut River Review,* and *War, Literature and the Arts*. An interview with him recently appeared on MinnPost. Two of his chapbooks were published in 2007: *November,* from Finishing Line Press, and *Grass Elegy,* from Red Dragonfly Press.

Pel Ray Moo is from Burma. She is married and has five children. Before she moved here, she lived in a Karen Refugee Camp in Thailand. She left her country because it had a civil war for a long time—since she was a child until right now. It was not safe for living, and it was difficult to get an education. She came to the U.S on February 17, 2009. When she arrived here it was very difficult because she didn't speak English or know how to get around. She has studied English at the Minnesota Literacy Council for over two years.

Jim Moore is the author of six collections of poetry, including *Lightning at Dinner, The Freedom of History,* and *The Long Experience of Love*. His poems have appeared in *American Poetry Review, The Nation, The New Yorker, The Paris Review, The Threepenny Review, The Pushcart Prize* anthology, and in many other magazines and anthologies. Moore has received numerous awards and fellowships from the Bush Foundation, The Loft, the McKnight Foundation, and the Minnesota State Arts Board. He teaches at Hamline University and at Colorado College, Colorado Springs, as well as online through the University of Minnesota Split Rock Arts Program. He is married to the photographer JoAnn Verburg. They live in Saint Paul and in Spoleto, Italy.

Louis Murphy is a creative writing student at Hamline University in Saint Paul. He is a member of the mentally disabled community, and works constantly to rise up from that position. Some of his works are published in *Haute Dish,* a publication of Metropolitan State University.

Michael E. Murphy grew up in Saint Paul. He spent his career as an international business lawyer with Faegre & Benson in Minneapolis. In retirement, he has been teaching part-time at the University of St. Thomas Law School, serving on the Ramsey Hill Neighborhood Association, and tutoring immigrant students at Linwood School.

Joe Nathan is a former Saint Paul Public School teacher and administrator, former PTA president, father of three Saint Paul Public School graduates, and director of the Center for School Change at Macalester.

Nneka Onyilofor is an up-and-coming writer looking for more writing opportunities!

Thomas Kevin O'Rourke has lived and worked on the Mississippi River for decades. His oral stories have been presented as part of the Rockefeller Folk Arts Exhibition and the TPT production *Tales of Minnesota*. He won the Scottish International Open Poetry Competition in 1991 and 1992.

Gerri Patterson was born in Saint Paul and has lived here for most of her life. She loves cooking, traveling, taking photos of interesting places, and eating good food; she also loves theater and writing. Wine is a plus.

Eli Pattison attends sixth grade in Saint Paul Public Schools. Eli learned a lot from his fifth grade teacher, Mr. Olmstead. His favorite book series is the Hunger Games trilogy. The best movie he's ever seen was *Avatar*, but he also likes comedies. Eli likes to play sports, and plays baseball and soccer on teams.

Lucy Pavlicek attends sixth grade in Saint Paul Public Schools. Lucy was born on December 2, 1999, in Saint Paul. Her favorite book is *The Miraculous Journey of Edward Tulane.* In her free time, she likes to sing, sew, and draw.

Carrie Pomeroy's writing has appeared in *Calyx, Literary Mama, The Laurel Review,* and the anthology *Riding Shotgun: Women Write About Their Mothers,* edited by Kathryn Kysar. She is working on a memoir about motherhood, and she blogs about family life at playschooling.blogspot.com. She lives in the Hamline-Midway neighborhood of Saint Paul with her husband and two small children.

J. Otis Powell! is a writer, performance artist, mentor, curator, consultant, facilitator of Open Space Technology, and arts administrator. He was a founding producer of *Write On Radio* while working at The Loft Literary Center. He has received The Loft Creative Nonfiction Award, Jerome Mid Career Artist Grants, and the Intermedia Arts Interdisciplinary McKnight Fellowship.

Jeri Reilly has lived in Saint Paul since emigrating from Minneapolis in 1987. She was, however, merely returning to her roots inasmuch as an ancestor, who had left Denmark to avoid the draft, built his house on Benhill Road. A writer and editor, she works at the Minnesota Historical Society.

Tom Reynen is a photographer who grew up in the Mac-Groveland neighborhood, attended St. Agnes High School and St. Thomas College, and currently lives in Shoreview. His work has been exhibited in a number of local shows, and he is a resident member of the AZ Gallery in Lowertown. Tom is also on the board of Gallery 96, a nonprofit arts organization that promotes art in the northern Saint Paul suburbs. See more of his work at tom-reynen.artistwebsites.com.

Mary Kay Rummel grew up and lived in Saint Paul for many years. Her sixth book of poetry, *What's Left Is the Singing,* was published by Blue Light Press of San Francisco in 2011. Other recent poetry books include *Love in the End* and *The Illuminations.* She has poems in the anthology *The Wind Blows, The Ice Breaks,* from Nodin Press, and short fiction in *Double Lives,* from Wising Up Press. She is a professor emerita at the University of Minnesota, Duluth, and teaches part-time at California State University, Channel Islands, dividing her time between California and Minnesota. Her website is marykayrummel.com.

Lily Rupp lives in the Summit Hill neighborhood of Saint Paul, where she sometimes walks her West Highland terrier, Stew. She is enrolled in the eighth grade at Laura Jeffery Academy. Lily enjoys drawing, painting, music, and writing poetry.

Michael Russelle is a scientist, spouse, father, grandfather, uncle, friend, neighbor, activist, Quaker, volunteer, bread baker, gardener, tinkerer, and sometime poet. He's grateful for having had a mostly sweet and fulfilling life so far, and is happy even when someone else catches the foul ball.

Paw Ree Say has been living in Saint Paul for three years and three months. She is from Burma, and grew up in a large, very poor family. She has two brothers and four sisters. She also has two children: a four-year-old boy and a six-year-old girl. She enjoys going to the park with her family when she has free time. Someday she hopes to earn her GED and attend college. She likes Saint Paul because this is the place where she rebuilt her new life.

Shiny Thunder Productions, a cinema production team based in Lowertown Saint Paul, was formed by Jeremy Hosterman and Karl Warnke. They believe that artistic collaboration fuels passion in projects. Their recent film, *The Great Work of Dr. D. Volos Tinkerpaw*, was shown at the Wisconsin Film Festival in 2011. Shiny Thunder collaborated with ocal McNally Smith music student Benjamin Kelly to create the film *My Milton*, in which Ben performed his original music with the film at his senior recital.

Anura Si-Asar was born and raised in the historic Rondo community of Saint Paul. He is the co-publisher of Papyrus Publishing Inc. with his wife, Rekhet. He coordinates the Imhotep Science Initiatives, an African youth development program at the Cultural Wellness Center. Anura is also a firefighter for Minneapolis and a father of three children.

John Sielaff spent thirty years as a union carpenter and member of Saint Paul Local 87. Just this year, Local 87 was incorporated into Local 322, which encompasses all carpenters in the Twin Cities.

Maria Luisa Simon was born in Ixmiquilpan, Hidalgo, in central eastern Mexico. She went to school until she was sixteen, and then took a part-time job and was married. One of the most beautiful moments in her life was when she had her daughter, one year after she moved to Saint Paul. She has been studying English at the Minnesota Literacy Council for one year, and enjoys playing soccer and baseball.

Julia Klatt Singer writes poetry and short stories, and is a coauthor of *Twelve Branches: Stories from St. Paul*, published by Coffee House Press. She works as a visiting writer in the schools through COMPAS, and hasn't found a river yet that she doesn't want to cross.

Bick Smith is a local filmmaker and writer who also works in radio and TV. He and his wife have a daughter.

Cynthia Schreiner Smith has turned her early fascination with Pig's Eye into a successful career as a historical tour guide for Down In History Tours at the Wabasha Street Caves. She can be seen most often portraying the 1930s gangster Edna Murray, a.k.a. the Kissing Bandit.

Sybil Smith is author of the *Twin Cities Fishing Guide*, *Brainerd-Mille Lacs Fishing Guide,* and *Twin Cities Shore Fishing Maps*. She is also owner of Smith House Press, FINS Publications, and the Ebook Consultants.

Susan Solomon is the editor/cartoonist of *Sleet Magazine*, an online literary journal.

Oliver Swingen loves to draw and write. His other hobbies are playing guitar, karate, and yo-yoing. He has a little sister, and a dog named Fanny.

Jennifer Syverson was, upon arrival into this world, given the *Optimize Your Life!* book. Being genetically inclined toward disorganization, she promptly mislaid it. She looks for it sporadically, but is frequently distracted by the *Saint Paul Almanac* and all the optimal happenings in Saint Paul.

Muriel Tate writes, "We all think of yesterday, but in reality if we didn't have progress we would become non-achievers. We must not forget that without dreams of walking on the moon, astronauts in space for weeks, electric cars, etc., there would be no progress. We must always reach for the stars, but still keep our feet on the ground. Yesterday was great but *today* is even better!"

Michael Teffera is originally from Ethiopia and moved to Saint Paul on August 31, 2006. He graduated from Metro State University with a bachelor's degree in accounting and is currently working at U.S. Bank as an accounting specialist. His hobbies include bike riding, writing short stories and poems, and watching movies.

Alexander J. Theoharides is a writer and teacher from the Linden Hills neighborhood of Minneapolis.

David Tilsen is still living in a rich fantasy world surrounded by family, friends, dogs, and squirrels. He doesn't particularly like the squirrels.

Tobechi Tobechukwu is originally from Baltimore, Maryland. A photographer and artist, he has specialized in social documentary photography for over eighteen years, receiving several awards for his work, including the McKnight Photography Fellowship for Artists in 2004. He resides in Saint Paul with wife, Zuri, and daughter, Akira.

Steve Trimble lives in the Dayton's Bluff neighborhood near Indian Mounds Park. He has researched, written, and taught Twin Cities and Minnesota history. He serves on the editorial board of the Ramsey County Historical Society and the St. Paul Heritage Preservation Commission. He has recently authored a large article in Ramsey County History on three East Side neighborhoods in the 1940s and '50s. He also collects novels set in Minnesota and plants heirloom tomatoes.

Twin Cities Brightest takes straight out of the camera long-exposure-light-painting-pictures using luminous tools such as LED lights and flashlights. No photoshop, just magic in front of the camera.

Katrina Vandenberg's first collection of poems, *Atlas*, was a finalist for the Minnesota Book Award. Her new chapbook, *On Marrriage*, is available from Red Dragonfly Press. She's received residencies from the Sewanee Writer's Conference, the Amy Clampitt House, and the MacDowell Colony, and her work has appeared in journals such as *The American Scholar*, *The Iowa Review*, and *Post Road*.

Diego Vázquez Jr. writes poems to flowers, birds, rocks, rivers, salmon, and people, too! Vázquez's stories were included in *Twelve Branches*, and his novels include *Growing through the Ugly* and *The Fat-Brush Painter*. You might meet him in your school through a COMPAS residency. He is proud to have his poem stuck in cement (in a Saint Paul sidewalk).

Kathleen Vellenga serves as chair of the Minnesota State Higher Education Services Council. Her lifelong passion is working to improve opportunities for all children. Kathleen continued her advocacy for children while representing her Saint Paul neighborhood in the Minnesota State House of Representatives from 1981 to 1995. She currently serves on the boards of Serve Minnesota and the Sexual Victims Center. Kathleen is now writing a historical novel. She and her husband are an active support team for their six grandchildren.

Saymoukda Duangphouxay Vongsay is a co-founder of The Unit Collective of Emerging Playwrights of Color, National Lao American Writers Summit chair, inaugural winner of the 2010 Alfred C. Carey Prize in Spoken Word Poetry from New York, and member of the advisory board to the 2010 Asian Film Festival.

David Vu was born and raised in Minneapolis and has been writing poetry for thirteen years. He started writing poetry for school, but after years of encouraging words from teachers and friends, he decided to take poetry a little more seriously and started writing as a way to express himself. He debuted in the 2010 *Saint Paul Almanac* Lowertown Reading Jam: Redefining Hmong Men, alongside many other Hmong writers. As a new and upcoming spoken word artist, Vu hopes to perform more and continue with his poetry.

Elena Walczak attends English classes at the Minnesota Literacy Center on the East Side.

Leslie Walters knows from experience that no Saint Paul institution is quite so laden with celebrities as the annual Winter Carnival—and she has rubbed elbows with some of the best of them, from local film impresario Mel Jass to renowned comedian Tommy Smothers to the Prince of the South Wind. Whether participating as a young carnival princess or Humboldt High School Indianette performing with the marching band, she's reveled with Saint Paul's *in* crowd at many a Torchlight Parade after-party.

Marilynne Thomas Walton earned a bachelor's degree in both English and library science from the College of Saint Catherine (now St. Catherine University). She has worked as a librarian in Saint Paul and in New York City, where she lived for many years. A winner of The Loft's Le Poeme contest, she also received honorable mention in the 2006 McKnight Artist Fellowshps for Writers, Loft Awards in Poetry. Her work has been published in such journals and anthologies as The Northland Review, Loonfeather, and Concert at Chopin's House.

Cary Waterman's most recent book, *Book of Fire,* was published by Nodin Press. She lives in the Hamline-Midway area with her daughter and her dog, George, and teaches creative writing at Augsburg College.

Greg Watson's work has appeared in numerous literary publications, including *The Seattle Review, Tulane Review,* and *Poetry East*, and has been featured on Garrison Keillor's *Writer's Almanac*. His most recent collection is *What Music Remains*, published by Nodin Press. He lives in the Mac-Groveland area of Saint Paul.

Susan Steger Welsh is a native Saint Paulite whose first poetry collection, *Rafting on the Water Table,* published by New Rivers Press in 2000, was a finalist for a Minnesota Book Award. She has been awarded two State Arts Board Fellowships, an SASE/Jerome fellowship, and a Jerome/Travel Study grant.

Linda White, a Saint Paul native, is a writer, editor, and publicist living on the edge of Saint Paul. She has been involved in working with words for over twenty years. She writes articles, reviews, and creative nonfiction, and teaches workshops. Her passion is the written word.

Mary Wlodarski is a native of Minnesota, and a lover of nature and all things animal. She lives in Oak Grove with her husband, three horses, and miniature daschund. She is working on her MFA at Hamline University in Saint Paul while teaching high school English in Andover.

Lucia Wroblewski was born and raised in Saint Paul, where she was appointed a Saint Paul police officer on March 20, 1989. She was honored as Saint Paul Officer of the Year in 2001 with patrol partner Officer Tim Bradley; and received the highest accommodation the department bestows, The Metal of Valor, on September 29, 1996. Lucia lives with her partner Jen Moore in greater Saint Paul.

Pa Yong Xiong, an undercover weirdo as she likes to call herself, just graduated from Gordon Parks High School. When she's not in school she likes to daydream about escaping from all the peas in the same ol' boring pod and into a fruit bowl of colors. But for now she enjoys the thrill of singing to her unbelievably great audience, shampoo and conditioner, and most of all, hearing the shutters of her banged-up Canon camera. Hungry to learn more about photography, she jumps at every opportunity she gets to expand her knowledge of this art form, so that one day everyone can see beauty in everything, as she does.

Ernesto 'Neto' Ybarra is an artist raised in America in a Mexican household, growing up with a strong connection to his heritage. After traveling through Mexico with local hip-hop act Los Nativos, he came back with an appreciation for the bright colors and the traditional appeal of his culture. Inspired by Mayan codices and everyday scenes, Neto Ybarra's latest paintings take on an ancient essence while still incorporating modern subject matter, creating images that tug and pull the viewer from one time and place to another.

Patricia Anita Young was born in Saint Paul and now resides in Minneapolis. She is an accounting technician who enjoys writing freelance articles.

Community Editors' Biographies

Daunell Barnwell (Nam) is a self-proclaimed nerd and aspiring writer and student at Gordon Parks High School who is proud to call the glorious expanse of Saint Paul his home. He manages to make time for working on the *Almanac* in between partially slacking in school, road trips to Mankato and Duluth, and fervent Yu-Gi-Oh matches with friends on weekends.

Maya Beecham, a second-generation native Saint Paulite, was born in the historic Rondo neighborhood, graduated from Cretin-Derham Hall High School, and earned a bachelor of arts in communication studies at Hamline University. Currently, she works for a national nonprofit organization in Saint Paul, and as a freelance writer.

Mary Davini has many loves; some of these include summer nights, foggy mornings, sand volleyball, and the city of Saint Paul. She and her husband like to spend their days in their East Side home watching movies, sharing the bed with their dogs, and playing with their adorable baby girl.

Nimo Farah loves orators and storytellers. Her ideal vacation is visiting remote villages in Somalia and listening to the stories of elders and children under the dancing stars and full moon while drinking tea. She has an inner child that recently turned four years old and can doodle and dream for hours (she looks forward to a day dedicated to dreaming). She lives in many places in Minneapolis and Saint Paul, including her car (she's always driving and up for any adventure) and thinks of herself as a Twin-Cities nomad. Being the ninth of eleven children allows her to live and eat at many homes and run around with lots of nieces and nephews to burn the calories from all that Somali food. She recently began writing and is an aspiring storyteller. Being a community editor for the *Almanac* is food for her soul.

Pamela R. Fletcher, writer, editor, teacher, and lover of life and social justice, believes that one blooms where one is planted; so, if you happen to see a California poppy blossoming in the Minnesota corn fields, that's her!

Shaquan Foster is a graduate from Highland Park High School readily awaiting the future and all the changes it will bring. Born in the great Saint Paul, he loves art and finds it in every aspect of life.

Andrew Hall is a graduate from Highland Park High School who attends the University of Minnesota. This is his third year with the *Almanac*, and he hopes to continue to work with the organization.

Barbara Haselbeck calls the East Side home, edits for a living, writes for discovery, and feels ambivalent about shoveling snow.

Charlotte Kazlauskas was in love the first time she picked up a pen. At a ripe sixteen years of age, she delightedly attends Perpich Center for Arts Education. She intends to have big plans when she graduates.

Patricia Kirkpatrick has worked as a writer, teacher, and editor around the country. She is the author of *Century's Road* and *Plowie: A Story from the Prairie*; her awards include fellowships from the NEA and Bush Foundation, and a McKnight Loft Poetry Award. She serves as poetry editor for *Water-Stone Review*.

Jewell Hill Mayer: News flash! Shy Southern belle (*not!*) gets transported to Yankee country (Minn.), lives here sixty years before discovering like-minded writers and intelligentsia, begins to learn how to edit and publish, and—*voià!*—becomes one of an elite group who choose stories for the *Saint Paul Almanac*.

Marianne McNamara, a third-generation Saint Paulite, has had her poems published in several anthologies and publications, including the 2011 *Saint Paul Almanac, County Lines, Dust & Fire, Read Write Poem NaPoWriMo Anthology, The Talking Stick,* and *Lake Country Journal,* and had one of her poems engraved on Saint Paul sidewalks in 2009, through the Everyday Poems for City Sidewalk project. She and her husband have two grown children and one amazing granddaughter, and have lived in Macalester-Groveland for over thirty-five years. She loves all things Saint Paul, from the State Capitol building to the State Fair.

Arthur Nguyen is a graduate of Johnson High School who is now attending Harvard. He is proud of both his academic accomplishments and his work as a community activist. Arthur played a pivotal leadership role in Saint Paul Project Homeless, which raised over $21,000 for the thousands of hungry and indigent in the city, and entered the world of politics by spearheading legislation. A passionate tennis player, he strives to get on the courts to hit some balls and rally. Often stressed over a multitude of assignments, he still manages to find time to take a break from deadlines and reports to savor life's subtleties.

Sandra Opokua was born in Ghana and came to Saint Paul in 2007, where she's now a senior at Humboldt High School. She used to have six dogs—and it's not that easy to take care of them. She is an only child, but don't think that makes her spoiled—she's not! Her favorite author is Jodi Picoult, and she especially likes the books *My Sister's Keeper, The Pact,* and many more. She also loves to dance and cook, and sometimes watch reality TV shows. She would like to travel to Spain and Britain some day.

Jennifer Syverson was, upon arrival into this world, given the *Optimize Your Life!* book. Being genetically inclined toward disorganization, she promptly mislaid it. She looks for it sporadically but is frequently distracted by the *Saint Paul Almanac* and all the optimal happenings in Saint Paul.

Diego Vázquez Jr. writes poems to flowers, birds, rocks, rivers, and salmon—and people too! Vázquez has been a visiting writer in the schools for many years. His novels include *Growing Through the Ugly* (W.W. Norton) and *Border Town Sky* (forthcoming). As a community editor for the *Saint Paul Almanac* he is constantly searching for new stories to publish. In 2008, he was selected as a Saint Paul Everyday Sidewalk poet. He is proud to have his poem cemented into the city's sidewalks. A long time ago, Vázquez hosted poetry slams in Minnesota.

Mai Yang Xiong plans to attend St. Catherine University, majoring in psychology. She enjoys composing music, challenging herself in academics, and living in the city of Saint Paul with her friends and family. On a quiet night, rather than imagining a calm and cool evening, she tends to think that a zombie will attack from behind at any minute. But like the brave hero in any zombie movie, she strives to survive with her busy and very complicated schedule. Adventurous and curious toward the world, Mai Yang is looking forward to a bright future.

Pa Yong Xiong likes to call herself an undercover weirdo. She is a graduate of Gordon Parks High School; when she's not in school, she likes to daydream about escaping from all the peas in the same ol' boring pod and into a fruit bowl of colors. But for now she enjoys the thrill of singing to her unbelievably great audience, shampoo and conditioner, and, most of all, hearing the click of the shutters in her banged-up cannon camera. Hungry to learn more about photography, she jumps at every opportunity she gets to expand her knowledge of this art form, so that one day everyone can see beauty in everything, as she does.

Gordon Parks High School Students Document University Avenue in Transition

Paul Creager

On May 26, 2011, the students, staff, parents, and community stakeholders of Gordon Parks High School (GPHS) celebrated the one-year anniversary of the launch of *Transitions: University Avenue,* a student-produced documentary project about the changes wrought by the central corridor LRT, with an event dominated by the theme "Hope and Possibility." *Transitions* captures the before, during, and after stages of central corridor LRT construction on University Avenue; it is made possible through a partnership with the Minnesota Historical Society, funded by arts and heritage amendment dollars. The event was a time of celebration and reflection, an exciting milestone in the emergence of this new school.

We celebrated because numerous GPHS students are walking in the footsteps of Gordon Parks, preserving stories with the camera and audio recorder that have the potential to effect social change. Students are talking about how the project promotes their career, makes school exciting, and led to a surprising discovery: that they are very good at interviewing—something they didn't realize about themselves before. The students have found a real audience for their work at the same time that it is available worldwide.

The event was also a time for reflection. The same University Avenue businesses that we interviewed for the project provided the catering for the event. Traffic delays and construction are now posing real obstacles for small businesses, particularly independent restaurants. The very character and identity of University Avenue will surely change in the coming years. Our hope is that current businesses survive and live on to thrive in the changed landscape of a light rail–dominated corridor.

As *Transitions* continues in the coming years of LRT construction, we ask the community to walk with us and to help us. Please visit our website, www.universityave.org, to be inspired by student storytelling. We hope that you are moved by the potential for "Hope and Possibility" that the students of Gordon Parks, the new generation of University Avenue residents, hold inside themselves and can bring to this city.

2012 Year Planner

	JANUARY	FEBRUARY	MARCH
1	SU — NEW YEAR'S DAY	W	TH
2	M	TH — GROUNDHOG DAY	F
3	T	F	SA
4	W	SA — MAWLID AL-NABI	SU
5	TH	SU	M
6	F	M	T
7	SA	T	W
8	SU	W	TH — INTERNATIONAL WOMEN'S DAY / PURIM
9	M	TH	F — PURIM
10	T	F	SA
11	W	SA	SU — DAYLIGHT SAVING TIME BEGINS
12	TH	SU	M
13	F	M	T
14	SA	T — VALENTINE'S DAY	W
15	SU	W	TH
16	M — MARTIN LUTHER KING JR. DAY	TH	F
17	T	F	SA — ST. PATRICK'S DAY
18	W	SA	SU
19	TH	SU	M
20	F	M — PRESIDENTS' DAY	T — SPRING EQUINOX
21	SA	T — MARDI GRAS	W
22	SU	W — ASH WEDNESDAY	TH
23	M — CHINESE NEW YEAR	TH	F
24	T	F	SA
25	W	SA	SU
26	TH	SU	M
27	F	M	T
28	SA	T	W
29	SU	W	TH
30	M		F
31	T		SA

2012 Year Planner

	APRIL		MAY		JUNE	
1	SU	APRIL FOOLS' DAY PALM SUNDAY	T	MAY DAY	F	
2	M		W		SA	
3	T		TH		SU	
4	W		F		M	
5	TH		SA	CINCO DE MAYO	T	
6	F	PASSOVER BEGINS GOOD FRIDAY	SU		W	
7	SA		M		TH	
8	SU	EASTER	T		F	
9	M		W		SA	
10	T		TH		SU	
11	W		F		M	
12	TH		SA		T	
13	F		SU	MOTHER'S DAY	W	
14	SA		M		TH	
15	SU		T		F	
16	M		W		SA	
17	T		TH		SU	FATHER'S DAY
18	W		F		M	
19	TH		SA		T	JUNETEENTH
20	F		SU		W	SUMMER SOLSTICE
21	SA		M		TH	
22	SU	EARTH DAY	T		F	
23	M		W		SA	
24	T		TH		SU	
25	W		F		M	
26	TH		SA		T	
27	F		SU	SHAVUOT	W	
28	SA		M	MEMORIAL DAY	TH	
29	SU		T		F	
30	M		W		SA	
31			TH			

2012 Year Planner

	JULY	AUGUST	SEPTEMBER
1	SU	W	SA
2	M	TH	SU
3	T	F	M LABOR DAY
4	W INDEPENDENCE DAY	SA	T
5	TH	SU	W
6	F	M HIROSHIMA/NAGASAKI REMEMBRANCE DAY	TH
7	SA	T	F
8	SU	W	SA
9	M	TH	SU
10	T	F	M
11	W	SA	T
12	TH	SU	W
13	F	M	TH
14	SA	T	F
15	SU	W	SA
16	M	TH	SU
17	T	F	M ROSH HASHANAH
18	W	SA	T
19	TH	SU EID AL-FITR	W
20	F RAMADAN BEGINS	M	TH
21	SA	T	F INTERNATIONAL DAY OF PEACE
22	SU	W	SA AUTUMN EQUINOX
23	M	TH	SU
24	T	F	M
25	W	SA	T
26	TH	SU	W YOM KIPPUR
27	F	M	TH
28	SA	T	F
29	SU	W	SA
30	M	TH	SU
31	T	F	

2012 Year Planner

	OCTOBER		NOVEMBER		DECEMBER
1	M	TH	ALL SAINTS' DAY / DAY OF THE DEAD	SA	
2	T	F		SU	
3	W	SA		M	
4	TH	SU	DAYLIGHT SAVING TIME ENDS	T	
5	F	WORLD TEACHER'S DAY	M		W	
6	SA	T	ELECTION DAY	TH	
7	SU	W		F	
8	M	TH		SA	
9	T	F		SU	HANUKKAH BEGINS
10	W	SA		M	INTERNATIONAL HUMAN RIGHTS DAY
11	TH	INDIGENOUS PEOPLES DAY	SU	VETERANS' DAY	T	
12	F	M		W	
13	SA	T		TH	
14	SU	W		F	CHRISTMAS BIRD COUNT BEGINS
15	M	TH	MUHARRAM BEGINS	SA	
16	T	F		SU	
17	W	SA		M	
18	TH	SU		T	
19	F	M		W	
20	SA	T		TH	
21	SU	W		F	WINTER SOLSTICE
22	M	TH	THANKSGIVING	SA	
23	T	F		SU	
24	W	UNITED NATIONS DAY	SA		M	CHRISTMAS EVE
25	TH	SU		TU	CHRISTMAS DAY
26	F	EID AL-ADHA	M		W	KWANZAA BEGINS
27	SA	T		TH	
28	SU	W		F	
29	M	TH		SA	
30	T	F		SU	
31	W	HALLOWEEN			M	NEW YEAR'S EVE

Looking for Writers

Want to See Your Story Published in the Saint Paul Almanac?

The *Saint Paul Almanac* is always looking for unique Saint Paul stories. Whether you're a professional writer or writing for the first time, we're interested in reading your work and publishing it.

- Please send us your stories, poems, or spoken-word pieces of 650 words or less.
- We pay small stipends on publication.
- All entries are reviewed by the community editors in a blind judging process.
- You may live anywhere in the world and send in your story of Saint Paul.

Thank you for wishing to participate in the *Saint Paul Almanac*'s experiment in democratic publishing. Please read the writers' guidelines below for further information on the content, tone, and format of submissions.

Submission deadline for 2012 Almanac

Dec. 1, 2011

Where to send your story

Attention: Kimberly Nightingale, publisher
Emailed stories are preferred.
Via email: stories@saintpaulalmanac.com

Via postal mail
(postal mail is strongly discouraged unless you have no access to email)

Stories
Saint Paul Almanac
275 East Fourth St., Suite 735
Saint Paul, MN 55101

Writers' guidelines

We receive hundreds of submissions every year, and we read each one carefully. To help you understand the *Almanac*'s format, please keep the following points in mind:

Make it personal

Daily and weekly newspapers and TV/radio news provide Saint Paulites with plenty of straight news and dry facts. What the *Almanac* is looking for is something much more personal. For example, we are more interested in a story on your reactions to the Saint Paul Saints' season than in one on the Saints—after all, we can open the sports page and find that. If you write about a Saint Paul person, make it clear to readers why this person deserves their attention. Similarly, if you work for an organization, don't just tell us about the organization—describe why working there is so fun or meaningful or challenging to you.

Be specific
It's the bright particulars that give stories their charm and uniqueness. Help your readers see, hear, touch, taste, and smell the experiences you're writing about. Specifics help you tell your story.

Don't advertise
The *Almanac* is published by a nonprofit organization. We don't publish advertisements in the guise of stories. If you want to sing the praises of your favorite bartender or grocery store, dig a little deeper—our readers want a living profile of a person or place.

Stay within word counts
One of the *Almanac*'s goals each year is to publish the broadest and deepest possible range of writing. For this reason, we must limit the length of pieces, and we may have to further limit them through careful copyediting. Most of our selections are 300 words (or less) or 650 words (or less). *If you want to submit a longer piece, please contact the editor by email first and describe the piece you want to submit.* We will let you know if you should send in the longer piece or not.

Be frisky
Have you written a poem, lyrics to a song, or a short scene that you'd like to submit? Essays aren't the only things we publish—we're happy to look at other formats, including graphic fiction.

Remember that we're in this together
Just as you bring unique experience to the submissions you send us, we bring something unique to publishing the *Almanac*'s selections. Our work is a collaboration. We may need to tighten or shorten what you've sent us; we may need to ask you to rewrite or add something to it. Please don't think of such editing as criticism of your writing—it is not. Editors are the midwives to your words, helping them to be born into the world of a specific publication.

Help us keep our costs down
Formatting selections is expensive. If you believe in and want to support the *Almanac*, please help us keep our expenses down by submitting your contributions this way:

1. Put your name and the title of your submission on the left instead of centered.

2. Double-space your lines.

3. After the period at the end of a sentence, use only a single space (not two spaces) before you begin another sentence.

4. When you email us your submission, please give the file a title that includes one or two words to describe the contents and your last name—for example, *MoundParkLee.doc.*

5. Include a short (50 words or less) biography at the end of your submission.

Thank you for observing our submission guidelines and good luck!

Community Editor Apprenticeship Project

Want to Become a **Saint Paul Almanac** *Community Editor?*

The next community editor project will begin in October 2011.

Community editor requirements: a love for writing, and you live/work/or attend school in Saint Paul. Potential community editors must submit a short application, including a brief essay on why they want to be an editor. Each community editor must commit to reading at least 100 selections. Small stipends are paid to community editors for their hard work. Persons age 15 or older are welcome to participate. Contact executive director Kimberly Nightingale at kimberly@saintpaulalmanac.com for more information.

During the course of 20 weeks and 14 two-hour meetings, between October 2011 and January 2012, community editors/apprentice editors will:

1. Learn how to gather poems and stories in their communities.

2. Help people they gather stories from send in their best work.

3. Determine collectively what goes into the *Saint Paul Almanac,* based on criteria of quality and inclusiveness.

4. Learn copyediting marks, tools, and resources.

5. Learn the steps in publishing a book.

6. Improve their own writing and editing through workshop sessions with professional writers.

7. Build confidence and trust in their abilities through participating in the community editor process.

8. Develop relationships with professional writers that may not have occurred in other contexts.

Photo © Payong Xiong

Community editors discuss writing at a 2010 meeting at the Black Dog Cafe

Notes

Notes

Notes

Notes

Subscribe!

Three annual issues
for $40

(price includes tax,
shipping, and handling)

To order

www.saintpaulalmanac.com

mail: Subscriptions
Saint Paul Almanac
275 East Fourth St, Suite 735
Saint Paul, MN 55101

If mailing, please fill out and send the info below.

Begin with *2013 Saint Paul Almanac*

Check or money order enclosed

Charge: __ Visa __ MasterCard

CARD NUMBER

EXPIRATION DATE

SIGNATURE OF CARDHOLDER

MAILING ADDRESS

EMAIL

For gift orders

SHIP TO NAME

MAILING ADDRESS